Gothic television

MANCHESTER
1824

Manchester University Press

Gothic television

Helen Wheatley

Manchester University Press

MANCHESTER AND NEW YORK

distributed exclusively in the USA by Palgrave

Published by Manchester University Press
Oxford Road, Manchester M13 9NR, UK
and Room 400, 175 Fifth Avenue, New York, NY 10010, USA
www.manchesteruniversitypress.co.uk

Distributed exclusively in the USA by
Palgrave, 175 Fifth Avenue, New York,
NY 10010, USA

Distributed exclusively in Canada by
UBC Press, University of British Columbia, 2029 West Mall,
Vancouver, BC, Canada V6T 1Z2

British Library Cataloguing-in-Publication Data
A catalogue record for this book is available from the British Library

Library of Congress Cataloging-in-Publication Data applied for

ISBN   0 7190 7148 8 *hardback*
EAN   978 0 7190 7148 5

ISBN   0 7190 7149 6 *paperback*
EAN   978 0 7190 7149 2

First published 2006

15 14 13 12 11 10 09 08 07 06   10 9 8 7 6 5 4 3 2 1

Typeset in Scala with Meta display
by Servis Filmsetting Ltd, Manchester
Printed in Great Britain
by Bell & Bain Ltd, Glasgow

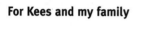

For Kees and my family

Contents

List of figures

Acknowledgements

I would like to thank everyone who read or listened to this work as it developed. This book originated in my doctoral thesis and I am particularly grateful to my PhD supervisors in the Department of Film and Television Studies at the University of Warwick: Jason Jacobs (now at Griffith University), who inspired me at the start of this work, and Richard Dyer, who was always insightful and generous in his guidance as I finished it. Christine Geraghty and Peter Hutchings examined my PhD and their perceptive comments on this work were invaluable at a crucial point in its development. Thanks also go to Elaine Lenton and Tracey Bale at the University of Warwick, who were always there to help. I am also indebted to the members of the Midlands Television Research Group, past and present, for providing intellectually stimulating diversions, and for listening to early work with patience and generosity. Indeed, thanks must go to all of my colleagues and students at the University of Warwick and the University of Reading, and to all at Manchester University Press.

I would also like to thank the staff at the following institutions: the University of Warwick library, the BBC Written Archives, the British Film Institute library, the National Film and Television Archive, the Canal+ archive, Pearson International library services, the British Newspaper Library, and the now sadly disbanded Independent Television Commission library. I gratefully acknowledge the support of the Arts and Humanities Research Board which funded the research project 'Cultures of British Television Drama, 1960–82' at the University of Reading. Sections of this book form part of this project's outcomes.

I am also grateful to all of my friends and family for being patient with me during the production of this book. I want to apologise to the following people for not seeing them often enough while I was completing it: Tom and Nicola Wheatley, Mary and Noah Wheatley, Claire Thompson, Kathryn Tennison and Julia Quillin. Thanks also to Karl

Franzen and Karen Blair for providing a fantastic, and much-needed, holiday in the middle of my research. My grandfather, William Francis, was particularly patient with me as I completed this book; I know he would have been proud to see it published. This book would not have been finished without the intellectual and emotional support of my two friends, Rachel Moseley and Helen Wood. I am particularly grateful to Rachel, not only for her advice and insightful comments on the seemingly endless drafts of this book, but also for being a great friend and an excellent personal shopper. I am indebted to my parents, Merryll Wheatley and Phil Wheatley, for their unerring support and encouragement. Finally, to Kees de Groot: I can't thank you enough.

Introduction: Gothic television – texts and contexts

What is the Gothic? What is Gothic television?

The last decade has seen a diffusion of the Gothic across a wide range of cultural sites, a relative explosion of Gothic images and narratives prompting a renewed critical interest in the genre. The attendant fields of study which engage with the Gothic are numerous: literary theory and history, musicology, history, art history, architecture and landscape studies, theatre studies, film studies, cultural studies, and so on. Rather surprisingly however, given this proliferation of Gothic narratives and imagery across popular culture and criticism, very little sustained attention has been paid to what we might term 'Gothic television' until this point. This book sets out to fill this gap, to offer an analysis of where and how the genre might be located on British and US television, from the start of television broadcasting to the present day, with a particular focus on Gothic television drama. While some have seen television as too 'literal' a medium to successfully present potentially affective Gothic fictions, I will argue that, conversely, television is the ideal medium for the Gothic. In this analysis, Gothic television is understood as a domestic form of a genre which is deeply concerned with the domestic, writing stories of unspeakable family secrets and homely trauma large across the television screen. The connections made between the Gothic text and television's reception contexts therefore lie at the centre of this book. This book also challenges the relative stagnation of the canon of television studies in the UK and abroad. While television's textual history is vast, stretching back from this point over seven decades, 'television', as it is constituted in the academy, is relatively tiny, represented by a small number of texts to which scholars of television return time and again. Thus, this book can be seen as a small part of a broader effort to widen our knowledge and understanding of television programming, charting a little known genre from its inception to more recent developments, and eschewing the realist paradigm which has dominated historical television scholarship.

A singular definition of the Gothic as a genre of fiction has, throughout the history of Gothic studies, been difficult to isolate, due in no small part to the fact that the Gothic has been alternately described as an aesthetic, mode or style, as a set of particular themes and narrative conventions, as a sub-genre of fantasy, and, initially, as an isolated historical movement. As Lenora Ledwon has argued, 'even among other genres, the Gothic seems particularly difficult to define. Part of the difficulty lies in the fact that, rather than speaking of one monolithic category of "Gothic", it is more appropriate to recognise that there are many *Gothics*[1] (Ledwon, 1993: 261). Some attempts at a categorisation of the genre have produced lists of characteristics (plot events, settings, characters, etc.) which the Gothic text may deploy. For example, David Punter proposes the following definition: '[the fictional Gothic is characterised by] an emphasis on portraying the terrifying, a common insistence on archaic settings, a prominent use of the supernatural, the presence of highly stereotyped characters, and the attempt to deploy and perfect techniques of literary suspense' (1980: 1). To this list we might add a tendency towards convoluted plotting and multiple narrators (what Eve Sedgwick identifies as 'the difficulty the story has in getting itself told' (1986: 13)), a frequent deployment of horror and/or disgust, and an obsession with motifs of the uncanny. Larry Gross, on the other hand, offers a more open definition of Gothic fiction as a 'literature where fear is the motivating and sustaining emotion' (1989: 1).

Defining Gothic television presents further problems. Unlike Gothic literature, Gothic television is not a category which is utilised by television industry professionals to define their programmes, nor one which exists in everyday parlance (and is therefore not regularly used by viewers in categorising their viewing habits). Nor is the term found in the generic shorthand employed in listings guides to describe new series (for example, 'the latest sci-fi thriller', 'a new situation comedy for Saturday night', and so on). However, none of this precludes us from discussing the Gothic as a recognisable and separate category of television fiction. As the example of *film noir* has shown within cinema studies, a genre may indeed be identified or generated through critical activity (see Altman, 1999; Naremore, 1998). The central aims of this book are therefore to define the genre as it appears on UK and US television, to unpack Gothic television as a critical category, and to provide some starting points from which to begin thinking about the specific relationship between the Gothic as a genre concerned with domestic spaces and narratives and television as an inherently *domestic* medium.

As in Gothic literary studies, it is possible to produce an initial taxonomy of Gothic television in order to distinguish the genre from the other generic categorisations which are applied to its texts (e.g. 'supernatural thriller', 'spooky drama', 'made-for-television horror', and so on). This preliminary attempt to define something called 'Gothic television' allows for intuitive starting points from which the investigation can then move on, testing and complicating the following definition. In some cases, such as the television adaptation of classic Gothic literature, it is clear to see the origins of the definition 'Gothic television'; however, more broadly, the programmes identified as Gothic television in this study can be linked together both thematically and stylistically. The Gothic television narrative is likely to feature many of the following: a mood of dread and/or terror inclined to evoke fear or disgust in the viewer; the presence of highly stereotyped characters and plots, often derived from Gothic literary fiction (e.g. the hero or heroine trapped in a menacing domestic situation by an evil villain, or the family attempting to cover up hidden secrets from the past); representations of the supernatural which are either overt (created through the use of special effects) or implied (suggested rather than fully revealed); a proclivity towards the structures and images of the uncanny (repetitions, returns, déjà vu, premonitions, ghosts, doppelgangers, animated inanimate objects and severed body parts, etc.); and, perhaps most importantly, homes and families which are haunted, tortured or troubled in some way. In addition, these narratives are likely to be organised in a complex way, structured around flashback sequences, memory montages and other narrative interpolations. Gothic television is visually dark, with a mise-en-scène dominated by drab and dismal colours, shadows and closed-in spaces. Programmes of this genre are also inclined towards camerawork and sound recording taken from a subjective perspective (from the 'spirit's-eye-view' of ghosts and supernatural beings, to the point of view of the victimised heroine in adaptations of the female Gothic novel). Gothic television is thus heavily impressionistic at times.

With a working definition that remains necessarily inclusive, we might now begin to think about which programmes fall into this category and the decisions that have been made in gathering together the texts at the centre of this analysis. A study of Gothic fiction on television in the UK and US which attempted to be encyclopaedic in its coverage would include (at the very least) consideration of the following programmes:[2]

UK

A Ghost Story (BBC, 1947)
Rebecca (BBC, 1947)
The Edgar Allen Poe Centenary (BBC, 1949)
Rebecca (BBC, 1954)
Hour of Mystery (ABC [UK], 1957)
Tales of Mystery (A-R, 1961–63)
Doctor Who (BBC1, 1963–)
Out of the Unknown (BBC2, 1965–71)
The Wednesday Thriller (BBC1, 1965)
Mystery and Imagination (ABC [UK]/Thames, 1966–70)
Woman in White (BBC1, 1966)
Haunted (ABC [UK], 1967–68)
Journey to the Unknown (ATV, 1968–70)
Late Night Horror (BBC2, 1968)
'Whistle and I'll Come to You' (BBC1, 1968)
Ghost Story for Christmas (BBC1, 1971–78)
Dead of Night (BBC2, 1972)
Thriller (ATV, 1973–76)
The Georgian House (HTV, 1976)
Count Dracula (BBC2, 1977)
Supernatural (BBC1, 1977)
The Clifton House Mystery (HTV, 1978)
Rebecca (BBC1, 1979)
Sapphire and Steele (ATV, 1979–82)
Hammer House of Horror (Cinema Arts International, 1980)
Woman in White (BBC2, 1982)
The Children of Green Knowe (BBC1, 1986)
Northanger Abbey (BBC2, 1987)
Moondial (BBC1, 1988)
Tom's Midnight Garden (BBC1, 1989)
Ghostwatch (BBC1, 1992)
Chiller (Yorkshire, 1995)
Ghosts (BBC2, 1995)
The Haunting of Helen Walker (Rosemont Productions Ltd, 1997)
Rebecca (Carlton, 1997)
Woman in White (BBC1, 1997)
Ultraviolet (World Productions, 1998)
The League of Gentlemen (BBC2, 1999–2002)
Turn of the Screw (United Film and Television Productions, 1999)
Christopher Lee's Ghost Story for Christmas (BBC1, 2000)

Urban Gothic (Channel 5, 2000–1)
The Wyvern Mystery (BBC1, 2000)
Dr. Terrible's House of Horrible (BBC2, 2001)
Strange (BBC1, 2002–3)
Garth Merenghi's Darkplace (Channel 4, 2004)
Hex (Shine, 2004–)

US

Lights Out (NBC, 1949–52)
Suspense (CBS, 1949–54)
One Step Beyond (ABC [US], 1959–61)
Thriller (NBC, 1960–62)
The Addams Family (Filmways, 1964–66)
The Munsters (Kayro-Vue Productions, 1964–66)
Dark Shadows (Dan Curtis Productions Inc., 1966–71)
Night Gallery (Universal TV, 1970–73)
The Night Stalker (ABC [US], 1972)
Frankenstein (ABC [US], 1973)
Kolchak the Night Stalker (Universal TV, 1974–75)
Twin Peaks (Lynch-Frost Productions, 1990–91)
Dark Shadows (Dan Curtis Productions Inc., 1991)
The X-Files (10:13, 1993–2002)
American Gothic (CBS, 1995–96)
Millennium (10:13, 1996–99)
Poltergeist: The Legacy (PMP Legacy Productions, 1996–99)
Profiler (NBC, 1996–2000)
Buffy the Vampire Slayer (20th Century Fox Television, 1997–2003)
Brimstone (Warner Bros. Television, 1998–99)
Angel (20th Century Fox Television, 1999–2004)
The Others (NBC, 2000)
Six Feet Under (HBO, 2001–)
Carnivàle (HBO, 2003–5)
Kingdom Hospital (ABC [US], 2004)
Point Pleasant (20th Century Fox Television, 2005)

However, while I examine a broad range of material in this book, it is not my intention to cover all of the programmes detailed above. Rather, the five case studies offered here are organised around sub-categories of Gothic television (as delineated at the end of this introduction), and thus I offer analyses of several interesting 'moments' in the history of Gothic television. Tzvetan Todorov describes this case study method, which he terms the 'scientific' method of genre study, in his insightful discussion of genre analysis and the fantastic:

> One of the first characteristics of scientific method is that it does not require us to observe every instance of a phenomenon in order to describe it; scientific method proceeds rather by deduction. We actually deal with a relatively limited number of cases, from them we deduce a general hypothesis by other cases, correcting (or rejecting) it as needs be. Whatever the number of phenomena (or literary works) studied, we are never justified in extrapolating universal laws from them; it is not the quantity of observations, but the logical coherence of a theory that finally matters. (1975: 4)

Todorov's delineation of this method thus allows us to proceed in utilising the case study to generate a tentative definition of the genre as it has developed on British and North American television, and to deduce a number of observations about its conventions and variations, building a 'logically coherent' theory of Gothic television throughout the course of this book.

Television and the uncanny

As stated above, any discussion of the Gothic as it appears on television must acknowledge the centrality of the uncanny as one of its defining concepts, though the flexibility of this term means that a definition of its particular meaning in this book needs to be outlined here. I take as my starting point Sigmund Freud's 1919 essay, 'The Uncanny' (1990), which brought to light the potential 'affectiveness' of uncanny fiction (the potential to disturb, to produce uncanny feeling), while simultaneously viewing uncanniness as a sensation experienced by his analysands. In the opening of this essay, Freud offers a lengthy discussion of the origins and definitions of the words 'heimlich' (literally familiar or homely) and 'unheimlich' (uncanny or, literally, 'un-homely') and concludes that the two terms are not mutually exclusive, but rather are inextricably linked: 'heimlich is a word the meaning of which develops in the direction of ambivalence, until it finally coincides with its opposite, unheimlich. Unheimlich is in some way or other a sub-species of heimlich' (Freud, 1990: 347). This linguistic genealogy, which illuminates the very closeness of the two terms, thus demonstrates that the uncanny cannot be found without the presence of the familiar.

Throughout his essay, Freud develops what Terry Castle has described as a 'theme-index' (1995: 4) of the uncanny,

> An obsessional inventory of eerie fantasies, motifs, and effects, an
> itemised tropology of the weird. Doubles, dancing dolls and automata,
> waxwork figures, alter egos and 'mirror' selves, spectral emanations,
> detached body parts ('a severed head, a hand out of the wrist, feet that
> dance by themselves'), the ghastly fantasy of being buried alive, omens,
> precognitions, déjà vu . . . What makes them uncanny is precisely the
> way they subvert the distinction between the real and the phantasmic.
> (Castle, 1995: 4–5)

In this categorisation of the Freudian uncanny, the blurred distinction
between the 'real and the phantasmic' as Castle sees it might also be
read as the dissolution of boundaries between the familiar and the
strange, or the everyday and the disturbing. Thus, the central proposition of Freud's essay is that '[t]he uncanny is that class of frightening
which leads back to what is known of old and long familiar' (1990: 340).
As Freud scrutinises the relation between the fictional and the real
within the literary text, he concludes that the uncanny can only be
achieved through a 'disruption' of an essentially realist text, rather than
a narrative more thoroughly couched in the realm of the fantastic or
marvellous.

This relationship between the imagined and the real, or the strange
and the familiar, highlighted by Freud in relation to the uncanny, is
significant in understanding the structures of feeling within Gothic television. This closeness accounts for Gothic television's simultaneous reference to its domestic reception context, in order to produce its lucid
sense of the uncanny. As will be argued in the following analyses of
Gothic television, we are constantly reminded that this is terror/horror
television which takes place, and is *viewed*, within a domestic milieu.
Other critics have also located the juxtapositioning of the familiar and
the strange within television's wider broadcast flow, contrasting the
uncanny with the more benign, everyday forms of television that surround the Gothic text (see Probyn, 1993). However, I will argue that the
familiar and the strange of uncanny fiction are also located within the
Gothic text on television, as well as in its relation to other forms of television. As I have argued elsewhere (Wheatley, 2002), in relation to the
Danish serial drama *Riget* (*The Kingdom*) (Danmarks Radio/Zentropa,
1994), the uncanny can be found in the very structure of Gothic television: it is located in its repetitions and returns, in an aesthetic which
combines traditionally realist, familiarising programme making and
non-naturalistic, disorienting filming and editing, in Gothic television's
familiar characters and plotting (the presence of doppelgangers, ghosts,
premonitions and flashbacks, and so on), and even in the generic
hybridity of the Gothic text.[3] The uncanny is therefore located in the

moments in Gothic television in which the familiar traditions and conventions of television are made strange, when television's predominant genres and styles are both referred to and inverted. This notion of the uncanny runs throughout my examination of Gothic television.

Of course, any study of television genre must acknowledge the problematic of generic hybridity, as suggested above. If *The Wyvern Mystery* is a Gothic drama, isn't it also a heritage or costume drama, a literary adaptation, perhaps even a romance? *Millennium*, on the other hand, might also be described as a serial drama, a cop show, a serial killer narrative, and even a piece of telefantasy. *The Addams Family* is as much a situation comedy as it is an example of Gothic television. As Graeme Turner has argued, '[i]t is pointless to insist on generic purity in relation to television programmes . . . Television genres are notoriously hybridised and becoming more so' (2001a: 6). This book does not, therefore, argue for the generic purity of Gothic television: rather, at various moments during the discussion of the following case studies, generic hybridity is brought to the foreground of the discussion in order to deepen our understanding of the characteristics and narrative preoccupations of Gothic television, particularly in relation to the notion of the uncanny.

Gothic cinema: critical approaches

While there is scant space in this introduction for an analysis of the wide-ranging critical literature on Gothic fiction in its literary forms, I wish to take a moment here to survey the field of Gothic cinema studies. Studies of the literary Gothic have suggested many of the directions established in Gothic film and television studies, from the development of Marxist and psychoanalytic approaches that explore the questions of what the Gothic genre might be 'working through' (and attendant questions of the genre's transgressive potential), to more recent debates surrounding the ways in which Gothic fictions address issues of identity and identification, with a renewed interest in readership and the potential uses and pleasures of the Gothic text. While the films considered within the field of Gothic cinema studies are diverse, the questions that unite this work relate to the notion of medium specificity, and the relationship between Gothic cinema and other forms of Gothic fiction (particularly Gothic literature). As with the study of Gothic literature, the study of Gothic film has also been led by the desire to reveal the 'underside' of more mainstream traditions of filmmaking, looking at Gothic film as antithetical to more 'respectable' cycles within a variety of national cinemas.

Stephen Farber's essay 'The New American Gothic' (1972) offered one of the first discussions of the cinematic Gothic, defining films such as *Lilith* (US, 1964), *Hush, Hush Sweet Charlotte* (US, 1964) and *Inside Daisy Clover* (US, 1965) as sharing 'arresting distortions in mood and cinematic technique' (1972: 95):

> All of these films deal, directly or indirectly, with horror, often with absolutes of Evil . . . This suggestion of demonic or nightmarish menace, often in the setting of lush, ominous decay . . . supplies a crucial thematic resonance in these gothic films . . . [which share] a very distinctive kind of baroque and self-conscious expressionism, relying on unusually over-ripe, even violent visual exaggerations and refractions. (1972: 95)

Farber's analysis thus highlights several visual elements as Gothic (such as black costumes and settings, 'weird' lighting and camera angles designed to unsettle the audience, exaggerated shadows, large, asymmetrical setting and shot composition, and so on), and asserts that the 'new American Gothic' in film is characterised by a certain tension between a glossy surface and a degraded interior. Farber's study thus offers an early example of the Gothic as a critically constructed genre, discussing films which were not readily marketed as 'Gothic' in the first instance.

Perhaps unsurprisingly, many of the other analyses of the Gothic in Hollywood cinema have focused on the adaptation of Gothic literary classics, most notably Mary Shelley's *Frankenstein* (1818) and Bram Stoker's *Dracula* (1897). For example, Roy Huss (1972) discusses the translation of Gothic theatre to Gothic cinema in the United States in the early part of the twentieth century. The question of medium specificity, or how to translate the gore of Gothic horror and the chilling suggestiveness of Gothic terror to the screen, has been a focal question for studies of Gothic cinema, and is also an issue raised in this study of Gothic television. For example, Huss criticises Todd Browning's version of *Dracula* (US, 1931) for being too theatrical and therefore 'un-cinematic', arguing that the film owes much to Balderston and Deane's 1927 New York stage adaptation of the novel: '[Browning] seems to regard the frame of his camera's viewfinder merely as a proscenium arch to be filled with performers and background décor' (1972: 51).[4] According to Huss, techniques of 'suggestion' need to be developed in order for the Gothic to be successful in the cinema; this sentiment thus reflects the attempts of the makers of early Gothic television to look for ways in which to translate the restraint of its literary and radiophonic heritage to television, using oblique techniques of shooting and editing to imply, rather than reveal, the presence of the supernatural (see chapter one).

The other major cycle of American Gothic cinema to receive critical attention is the Gothic woman's film of the 1940s. While there have been a number of studies dealing with this sub-genre (cf. Modleski, 1982b; Waldman, 1983; Gallafent, 1988; Walker, 1990; Hollinger, 1993; Fletcher, 1995; Hanson, 2000), Mary Ann Doane's *The Desire to Desire: The Woman's Film of the 1940s* (1987a) is perhaps the most sustained analysis. Doane's particular interest is in female spectatorship and her analysis configures the female moviegoer as an 'over-involved' viewer. Locating the Gothic in the cycle of paranoid woman's films of the 1940s (e.g. *Rebecca* (US, 1940), *The Spiral Staircase* (US, 1946)) she argues that these films utilise many of the visual and narrative tropes of the Gothic genre to instil a sense of unease in the spectator. Doane relates this cycle to women's Gothic 'pulp fiction', arguing that these films allow the female spectator to confront her fears and desires, and her paranoia, as they relate to her daily life (specifically, women's wartime experiences and the anxiety surrounding the return of husbands and fathers after the second world war). Subsequently, Doane depicts the home as an uncanny space and a site of great anxiety within the Gothic woman's film, prefiguring the focus on domesticity, and the close and meaningful relationships between viewer and text, in this exploration of Gothic television.[5]

More recently, there have been a number of horror film 'readers' which have, in part, taken up a discussion of Gothic cinema (Gelder, 2000a; Jancovich, 2002). Of particular interest is Brigid Cherry's work (2002), which deals with Gothic cinema as a group of texts with a very specific set of viewing practices for the female viewer. Cherry found that the pleasure of watching Gothic horror films for the women in her survey was very firmly identified with the pleasures of consuming the heritage text/costume drama:

> For many viewers, the appeal of vampirism seems to be tied into a romanticism of the past. The taste for Gothic horror is often linked to a liking for historical and costume dramas, with Hammer and other horror films providing a key source of images for this imagined past, which one 23-year-old respondent described as 'a stylish image of dark beauty . . . The classically Gothic full-length dresses and cloaks, the numerous high-ceilinged rooms full of dark wood and velvet curtains are now, without a doubt for me synonymous with grace and charm'. (Cherry, 2002: 172)

Cherry's research thus appears to confirm the notion that the Gothic drama is closely related to the heritage text, as proposed in the following exploration of Gothic television.

The Gothic tradition in national cinemas beyond Hollywood has also received scant critical attention, with a few notable exceptions. For example, German Expressionism has been seen as a key site of the Gothic in cinema (see Eisner, 1969; Coates, 1991). The critical analysis of the Gothic horror film as an important cycle within British cinema has also been sporadic and disjointed (compared, for example, to the more established bodies of scholarship on the social-realist tradition in British cinema, or the heritage film), meaning that the main focus of work on British Gothic cinema has been the 'rediscovery' of the key auteurs and studios producing this cycle. This work was inaugurated by David Pirie's book *A Heritage of Horror* (1973), which offers the reader an extended discussion of the Gothic output of the Hammer studio and some other notable examples of British horror cinema of the period 1946–72. Contrary to previous depictions of British cinema as the realm of kitchen-sink realism and anodyne costume dramas, Pirie offers a revisionist history of the *grand guignol* tradition in British cinema, rediscovering many of the 'auteurs' of British Gothic filmmaking (Fisher, Francis, Hamer, Cavalcanti, etc.). Despite Pirie's attempt to bring a widespread tradition of British filmmaking to light, it was another twenty years until Peter Hutchings (1993; 2002a; 2002b; 2003) took up Pirie's call for further research to be undertaken on the Gothic in British cinema. Hutchings furthered the study of this genre in the UK by situating his analyses more carefully in a social and industrial context, arguing that British Gothic cinema reflected era-specific concerns surrounding issues of masculinity, authority and the family (1993). Indeed, Hutchings would later argue that Pirie had somewhat misrepresented British Gothic cinema, characterising the cycle through an over-emphasis on the Hammer studios and ignoring the distinctiveness of the output of the Amicus studios, for example (2002b). Of particular interest to this study of Gothic television is Hutchings' analysis of the ways in which familial authority is reflected in British Gothic cinema. Informed by psychoanalytic theory, Hutchings argues that setting these films in the past allows for an exploration of the 'psychological effects of the family structure' (1993: 167), away from the familiarity of the more recognisable modern world. The argument might suggest that the following reading of Gothic television as a domestic form of a domestic genre taps into deeper psychological structures concerning the home and family. While this book is not informed by psychoanalysis as Hutchings' analysis of British Gothic cinema is, it does identify similar concerns about power and authority within the parameters of the domestic space. The other key addition to the field of British Gothic film studies has been Steve Chibnall and Julian Petley's collection on *British Horror Cinema* (2002a), which, they argue, builds on the work of Pirie and Hutchings by offering a number of key contextual analyses. They are 'concerned not simply with films as texts but with the institutions and discourses within which those texts are produced, circulated, regulated and consumed' (2002b: 3), and introduce new work on British horror cinema looking at key studios (e.g. Amicus), directors (e.g. Pete Walker and Clive Barker) and sub-genres of the Gothic cycle (the psycho-thriller, the occult horror film).

Gothic television: critical approaches

If the critical work on Gothic cinema is patchy, then research into the Gothic as it appears on television is virtually nonexistent. However, from 1980 onwards, some of the more general accounts of Gothic fictions have described a widespread diffusion of the mode into areas other than literature and film (see Botting, 1996; Edmundson, 1997; Grunenberg, 1997; Davenport-Hines, 1998), with television noted as an important new location for the Gothic in the twentieth century. Studies such as these have called for the kind of sustained analysis of Gothic television as that which is offered in this book. As with Gothic film studies, critical discussion of Gothic television is highly indecisive about the kinds of texts which may be considered under this generic umbrella term: programmes as diverse as chat shows, soap operas, serial drama, made-for-TV movies and the news have all been described as Gothic, or as having Gothic elements. The label 'Gothic', when applied to the television text, has been variously used to identify either those programmes which utilise a Gothic *narrative form*, featuring key figures and/or events associated with the genre (e.g. the victim-heroine and villainous anti-hero, or the presence of a disturbing secret from the past), or those which deploy a Gothic *style*, which exploit key elements of the Gothic image repertoire and which are characterised by a certain darkness or gloominess. As a way to limit its corpus, this study of Gothic television has concentrated on those television fictions which offer both of these identifying features; however, it is important to acknowledge that the Gothic might also be understood as a mode or style on television, as well as a coherent genre, and that traces of the Gothic can be found in a wide range of programming.

The first instance of a brief discussion of what I have subsequently understood as Gothic television is found in S.S. Prawer's book on the terror film (1980), a label that Prawer applies to those films which we might also understand as 'Gothic'. In this study, Prawer notes the importance of television within the 'terror' cycle, and suggests that the medium has 'evolved its own variations' (1980: 20) of this genre for the smaller screen:

Examples are legion; they range from ghost-stories based on the tales of M.R. James or specially written by Robert Muller and others to TV movies like Dan Curtis's *The Night Stalker* . . . The continuities between such works and the old B movies are not only thematic: they are made under similar restraints of money, location, and shooting time, though flexible and sophisticated technical equipment, specially adapted to the lower definition of the TV screen is apt to disguise this. (1980: 20)

Here Prawer points towards the anthologised ghost story (such as *Ghost Story for Christmas* (M.R. James adaptations) and *Mystery and Imagination* (featuring the writing of Robert Muller)) and the work of Gothic television 'auteur', Dan Curtis, as particularly prominent examples of 'terror television'. By drawing parallels between the production conditions of low budget cinema and television in the 1960s and 1970s, Prawer highlights the relationship between this genre and the development of new/innovative production technologies for television. He suggests that television as a medium is responsible for 'the rediscovery of avant-garde devices – violently clashing images, unusual angles of vision, frozen frames, shooting through gauze, negative prints, etc.' (1980: 21), drawing attention to the innovative techniques which were utilised to enable the visualisation of the supernatural within the anthology series of the 1960s. Prawer thus initiates a discussion of Gothic television that prefigures more recent analyses of the relationship between the genre and innovation in early cinema (see Castle, 1995; Mannoni, 2000; Gunning, 2001). Prawer also suggests that the viewing context of television is of central importance to the reception of terror on this medium, suggesting that the viewer's response will be '*significantly conditioned* by the domestic setting in which they – unlike cinema goers – watch such works' (1980: 20).[6] The notion that the domestic setting is instrumental in producing the medium-specific sensations of terror and uncanniness in the television viewer is also central to this analysis of Gothic television.

While Prawer's preliminary thoughts on terror on television would seem to call for a lengthier analysis, the following years did not produce such an enquiry. Rather, just as Gothic fictions on broadcast television declined in number during the 1980s, so scholarly interest in the genre failed to develop. What little discussion there was during this period was centred on the horror series/made-for-television horror film in the US as an inferior version of the theatrical horror film, and the medium's inability to produce a truly satisfying horror story. For example, in his overview of horror in the US, novelist Stephen King (1981) notes the impossibility of producing this genre on television (ironic, given the popularity of adaptations of King's work on US TV later in the 1980s and 1990s). King argues that the censorial restraints of commercial television meant that it was impossible to produce true horror on the medium, stating that the restrained, suggestive ghost story failed to compete with the real horrors shown on television news programmes:

> Horror has not fared particularly well on TV, if you except something like the 6 o'clock news, where footage of black GIs with their legs blown off, villages and kids on fire, bodies in trenches, and whole swatches of jungle being coated with good old Agent Orange . . . it is very difficult to write a successful horror story in a world which is so full of real horrors. A ghost in the turret room of a Scottish castle just cannot compete. (1981: 212–13)

According to King then, fictional horror on television stands a poor second to the *real* horrors on television and, in particular, the broadcasting of the Vietnam War.

Like Stephen King, Gregory A. Waller, in his study of the American horror film (1987a), argues that television cannot succeed in producing horror. However, unlike King, Waller's argument centres on the medium's inferiority to film rather than its inability to surpass the real horrors presented on television: 'on most television sets, shadows and darkness become murky, textureless areas that lack the ominous blackness so often favoured by horror film directors' (1987b: 159). While the historical specificity of Waller's analysis ought to be acknowledged, given that he is writing in an era before the full impact of television's future digital technologies had been realised, he directly counters Prawer's suggestion that the aesthetic limitations of television's production and broadcast technologies prompted exciting and innovative experimentation in the field of the horror film made for television, seeing television versions of the genre merely as poor cousins of their cinematic counterparts.

Waller also suggests that as a domestic medium, television is too cosy and reassuring to successfully present affective horror drama, and that television's broadcast flow of advertising, news and so on negates the horror being shown in the tele-film:

> Having been to hell and back the viewer can also proceed with life as usual, staying tuned for the 11 o'clock news . . . Even more than the happy reconciliatory, restorative endings of virtually all the tele-films . . . the commercial breaks in made for television movies serve to dissipate – to deny – horror by predicting the future and insisting that the problems are solvable, and happiness, safety, health, security, and pleasure are attainable. (1987b: 159)

To some extent Waller counters his own argument by noting that a certain frisson is created by the domestic subject matter of the made-for-television horror film: '[these tele-films are] focused on the personal and the intimate, and are particularly given to narratives that feature an isolated victim . . . endangered young wife, or threatened middle-class family' (1987b: 145). He goes on to state that 'horror comes from outside the house and the family, infiltrating normality just as effortlessly and invisibly as the television programmes that appear in our living rooms' (1987b: 159). Therefore, Waller contradicts his own argument, proposing that, on the one hand, television is incapable of producing the desired 'affect' of the horror narrative, but, on the other, made-for-television horror emphasises a potential threat towards the very space in which it is being viewed. Furthermore, the repetitive nature of the broadcast text, and the fact that the tele-films which Waller discusses are likely to be shown within a season of such material, suggest that the restorative sense of closure which he isolates might, in fact, be a lot less final than he proposes. When each new week brings a new home-based horror, a sense of comfort or closure could be potentially hard to find.

As well as exploring Gothic (or terror/horror) fictions on television, a number of critics have understood various non-fictional forms of programming on television as deploying the Gothic as a mode or style. Elspeth Probyn (1993) and Mark Edmundson (1997) both briefly discuss the popular US chat show, *The Oprah Winfrey Show* (Harpo Productions, 1986–) as Gothic, for example. Probyn, writing about women's television viewing and the fear of crime, discusses the juxtapositioning of Oprah's probing into – and reconstructions of – rape, family crisis and/or violence against women with more benign, everyday moments of daytime programming within television's broadcast flow. Contra to Waller's argument that advertising potentially dispels a sensation of fear or unease which may be associated with viewing the Gothic on television, Probyn suggests that this juxtaposition creates a feeling of uncanniness and makes the domestic viewing space 'unheimlich' in Freud's terms:

> One of the most horrifying potential situations for women, rape, is articulated with mundane images of women and home – mad housewives in the supermarket, competition over hair colour, lovely young women conjuring up strange hunks to share their diet drinks – making the home unheimlich (uncanny). (1993: 271)

Mark Edmundson on the other hand states that *Oprah* (as well as the television news coverage of the OJ Simpson case, the Michael Jackson child abuse case and others) has been suffused with Gothic discourse (conventions, characters, plots) and focuses on the character conventions of the victim and villain:

On to Oprah's stage troop numberless unfortunates, victims and villains. The victims have been pursued, harassed, mistreated. They are sublimely innocent (as any reader of Gothic novels knows they have to be). The villains present a more interesting case. At first they come across as evil incarnate, or simply as monstrous creatures who have gone beyond evil and good. But eventually we learn that they themselves have been victims. They too are haunted by some past abuse, so that their bad behaviour takes on an air of inevitability. (1997: xiv)

According to Edmundson then, the Gothic on television is a melodramatic mode which may be appropriated in non-fictional programming in order to characterise certain figures: to demonise the bad guy and to valorise the victim.

This use of Gothic characterisation is also noted by Nicola Nixon in her essay 'Making Monsters, or Serializing Killers' (1998). While Nixon does not exclusively discuss television news and documentary (she also examines autobiographical 'true-crime' literature and transcriptions of court proceedings), she does suggest that the rather boring, everyman-type of serial killer is made more exciting, charismatic or terrifying by a semi-fictionalising or Gothicising process on television. Nixon states that in order to turn the serial killer into the mythical folk-devil figure it has become in the latter part of the twentieth century, Gothic discourse has been applied to these figures, turning them into anti-heroes and locating in them 'the possibility of horror and madness beneath . . . beauty, charm or charisma . . . the potential for an uncanny, supernatural or monstrous transcendence of the ordinary' (1998: 224).

As more broad discussions of Gothic culture began to circulate, some of these studies also turned their attention to television, albeit briefly. Fred Botting (1996) offers a history of Gothic literature and cinema, and a discussion of the central paradigms of Gothic studies, giving a general account of the ways in which the Gothic has shifted or 'diffused' across media. He sees the appearance of Gothic television as a product of postmodernity, citing both the parodic Gothic on television (particularly *The Addams Family* and *The Munsters*), and *Twin Peaks*, as examples of the complex, postmodern Gothic text. Also focusing on the cultural diffusion of the Gothic in late twentieth century culture, Christoph Grunenberg (1997) looks at an eclectic mix of texts/media in which the Gothic has become significantly present. These diverse media include visual/installation art, literature, film, computer games, the internet, music, fashion, style, advertising, 'real life', video art, photography and television, focusing particularly on Chris Carter's *The X-Files* and *Millennium* as 'mod-Gothic melodramas' (1997: 210).

In another recent eclectic cultural study of the Gothic, Richard Davenport-Hines (1998) has attempted to write a biography of the Gothic, tracing its progress through visual art, landscape gardening and architecture, literature, film and ultimately television. Davenport-Hines' brief discussion of television primarily centres on the soap opera as a Gothic genre. He reads the North American soap operas *Melrose Place* (Darren Star Productions, 1992–99) and *Sunset Beach* (Aaron Spelling Productions Inc., 1997–99) as Gothic, arguing that they offer 'no homeliness or reconciliation, only serial disruption' (1998: 10), and noting the presence of Gothic character types and narrative conventions within these soap operas: '*Sunset Beach* even had a long-running storyline about a villainous "top" trapping a victimised "bottom" in traditional Gothic subterranean confinement, and another about a generous millionaire called Ben haunted by an evil doppelgänger named Derek' (1998: 10). Davenport-Hines goes on to argue that the British soap opera *Coronation Street* (Granada, 1960–) might also be characterised as Gothic, given that its storylines frequently feature 'confused paternities, improbable coincidences, melodrama, sudden death, cheap ideas, [and] trivially stereotyped characters' (1998: 143). Ultimately, he argues that 'television – more than films, CD-ROM games or *Warhammer* role-playing – has been the most important medium of Gothic infiltration' (1998: 376), though his analysis of this phenomenon remains necessarily brief within the confines of his much broader study.

A more satisfying, if brief, account of Gothic television is offered by Lenora Ledwon (1993) in relation to the North American series, *Twin Peaks*, which Ledwon sees as the first series to 'tap the full potential' of this particular genre on the domestic medium: 'television would seem to be the ideal medium for Gothic inquiry. It is, after all, a mysterious box simultaneously inhabited by spirit images of ourselves and inhabiting our living rooms' (1993: 260). While Ledwon's work will be discussed at greater length in the final chapter of this book, it is important to note here that her argument supports the central proposition of this book: that television, even more than film, is inherently suited to the Gothic. Indeed, I would concur with Ledwon's suggestion that television's full potential as a medium of Gothic fiction is achieved in that most televisual of forms, the long-form serial drama: 'Film does not have the same Gothic potential as television precisely because of the finite time period for a film. A film must end, while a television series has a seemingly infinite potential to continue telling the story and to continue multiplying messages' (Ledwon, 1993: 267).

There is certainly a sense of timeliness to this study of Gothic television, in relation to a broadening academic interest in the study of generic, and non-naturalistic, television drama. One need only look towards the wealth of critical literature being currently produced on the teen-horror crossovers, *Buffy the Vampire Slayer* and *Angel* (e.g. Kaveney, 2001; Wilcox and Lavery, 2002; Parks and Levine, 2002; Jowett, 2005; Abbott, 2005), or recent monographs and collections on other instances of 'telefantasy' (e.g. Harrison, Pojansky, Ono and Helford, 1996; Lavery, Hague and Cartwright, 1996; Chapman, 2002; Bignell and O'Day, 2004; Johnson, 2005), or indeed the 'Generic Television Drama' strand of the Arts and Humanities Research Board-funded research project, 'Cultures of British Television Drama, 1960–82',7 to chart the increase in critical interest in what might be described as the 'underside' of television drama. Describing a similar shift in interest in British cinema outside of the realist paradigm, Julian Petley termed this work a redis-covery of a 'lost continent' (1986), arguing that,

> these films form another, repressed side of British cinema, a dark, dis-dained thread weaving the length and breadth of that cinema, crossing authorial and generic boundaries, sometimes almost entirely invisible, sometimes erupting explosively, always received critically with fear and disapproval. Like repressed libidinal forces these films form a current running underground, surfacing only intermittently. (1986: 98–9)

Petley's eloquent metaphor, of the underground stream erupting spec-tacularly at various points along its route, might equally be applied to the history of Gothic television in Britain. These programmes both 'erupt' into the flow of broadcast television at sporadic intervals, challenging perceptions of the type of drama suitable for television broadcast, and are also beginning to 'surface' within the academy at a moment in which the dominant historical narrative of television drama as a predom-inantly realist form is being challenged.

The model viewer: reading the text

As suggested above, one of the definitive aspects of Gothic television is its awareness of the domestic space as a site loaded with Gothic possi-bilities. It is television's ontological status as a domestic medium which potentially emphasises this Gothic rendering of homes and families, drawing parallels between the domestic spaces on screen and those homes in which the dramas are being viewed. As Lynn Spigel has argued in her analysis of television and domestic space in the US in the 1950s (1992a), the 'television as a mirror of family life' argument is an over-simplification of the ways in which representations of domestic space on television highlight certain aspects of the familial and domestic experience at any particular moment. For example, for Spigel, in the context of situation comedies of the 1950s, television reflects back the theatricality of middle-class suburban living in the United States (1992a; 1992b). In Gothic television, on the other hand, television fiction emphasises the anxieties and paranoia of family life. Throughout this book I explore the possibilities of locating an image of both the reception context of television and the identity and concerns of the television viewer, by analysing the television text itself. Therefore, I construct what Umberto Eco might call a 'model viewer' by reading the Gothic television drama's modes of address and by scrutinising its semantic and syntactic elements. The term 'model viewer' is adapted from Eco's work on the 'model reader' (1979; 1994) and his proposition that 'in a story there is always a reader, and this reader is a fundamental ingredient not only of the process of storytelling but also of the tale itself' (1994: 1). In the context of television, this would suggest that both the viewer and the context of viewing (the home) are fundamental ingredients within the programmes in hand, and are therefore present and locatable within the television text. This argument is absolutely central to my study of Gothic television, in that it proposes a method for looking at the ways in which television drama reflects upon its reception, recording the viewer and the act of viewing into the programmes at hand. It is subsequently hoped that this analysis of the textual inscription of viewing might be more broadly applicable to a wider understanding of the textual processes of television fiction. As Graeme Turner argues,

> for those who study television, genre is a means of managing television's notorious extensiveness as a cultural form by breaking it into more discrete and comprehensible segments . . . Researchers have found that to understand the characteristics, conventions and pleasures of a particular television genre is also to understand a great deal about television as a cultural form. (2001b: 5)

This analysis of Gothic television might therefore enable us to think about the ways in which television fiction is distinct from the dramatic output of other media and, more specifically, to think about the ways in which television drama and comedy reflect upon the status of the medium itself.

These observations raise questions of methodology, in that the method of analysing television's relationship with the domestic viewer proposed here runs contra to television studies' long-standing interest in engaging empirically with 'real', rather than imagined, viewers. From the very earliest attempts to make sense of the phenomenon of television, right up to current debates about the nature of the medium in a technologically transitional moment in its history, the home has been a contested and divergently depicted site within television studies. Characteristically, given television studies' position as the hybrid product of a number of disciplines (see Brunsdon (1998) for a discussion of this hybridity), the questions asked of and about domestic space in relation to the study of television are manifold and diverse. Whereas the concerns of this book lie largely in the description and analysis of how the domestic is acknowledged by or reflected in the television text (and how those producing Gothic television define the relationship between the domestic viewer and their programmes), other scholars of television have sought to examine the relationship between television and domestic space in different ways. For example, Lynn Spigel (1992a; 2001) and others have examined television's central location, the home, through an analysis of intertextual discourses of domesticity, primarily located within contemporary journalism, lifestyle magazines and advertising, which construct an image of what television is, or might be, within the broader context of 'lifestyle' discourses.

Looking at the domestic from an empirical perspective, television scholarship coming out of cultural studies has also utilised ethnographic research methods to ask questions about the ways in which television interacts with the home, and, in turn, the ways in which the domestic viewer interacts with television (e.g. Morley, 1986; Gray, 1992; Gauntlett and Hill, 1999; Tufte, 2000; Wood, 2001). Furthermore, Thomas Tufte's work on Brazilian television viewing (2000) challenges the conception of television as a wholly domestic medium by noting the hybrid position of television as both public and domestic in Brazil. Similarly, Anna McCarthy's recent study of forms of 'ambient' television in the US (2001) takes this point one step further by researching television's public manifestations outside of the home. However, this study of Gothic television asks whether it is equally valid to make assumptions about who might be watching a piece of television (and indeed, where and how that act of viewing might be taking place) by looking to television itself, and by seeking out textual evidence, supported by production research, of the ways in which television is inherently preoccupied by its domestic viewers and an assumed image of 'home'.

Gothic Television therefore seeks to re-engage with television's textuality, looking at, for example, the ways in which Gothic television's heavy emphasis on the translation of character subjectivity implies a sense of connection, a simultaneity, between protagonist and viewer. As will be argued throughout this study, Gothic television is a particularly striking example of a genre of television programming which asks *to be looked at,* which demands concentrated attention from viewers (both domestic and scholarly), through its emotional intensity, its complex plotting, and its highly dense and detailed mise-en-scène. Alongside other recent studies of television (e.g. Caldwell, 1995; Jacobs, 2003; Creeber, 2004; Lury, 2005), this study of Gothic television refutes previous claims that television is a medium which defies intense analysis, and which is subject to a distracted glance, rather than a more concentrated gaze, from its viewers (see Ellis, 1982). As Jason Jacobs recently argued (2005), one of the central purposes of television studies needs to be the close and sustained critical analyses of television texts, dwelling on illuminating moments in the history of television programming. While Jacobs also proposed a project of value judgement in television analysis which this study of Gothic television pointedly does not take up as one of its central aims, his insistence on the legitimacy of close textual analysis within television scholarship is significant in relation to the methodological design of this study. To quote, at length, Glen Creeber's defence of this method:

> While some critics may dismiss such 'readings' as entirely subjective, . . . they are not meant to be understood as concrete factual suppositions. I do not pretend for one moment that I have discovered the final 'meaning' or 'truth' behind the programmes and debates I address. Instead, what this book aims to do is simply add to an ongoing *dialogue* around television drama, one that puts certain hypotheses up for debate and discussion without ever attempting to insist that any one of these readings is more valid or justifiable than any other that may (or may not) be in circulation. (2004: 17)[8]

Rather than conducting detailed interviews with the producers of the programmes at hand as other studies of television production have done (see Gitlin, 1994; Born, 2004), the production research in this analysis of Gothic television has been mainly reliant on the holdings of a number of written archives: the BBC Written Archive, the British Film Institute library and the now sadly disbanded Independent Television Commission library. By conducting extensive research at these sites, looking at material such as production files, drama policy documents, industry-based audience research (both quantitative[9] and qualitative[10]), publicity and marketing material, press cuttings and listings guides, and other tie-in material, I have attempted to reconstruct a picture of the attitudes to the genre held by industry professionals and others associated with the industry, such as television reviewers and journalists, and the discourses that surrounded their production and broadcast. This research has allowed me to contemplate the pleasures and attractions offered by Gothic television as understood by those producing the programmes in question, and has drawn my attention to the issues surrounding the problems and the potential impropriety of presenting the genre on television as faced by the producers of Gothic television. Furthermore, this production research has enabled me to interrogate the ways in which those producing the dramas in question acknowledge or implicate certain forms of viewing and reception within the discourses surrounding the television text. This follows an argument proposed by Charlotte Brunsdon in her analysis of the British soap opera, *Crossroads* (ATV, 1964–88): that programme publicity, scheduling and advertising all imply a certain kind of expected audience for television programming (in the case of *Crossroads*, the female viewer (Brunsdon, 1981)). Looking at the written documents which accompany and, in some cases, survive the Gothic television dramas under scrutiny here, I was also struck by the fact that Gothic television also offers insight into the changing modes of production within television drama at various pivotal moments in the history of UK and US television.[11] It is therefore hoped that the production research in this study will illuminate the ways in which notions of genre are formulated within the television industries under examination.

The chapters of this book are organised into a series of nationally and historically specific case studies, in order to explore the issues raised and definitions offered in this introduction. These case studies have been chosen for the set of interrelated, but different, questions they pose about the nature of the Gothic on British and North American television; these instances both highlight a set of specific discourses circulating within the Gothic genre on television, and focus our attention on industrial change and developments in television production in a number of significant instances, seeing the Gothic as a genre which pushed the possibilities and limitations of television production. As Cathy Johnson has argued in her study of telefantasy:

> while it is problematic to generalise too freely from a small number of case studies, the case study approach enables a combination of the synchronic and the diachronic, and a recognition of detail and the complexity of the historical moment . . . As such, case studies offer a useful counter to the totalising tendencies of grand theory, and open up history and theory to new questions and new lines of enquiry. (2005: 16)

Chapters one and two focus on two divergent strands of Gothic television that developed in the UK during the 1960s and 1970s, charting the emergence of the restrained, suggestive ghost story in chapter one (e.g. 'Whistle and I'll Come to You', *Mystery and Imagination, Ghost Story for Christmas*), and the effects-laden, supernatural horror tale in chapter two (e.g. *Mystery and Imagination* again, *Late Night Horror, Hammer House of*

Horror). I relate these two separate, but interrelated, Gothic traditions to a series of representational heritages in Britain – the literary, radiophonic, theatrical and cinematic Gothic traditions – thus arguing for the development of a number of *Gothics* on British television, rather than a single definitive version of the genre. Chapter one also offers an exploration of the genre's early history on British television, discussing the particular problems that the Gothic raised for the BBC as a public service broadcaster in the 1950s, with institutional anxieties about 'good taste and decency' attached to the broadcasting of horror/terror on television in the post-war years. Out of this hesitation, I argue, came the desire to 'show less and suggest more' in the anthologised ghost story, and the development of a 'gentlemanly', 'restrained' aesthetic for early Gothic television. This chapter also considers the Gothic adaptation as a subgenre of the heritage drama, exploring the notion that Gothic television offers something akin to a 'feel bad' heritage text.

Chapter two, on the other hand, outlines the emergence of what David Pirie has defined as 'an equally respectable Gothic line . . . which precisely depends upon the clear visual portrayal of every stage of action' (1973: 41), charting the spectacular representation of the grotesque and the horrific in the British Gothic anthology series. The analysis offered in this chapter is particularly concerned with the ways in which the Gothic genre on television enabled the showcasing of production innovations, with programme makers offering creative, and often visually spectacular, responses to the challenge of representing the supernatural on this medium, pushing the possibilities of television drama production. This analysis also highlights the particularly productive relationship between British Gothic television and both theatrical melodrama and popular British horror cinema in the 1960s and 1970s, noting a kind of aesthetic 'borrowing' rife in the anthology series at hand. In the latter part of this chapter, an exploration of the turn towards a more mimetic or domestic brand of Gothic horror in the late 1970s and early 1980s is offered, in relation to a detailed discussion of the anthology series, *Hammer House of Horror*. Thus, this chapter closes by reintroducing one of the central concerns of this book: that Gothic television is deeply concerned with 'home' and 'family' as sites of 'trouble' or anxiety.

Picking up the discussion of the Gothic as heritage text offered in chapter one, chapter three focuses on the adaptation of what has been termed 'female Gothic' or 'women's Gothic' novels, and, specifically, the big-budget, internationally co-produced, 'Sunday night' costume drama's own brand of Gothicism. This chapter looks in more detail at the ways in which a (gendered) spectator is 'recorded into' adaptations of female Gothic classics, such as *Rebecca*, *The Woman in White* and *The Wyvern*

Mystery: it does this by drawing out the connections between text and viewer in Gothic television, analysing the representation of domestic space in these adaptations, and paying particular attention to the ways in which structures of identification between heroine and viewer are laid in place by an emphasis on subjective audio-visual perspective. This perspective, I argue, allows for potentially affective points of recognition for the domestic, female viewer, as she recognises the terror and anxiety of familial trauma and domestic entrapment as experienced by a central heroine. I also spend some time discussing the generic hybridity of these programmes and understand these adaptations as heritage texts which deny the more usual pleasures of the television costume drama, offering a degraded version of the past which negates idealised representations of home and family more usual in heritage drama.

The final chapters of this book offer discussion of Gothic television in the US context, exploring the notion that home and family are perhaps even more central to the American Gothic narrative. Chapter four centres on a discussion of two hybrid forms of Gothic drama in the 1960s, firstly the Gothic family sitcoms *The Munsters* and *The Addams Family*, and latterly the Gothic soap opera *Dark Shadows*. Focusing on the representation of the home and extended family in these programmes, this chapter offers an analysis of the ways in which these texts expose prevalent anxieties in the 1960s around the instability of the familial unit and normative gender identities. As comedy, the Gothic sitcom offers a particularly interesting example of the ways in which the Gothic genre has been mobilised to 'work through' (Ellis, 2000) or 'worry at' (Wheatley, 2005) domestic life within a specific socio-historical moment (the mid-1960s in this case), within the context of a television genre (the sitcom) already understood as providing the *ideological flexibility* (Feuer, 2001) to explore social issues and problems. On the other hand, my analysis of *Dark Shadows* draws on the work on soap opera which reads this genre as a space for viewer identification and fantasy (see Ang, 1997, for example) on a personal or emotional level, and again I argue that subjective filming techniques create the textual potential for viewers to relate to the perils and domestic anxieties of Gothic television in an affective way.

To close this book, chapter five looks at some more recent examples of Gothic television in the United States, starting with a discussion of the long-form serial drama, *Twin Peaks*, as the initiator of a trend for dark, uncanny drama on North American television. The uncanny is particularly evoked in this chapter in relation to the repetitive structures and returns of the serial drama form. In this concluding chapter I synthesise the themes and concerns of this book, firstly by returning to the question of how the Gothic genre enabled the exhibition of innovations in television production in the US in the 1990s (in shows such as *American Gothic* and *Millennium*), drawing on the work of US television scholar John Thornton Caldwell and his notion of 'televisuality' (1995), and secondly by analysing the connection between domestic text and viewing context in the new American Gothic. This chapter is concluded by returning to images of home and family in these latter two serials, and the observation that the threatened domestic space and traumatised family are, in turn, central to a national Gothic narrative in the United States, pivotal in the specific identity of Gothic television, and implicated within anxieties surrounding the propriety of broadcasting the morbidity and horror of the Gothic into the homes of its viewers. Throughout this book then, I track the appearance of the most domestic of genres on the most domestic of media, examining the ways in which the two houses of Gothic television come together.

Notes

1 My emphasis.
2 Please note that throughout the book all transmission dates supplied pertain to the original transmission of the programmes in their country of origin, unless otherwise stated. Company credits within the text refer to either the station that broadcast the programme or one of the lead production companies. Fuller references are given in the teleography at the end of the book.
3 In the case of *Riget (The Kingdom)*, this generic hybridity is found in the blending of the hospital drama and Gothic horror, as also noted recently by Jason Jacobs (2003: 67) and Glen creeber (2004: 59).
4 This criticism resonates with the critical denigration of early television drama (as discussed in the following chapter).
5 A more thorough discussion of this branch of Gothic film studies is offered in chapter three of this book, in relation to the female Gothic adaptation for television.
6 My emphasis.
7 Recently conducted at the University of Reading, 2002–5.
8 As I completed this study of Gothic television, Karen Lury's book, *Interpreting Television*, was published (2005). Lury's detailed and painstaking description of television textuality offers scholars of television the critical tools to carry out medium-specific textual analysis, and will be an invaluable resource for those undertaking a text-based study of television, such as the one offered in this book, in the future.
9 For example, Audley, Gapper and Brown (AGB) Programme Ratings now held at the BFI Library.
10 For example, BBC Audience Research Reports held at the BBC Written Archive, Caversham.
11 See the discussion of *Late Night Horror* in chapter two, for example.

Showing less, suggesting more: the ghost story on British television

'A basic policy of ultimate good taste': the television ghost story

One of the key challenges in the presentation of the Gothic on television has to be the representation of the unrepresentable. Whether that be an invisible ghost passing through a room, manifesting as a change of temperature or a barely perceptible shadow in the corner of one's eye, or an indescribable feeling that something is 'not quite right' about a particular place or character, the makers of Gothic television have to find some way of transcribing these senses or feelings on to the screen without 'giving the game away'. As discussed in the introduction of this book, it is the feeling that television is too literal a medium, too obvious, too blatantly *visual*, which has challenged programme makers and troubled reviewers: how can one translate the kind of supernatural ghost stories produced by M.R. James or Joseph Sheridan Le Fanu for example, on to the small screen, while retaining their sense of the unknown? It was precisely this brand of the Gothic narrative (the restrained, atmosphere-led ghost story), which initiated Gothic drama on British television, and which saw the BBC, and later the commercial companies, struggle to maintain a sense of propriety and decency while offering their audiences the spine-chillingly supernatural as entertainment.

The history of television drama in Britain has been told as a decline in the single teleplay, as a progressive, culturally valued, but time and budget consuming television genre (see Gardner and Wyver (1983), in particular), and as the ascension of the serial drama, a denigrated form which nonetheless has been characterised as responding to the unique ontological status of television (see Creeber (2001b; 2004) for a clear delineation of this argument). However, sitting somewhere between these two poles is the generic anthology drama, single-teleplays grouped under a particular generic heading which were popular with

both audiences and producers in the formative years of British television. In the 1960s and 1970s in particular, the anthology format on
British television acted as a kind of 'halfway house' between the
respectable but expensive single play and the popular but predictable
serial drama. Writing about this format in his history of ITV programming, Jeremy Potter acknowledges:

> For drama departments anthologies of this kind had several advan-
> tages . . . [They] were likely to have wider audience appeal because the
> viewer could feel confidence in 'what the play was about' . . . IBA
> research in 1975 confirmed that plays presented within anthologies
> gained not only larger audiences but also greater appreciation than single
> plays on their own. For producers there was the advantage of being able
> to commission scripts from a circle of predictably professional contribu-
> tors able to embroider and develop a given theme with originality. To
> schedulers came the convenience of a block of programmes of similar
> length and similar audience appeal. (1990: 222)

Thus genres as diverse as the romance, the detective story and the heritage drama were broadcast under anthology series 'umbrella' titles,
responding to a need to produce economically viable television drama
which would attract the same core audience week after week (see
Wheatley (2004) for further discussion of this phenomenon). Such a
response was seen in the development of the Gothic anthology series in
the 1960s and 1970s, which fulfilled a dual remit for popular, entertaining television which would, it was hoped, attract a large and dedicated
audience, and for respectable, culturally valued television drama, often
adapted from the Gothic 'classics' (M.R. James, J.S. Le Fanu, Mary
Shelley, Bram Stoker, etc.) which would appeal to television's regulators
as well as its viewers. The opening chapters of this book therefore
chart the changes and developments in this particular generic anthology
format, from early experimentation in the 1940s and 1950s, to a relative
proliferation in the following two decades, when a plethora of
Gothic dramas were produced under such umbrella titles as *Tales of
Mystery* (A-R, 1961–63), *Mystery and Imagination* (ABC [UK]/Thames,
1966–70), *Late Night Horror* (BBC2, 1968) and *Ghost Story for Christmas*
(BBC1, 1971–78), to the generic anthology's disappearance in the 1980s
and its brief revival in the 1990s. In addition to this, these chapters will
also look at examples of key single plays which had an impact on the genre
(such as Jonathan Miller's play for the *Omnibus* series, 'Whistle and I'll
Come to You' (BBC1, 1968)), as well as comedic Gothic series which
demonstrate a clear debt to, or rather affection for, the Gothic anthology
series of the 1960s and 1970s, as in *The League of Gentlemen* (BBC2,
1999–2002) and *Garth Merenghi's Darkplace* (Channel 4, 2004).

In addition to providing an early history of the Gothic on British television, the first two chapters in this book also offer an insight into the
different ways that these anthology programmes approached the
difficulties of presenting Gothic or supernatural fiction on television.
These programmes demonstrated a clear consciousness of their domestic reception context, not merely in their repeated return to the home as
dramatic location; we can also see a clear address to a domestic viewer
through close analysis of the programmes in hand and through discussion of their intertexts (particularly the discourses surrounding key programmes in UK listings guides such as the *Radio Times* and *TV Times*).
The ways in which anthology series of the 1960s and 1970s negotiated
the possibilities and limitations of television production and reception in
creating satisfactorily 'affective' Gothic dramas are addressed in detail in
the following chapters, which chart the shift between two distinct modes
of Gothic representation: the suggestive, restrained ambiguity of the television ghost story, presenting mere hints and traces of the supernatural,
and, in chapter two, the excessive, spectacular, effects-laden supernatural
Gothic drama. Perhaps what these two distinct modes offered their
viewers was a distinction between terror and horror on television.

The evolution of these two modes of Gothic television is comparable
with the development of the genre in British cinema. Discussing the
broader tradition of British Gothic fiction, David Pirie characterises this
distinction in the following terms:

> In certain kinds of horror – especially the Victorian ghost story . . . to
> reveal your hand is to destroy a carefully wrought effect . . . But there
> is another equally respectable Gothic line . . . including M.G. Lewis,
> Mary Shelley, Bram Stoker and all Grand Guignol theatre which pre-
> cisely depends upon the clear visual portrayal of every stage of action.
> (1973: 41)

In the context of British Gothic cinema, we might see these two oppos-
ing poles of Gothic fiction as represented by, on the one hand, Jack
Clayton's *The Innocents* (UK, 1961) or most of Jacques Tourneur's *Night
of the Demon* (UK, 1957) (without the revelation of the 'demon' at the end
of the film, added at the insistence of the film's producers), and, on the
other hand, the prolific horror output of the Hammer and Amicus
studios.[1] In the following chapters, the multiple heritages of British
Gothic television will be addressed, challenging the theoretical assumption, for example, that a discussion of adapted television drama must
look back to its original literary source only. It will be argued that the
Gothic anthology dramas of the 1960s and 1970s borrowed from a
range of literary, radiophonic, theatrical and cinematic styles, a fact

which also contests the misguided assumption of earlier studies that nascent television drama was singularly theatrical in origin. Jason Jacobs, in his extensive analysis of the early development of British television drama, has successfully redressed the notion that all early television drama was simply 'static, boring, theatrical' (2000: 3), arguing that

> [t]he development of television drama is not a story of the steady emancipation from theatrical values toward the cinematic, but one where producers were able to choose from a range of stylistic features, some of them associated with theatre, some with film styles, and some with the narrative forms of literature. (2000: 117)

It is this notion of choice, this sense of 'textual borrowing' from a range of other media, which is integral to an understanding of the ways in which the Gothic drama developed on British television in the 1960s and 1970s.

In his recent overview of British television drama, Lez Cooke notes an increase in the production of 'horror plays' towards the end of the 1940s and the beginning of the 1950s, fuelled in part by the wish to explore the possibilities of the relatively new medium and the 'desire to develop a new aesthetic' (2003: 16). Drawing on Jason Jacobs' analysis of early British television drama (2000), Cooke argues that the adaptation of classic ghost stories 'encouraged producers and writers to experiment with the form of television drama in a way that the restaging of classics from literature and theatre generally did not' (2003: 16). Indeed, referring to memos held in the BBC Written Archives, Jacobs locates this shift in genre within the broader context of drama policy at the BBC, quoting a memo from Robert MacDermot written in February 1948 in which the Head of Television Drama suggests the adapted ghost stories (of M.R. James, E.F. Benson and Algernon Blackwood) as suitable and economically sensible material for an anthology series:

> As far as I know this hasn't been done before, either in sound or television, and would make a good contrast to our dramatic output of drama, comedy and straightforward mystery thrillers. I believe that television could create a very effective eerie atmosphere in this way and suggest that, if you agree, the plays are placed at the end of the evening transmission only and are advertised as being unsuitable for children. (Jacobs 2000: 97)

Jacobs' analysis therefore offers an insight into the BBC executives' sense of trepidation in broadcasting the genre (relegating 'horror plays' to late in the evening's schedule and demarcating them as 'unsuitable for children'). Jacobs traces this sense of anxiety to a memo sent the following year by Norman Collins (Controller of Television) to Cecil McGivern (then Deputy Head of Television) in which the problem of broadcasting horror in the home is explicitly addressed:

> It would be footling to say that we should never do any horror plays in television, but I think that, on the other hand, we have got to be careful not to overdo the terror and to recognise that what is seen on the screen in a person's home makes a very different impact from the impact made in cinema when a stridently advertised horror film is shown . . . we must remember that there will always be large numbers of unsuspecting persons who, as in Sound radio, simply turn to their set during trans-mission to see what is on. (Jacobs, 2000: 98)

These fears, that the BBC's viewer might be 'at risk' from and upset by inadvertently stumbling across horror and the supernatural during the course of an evening's viewing, would prove, to a certain extent, to have some foundation in less than a year's time.

During the fourth year of post-war production, in March 1950, the issue of broadcasting Gothic teleplays again became a contentious one for the BBC. While the long-running Gothic anthology drama was not yet in production, single plays such as those produced by Douglas Allen under the title of *The Edgar Allen Poe Centenary* in October 1949,[2] had begun to cause concern. Prompted by an unprecedented number of complaints about the unsuitable nature of television drama at the end of 1949,[3] an exchange of memos between key figures at BBC television took place in which the problems of broadcasting Gothic horror on tele-vision were debated. This debate was initiated by D. Singer, the Clerk to the Board of the BBC, who sent a memo to Basil Nicholls, Director of Home Broadcasting, questioning the propriety of this kind of drama:

> What I am trying to establish is whether the BBC – assuming it be a force in the land – ought to do what it can to rehabilitate this country . . . without being propagandist, I think we should always bear in mind that we, as a nation, are very sick. Seen in this light, a string of our horror plays seem to me to be escapism at its worst – hugging the knife that stabs you sort of thing. (Singer, 1950)

This need to 'rehabilitate' the country refers to the fact that Singer and the Board believed that Britain as a nation had been exposed to too many *real* images of death and horror during the Second World War, and there-fore ought not to be exposed to any fictional horrors as entertainment on television, a sentiment very much in keeping with the Reithian concep-tion of the corporation as a benevolent public nanny. Indeed, this attitude towards the immediately post-war broadcasting of Gothic horror drama is both similar and in direct contrast to those arguments surrounding the transmission of the same kind of material over twenty years later in the

United States, after the Vietnam War (a conflict which famously became known as 'the first television war'). This approach is exemplified by the theory on horror television espoused by the horror writer Stephen King (discussed in the introduction to this book), who proposed that dramatic horror would no longer have any effect on American television viewers who had been exposed, through the medium of television, to the real horrors of Vietnam, and that death and abomination had themselves become commonplace and everyday as forms of television entertainment. However, in Britain in the 1940s and 1950s, the desire, as represented by Singer's memo, was clearly to protect the viewer from *further* exposure to the horrors of war, rather than to keep them from the ennui of over-exposure.

A month after Singer's memo was sent, Val Gielgud, Head of the BBC's Drama Department, responded to these criticisms in a memo entitled 'Reflections upon the present state of television drama', which took to task those members of the viewing public who had criticised the corporation's dramatic output.

> Observe, for example, the recent explosion anent morbidity-and-horror in television plays: we were, I am sure, all perfectly aware of the situation, of its causes, and of the need to make changes, before we received the unsolicited assistance of . . . the famous 187 correspondents from the neighbourhood of Sutton Coldfield. This sort of outcry will always occur from time to time in the earlier stages of the establishment of a service . . . It unfortunately appears to be a fact that the majority of new purchasers of television sets seem to have remarkably low dramatic tastes – which may be largely due to the fact that many of them have had little or no experience of the living theatre. (Gielgud, 1950)

This correspondence, while acknowledging a need to address the suitability of the horror genre for television, clearly demarcates a certain attitude towards new television viewers in the regions as lacking in sufficient cultural capital to 'deal with' this kind of programming. The first provincial television transmitter, which had been installed in Sutton Coldfield in the autumn of the previous year, bringing the BBC to viewers in the Midlands for the first time, clearly also brought new problems relating to a more culturally diverse audience in the eyes of the London-centric BBC. More importantly, this memo highlights the key point of contention that ran throughout the debate: that the Gothic was an unsuitable genre for domestic transmission. According to Gielgud, the horror and morbidity of the genre were seen as acceptable within a public reception context, with the distancing effect of separation between audience and action inherent in the theatrical space, reinforced by the 'detached' attitude of the culturally informed theatre-goer. However, when performed within the bounds of private, domestic space, to a supposedly undiscerning 'mass audience', the same genres (horror, the supernatural, the Gothic, etc.) became far more problematic for the BBC. Relating back to Singer's remarks about avoiding bringing horror back into the nation's homes, Gielgud's rather superior attitude towards the new and decidedly 'un-metropolitan' viewers of Sutton Coldfield betrays the BBC's concerns regarding television's uneasy place within the provincial home. Several days later, in a note on drama policy written by Basil Nicholls, the problem of adapting moments of horror in 'classic' literature (specifically the gouging of Gloucester's eyes in Shakespeare's *King Lear*) for both radio and television was also addressed:

> It is not possible to lay down a detailed policy in the matter of horrific or sordid plays or plays dealing with unpleasant subjects. Such a policy would have to be framed in the most general terms – terms that would admit the blinding of Gloucester in *King Lear* while excluding some possibly lesser horror in some worthless play. Each play must be considered individually in terms of good taste and values. The above remarks apply in the first instance to sound broadcasting, but the basic policy of ultimate good taste must apply to television as well, although obviously the gouging out of Gloucester's eyes before a camera, however discreetly treated, raises a different class of problem to the broadcasting of the words, 'Out, vile jelly'. (Nicholls, 1950)

This 'basic policy of ultimate good taste', implying an aesthetic of suggestive restraint rather than 'improper display' in the adaptation of classic literature, subsequently shaped the BBC's attitude to Gothic drama for some time to come. Nicholls' discussion of the different problems of adapting for television and radio is also illuminating in that it exposes one of the early heritages of Gothic anthology drama. The following analysis thus outlines some of the ways in which such series looked back to their radiophonic ancestry in negotiating these issues of 'ultimate good taste'.

The extended Gothic anthology drama in British broadcasting did not begin on television but in a popular, long-running radio show. Fronted by Valentine Dyall, also known as 'The Man in Black',[4] ten seasons of Gothic plays under the umbrella title *Appointment with Fear* were broadcast on the Home Service between 1943 and 1944 and on the Light Programme between 1945 and 1955, produced by Val Gielgud and Martyn C. Webster. Dyall, who was best known for his sonorous, spine-chilling voice, acted as the host for the show, introducing the story (often the written-for-radio work of the American writer John Dickson-Carr, but also the adapted work of Poe, Stevenson and others), commenting on the narrative afterwards, and sometimes becoming absorbed into the action himself. However, conversely the Gothic anthology series did not appear on BBC television in the 1950s, perhaps reflecting the uneasiness felt towards the genre during the post-war decade. In fact, in Britain, it was not until the introduction of commercial television that the Gothic anthology series was again reconsidered as a viable form of television entertainment.

Even before the start of the commercial service in September 1955, both the BBC's and ITV's strategies for competition took the production of television drama as being the indicator of popularity and quality, and the anthology format was to become an integral part of this competition for viewers and cultural kudos.

> In drama the BBC persisted long after the arrival of ITV with a policy which one might expect of a public service broadcaster: it tried to be as eclectic as possible, offering classic plays, adaptations of great novels, original series and serials, and single plays by modern authors . . . Commendable as the BBC's drama policy was, it perforce became more sharply focused when in the late 1950s ABC introduced a Sunday night series shrewdly entitled *Armchair Theatre*. (Crisell, 1997: 95)

As is well documented, *Armchair Theatre* (ABC [UK]/Thames, 1956–74) became one of the most popular and long-running drama anthology series of the 1950s and 1960s, featuring both original and adapted teleplays. This series, not bound to a particular genre but to the remit for innovative, challenging television drama, showcased the best in television writing and production, and saw the anthologised television play on ITV developing a clear reputation for quality; the makers of *Armchair Theatre* also became known for making dramas more specifically suited to television as a medium. On the strength of *Armchair Theatre*, the drama department at ABC Television became celebrated as the home of groundbreaking drama, particularly after 1958 under series producer Sydney Newman. Famously, Newman had arrived at ABC from Canada with the desire to revolutionise television drama and produce teleplays which were more closely suited to the experiences and tastes of a mass audience; ABC's anthology drama series subsequently enjoyed a considerable popularity and success in the 1950s and 1960s.

In addition to the fact that the making of weekly anthologised teleplays suited the production structures of the television industry (they were relatively cheap and quick to make, using small, self-contained production teams), these 30 to 120 minute plays offered the opportunity for experimentation with the possibilities (and limitations) of television drama. Without the pressure of producing a serial drama which needed to maintain audience interest over a number of weeks, the producers, directors, writers and designers of ABC's anthologised teleplays were at more liberty to innovate, both in the style and content of the plays produced for the series (see Wheatley (2004)). It is therefore no surprise that in the franchise award competitions of the 1960s, anthology drama became one of ABC's key selling points; in April 1967 a document produced to accompany ABC Television's application for appointment as a programme contractor for the ITV network stated that 'ABC Television has always seen anthology drama as an opportunity for stretching the minds and feelings of peak viewing audiences beyond the narrow confines of variety acts and storytelling' (ABC Television Ltd, 1967: 2).[5]

As *Armchair Theatre* continued, Newman decided that the series would benefit from 'specialising' by focusing on a particular genre within a season of plays; this generic turn would also offer Newman a holiday from producing *Armchair Theatre* as he handed over the reins to his eventual successor at ABC, Leonard White, in the summer months. Thus in the summer of 1960, overlapping with the fourth season of *Armchair Theatre* plays, *Armchair Mystery Theatre* (ABC [UK], 1960–65) began its first season. This branch of the series set out to produce psychological thrillers and mysteries, and led the way for later generically identified anthology series (see Wheatley (2004) for a fuller discussion of this series). However, while *Armchair Mystery Theatre* offered an early and striking example of the generic anthology series in the early 1960s, there were still few examples of the Gothic anthology series on British television during the first few years of competition, with ABC television also producing the only notable exception to this: *Hour of Mystery*, broadcast in the summer of 1957. *Hour of Mystery* was a thirteen-week series produced by John Nelson Burton, in which episodes were linked by Donald Wolfit, playing a narrator in the guise of a connoisseur and collector of 'crime objects'. While little is known of this series (due to the significant gaps in the archiving of the early output of independent television), listings guides show that *Hour of Mystery* featured adaptations of classic Gothic stories (such as Wilkie Collins' 'The Woman in White' (ABC [UK], 1957)), thus deploying the strategy of encroaching on the BBC's dramatic territory by producing 'quality', popular literary adaptations. An article by Howard Thomas (then Managing Director of ABC) in *The Television Annual for 1958*, reports on *Hour of Mystery's* integral part in the company's competition with the BBC:

> So the battle goes on. With their sheets of daily programmes marked out hour by hour . . . ABC and ATV throw in *The 64,000 Question* and *Hour of Mystery* against the BBC's Saturday-night comedy hour . . . All this is for you, bringing you a choice, and offering more carefully planned programmes than when television was a monopoly. And your tastes are ever

changing. Today's favourite is tomorrow's bore. Where is the exact point at which a popular programme begins to pall? The programme planners' job is to anticipate your change of taste months before you do, and then take the programme off the air before you will not want it. (Thomas, 1957: 35)

Thomas' claims therefore support the notion that the Gothic anthology drama was beginning to be viewed as a viable weapon in the duopolistic war for ratings, a fact that is also acknowledged in a letter from Cecil Madden (Head of Programmes, BBC) to Michael Barry (Head of Drama), written after a Television Programme Planning Committee Meeting in 1959, in which Madden discusses the suggestion that the BBC introduce a generic season:

> I made a suggestion that if we are to compete in this way with feature films [on ITV], however old, the best method to adopt is possibly to make the plays conform to certain overall popular titles which will attract the viewer in themselves, such as, at random, 'Mystery Playhouse' . . . There is no doubt that 'Mystery Playhouse', 'Armchair Theatre' . . . do have a word of mouth and paper appeal. (Madden, 1959)

The BBC's hypothetical 'Mystery Playhouse' clearly shows an awareness, on the part of the corporation's executives at least, of the possibilities and attractions of generic specialisation in the drama anthology series, perhaps in direct reference to *Hour of Mystery* and pre-empting ABC's *Armchair Mystery Theatre* season in the following year.

While the BBC continued to eschew the Gothic anthology series in the early 1960s, perhaps on the grounds of their 'basic policy of ultimate good taste', the commercial television companies continued to experiment with the format more extensively from the early 1960s onwards. For example, London contractor Associated-Rediffusion produced the series *Tales of Mystery* between March 1961 and 1963, which featured twenty-nine episodes of the adapted stories of Algernon Blackwood.[6] The series was hosted by a sombre John Laurie and met with mixed reviews in the popular press. While some reviewers, such as Maurice Wiggins in the *Sunday Times*, felt the programme developed well on Blackwood's ghoulish storytelling from earlier years of broadcasting, others, such as Denis Thomas in the *Daily Mail* suggested that, 'Television being a strictly literal medium . . . can add nothing to a cosy tale of death and diabolism without overdoing it. One way to cope with this difficulty is to show less and suggest more' (Haining, 1993: 189). This kind of criticism, displaying a resistance to the representation of the supernatural on television, clearly rested on a certain nostalgia for the ghost story as told on radio, by Blackwood, Dyall and others, a medium which quite obviously 'showed less and suggested more' than television. The challenge for the directors, writers and producers of Gothic anthology drama was therefore established as a need to create *atmosphere*, to audio-visually evoke the supernatural in mood and feeling rather than to clearly visualise the genre's associated ghosts and monsters, and therefore to develop a restrained, suggestive aesthetic which remained more faithful to radio versions of the Gothic than to its cinematic and theatrical ancestors. To a certain extent, the producers of ABC's long-running Gothic anthology series, *Mystery and Imagination*, took up this challenge.

Mystery and Imagination

Mystery and Imagination ran in five seasons from January 1966 until February 1970, and was produced by Jonathan Alwyn for ABC Television (1966–68) and then Reginald Collin for Thames Television (1968–70). Based entirely on the adaptation of classic Gothic novels, short stories and plays, it most successfully marks what S.S. Prawer describes as the 'evolution' of television's own variations of the terror film for the small screen (1980: 20) in his extensive analysis of the cinematic 'terror film'. *Mystery and Imagination* was produced during an innovative time in the history of British television, often referred to as the 'Golden Age' of television drama (Caughie, 2000), and saw the Gothic drama on television being used to 'showcase' new production technologies and the talents of ABC's creative personnel. Furthermore, and most interestingly for this analysis of the Gothic anthology series, *Mystery and Imagination* shifted between two distinct modes of Gothic representation throughout its five season run: the suggestive, restrained ambiguity of the supernatural ghost story and the excessive, spectacular supernatural horror drama.

Production of *Mystery and Imagination* can, in part, be understood as a reaction to the criticisms levelled at Independent Television in the early to mid-sixties. When the Pilkington Report into television broadcasting was published in June 1962,

> The BBC was vindicated and ITV blamed. Pilkington retained its pristine objections to commercial television, judging it by Reithian standards and refusing to allow it any of its own . . . Claiming that the public service aims enshrined in the 1954 Television Act had never been fulfilled, the report proposed that ITV should start all over again. (Crisell, 1997: 111)

ITV was thus forced to re-examine its attitude towards 'quality programming' and 'public service' in relation to the broadcasting output offered by the BBC, and the contractors, particularly ABC, 'renewed their efforts at high quality drama' (Crisell, 1997: III). *Mystery and Imagination* can be seen as part of this response, attempting to produce a Gothic anthology series which was both 'quality' and 'popular' (in the Reithian sense of the words), using teams whose reputations had been established in other television drama, notably *Armchair Theatre*. Television writers such as Robert Muller and George F. Kerr, directors such as Patrick Dromgoole, Philip Saville and Joan Kemp-Welch, and a host of classically trained actors (Denholm Elliott, Freddie Jones, Joss Ackland) all contributed regularly to the series, as did a variety of well-respected production personnel. The series also brought with it the cultural cache of adapting a number of literary Gothic 'classics'.

In a *TV Times* interview given to coincide with the start of the series in 1966, *Mystery and Imagination*'s story editor, Terence Feely, commented on the medium's suitability for Gothic adaptations, and drew a parallel between domestic parlour storytelling at the end of the previous century and the activity of watching television in the 1960s:

> The Victorians were willing victims of the pleasurable shudder that makes the lamp light mellower, the fire warmer. These stories were written, in my view, as a protest against the increasing dominance of the machine . . . Yet, ironically, it is the machine – in the shape of television – which has restored these tales their original magic and power. They were written to be read aloud in the security of the family circle. In re-establishing the family audience, television has enabled us to re-create almost exactly the conditions in which their long gone authors intended these stories to be heard and to have their effect. (Feely, 1966: 4)

This clearly outlines the intention of the series: to use television to *return* to the domestic consumption of Gothic stories and tales, those narratives which sought to chill or terrify their readers (or, in this case, viewers) within the family group. Implicitly, the act of television viewing is being given a sense of cultural kudos here when compared with the reading of literary fiction. In the interview with Feely, as with the framing of the series elsewhere in the *TV Times*, the programme's 'literariness' was emphasised, 'authenticating' the series and assigning *Mystery and Imagination* a degree of quality and prestige:

> To prepare the . . . series, the producer, Jonathan Alwyn and I had to read through more than 400 Victorian tales of the bizarre and the supernatural looking for suitable ones to dramatise . . . We read so many stories to be sure we used the best and to soak ourselves in the Victorian writers' craftsmanship. (Feely, 1966: 4)

These comparisons, between the reading and viewing of Gothic fictions in the home, and the writing and televising of Gothic fictions for a domestic audience, speak much of the medium's anxiety about its own status as drama provider in the mid-1960s, and, in particular, about ITV's position within the institutional structures of British television. By drawing on these comparisons, the producers of *Mystery and Imagination* could fend off the criticisms of regulatory bodies and the press alike, by insisting on a literary ancestry for their series. As Jane Root has argued, 'above all, it is the literary adaptation which has come to represent the most central component of "good television"' (1986: 75). It is, of course, important to note here that the Gothic as a literary genre had had its own history of treading the fine line between popular sensationalism and the literary highbrow. As David Punter notes, the literary Gothic has a history of being seen as 'crude, exploitative, even sadistic . . . [pandering] to the worst popular taste of its time' (1980: 9). However, perhaps this notion of the Gothic as a populist or sensationalist genre meant that the Gothic might be seen as an appropriate choice of literature to adapt on commercial television in the mid-1960s, satisfying both the tastes of the viewing public and ITV's critics.

Feely's comments on *Mystery and Imagination*'s return to domestic Gothic storytelling are also reflected in a certain awareness of the viewing context present in the stories chosen for adaptation. More often than not, the teleplays chosen for adaptation centred around a haunted house or some kind of family trauma: these narrative concerns are seen in at least sixteen out of twenty-three episodes. The importance of the domestic location was reiterated by the 'taglines' published at the bottom of each episode's *TV Times* listing, often a piece of dialogue taken from the week's teleplay. Playing upon the idea that houses formed the cathexis of fear and unease in *Mystery and Imagination*, typical taglines included: 'Fear haunts this house – it lurks beyond the candle flame – it whispers down the corridors. Fear of living, fear of dying – Fear, Fear, Fear'('Fall of the House of Usher'); 'Please hurry home father – mother and I are frightened out of our senses' ('The Open Door'); 'I have seen things in this house with my own eyes that would make your hair stand on end' ('The Canterville Ghost'); or 'The house is silent now . . . and in the silence someone is listening' ('The Listener'). The programme's producers, and those responsible for its marketing, clearly wished to draw parallels between the Gothic text on television and the homely space of its reception, perhaps to increase the potential of their teleplays to produce *affect* in the viewer. It is also telling that each episode of the first three seasons of *Mystery and Imagination* was framed by the presence of a storyteller, Richard Beckett (played by David Buck) in the guise of a Victorian romantic, who not only introduced the episode but on several occasions became part of the drama itself. For example, in 'The Fall of the House of Usher' (ABC [TV], 1966),

Beckett took on the role of the nameless narrator in Poe's story, an old school friend of Roderick Usher's, and became very much involved in the narrative events, falling in love with Madeleine Usher and narrowly escaping death at the final spectacular collapse of the rotting house. This level of narrative interpolation by an 'involved' narrator is a classic device of the Gothic novel, and was also deployed in the ghost story as presented on radio (as in *Appointment with Fear*, discussed above). Beckett/Buck acted as an intermediary between story and audience, drawing the viewer 'into' the diegesis and therefore bridging the gap between the Gothic drama and the home. The presence of the storyteller was an established device in other Gothic or mystery television anthology series of the time (for example, Donald Pleasance introducing *Armchair Mystery Theatre* or John Laurie doing the same for *Tales of Mystery*), but *Mystery and Imagination* was, to my knowledge, the only British series in which, on occasion, the storyteller became fully integrated into the action of the narrative.[7]

'The Open Door'

In order to explore the first of the two previously outlined trajectories of the Gothic drama on television (the suggestive, restrained ghost story), and the debt which the Gothic anthology series owed to its radio prede-cessors, the following analysis looks at a single episode of *Mystery and Imagination* in more detail. The fourth episode of the first season, an adaptation of Margaret Oliphant's 'The Open Door' (ABC [UK], 1966), provides the case in point. As an episode which clearly sought to respond to criticisms levelled at the presentation of the Gothic on tele-vision, the following analysis will explore the ways in which a television adaptation of a ghost story might begin to sound and look like a 'radio play with pictures'. It would be problematic to argue that 'The Open Door' was somehow backward or primitive in its relationship to radio-phonic forms of the Gothic ghost story; rather, the complex sound design will be discussed as a creative response to the criticisms levelled at television's ability to 'tell a good ghost story', as well as a negotiation of the limitations of television production during the 1960s.

'The Open Door', adapted by George F. Kerr and directed by Joan Kemp-Welch, is a ghost story set in the late nineteenth century, based in the grounds of a Scottish country house (owned by Colonel Mortimer (Jack Hawkins)). The narrative centres around the haunting of a ruined house in the grounds of Colonel Mortimer's house which is first noticed by Colonel Mortimer's son, Roland (Henry Beltran). When the Colonel returns from a trip to London after hearing of his son's 'disturbance', the Colonel himself investigates the sound of the haunting (a child sobbing), firstly with an army companion (Derek Tansley), then with the sceptical local doctor (Mark Dignam), and finally with a priest (John Laurie) who recognises the ghost as Willy, a local lad killed during service as a drummer boy in India, and who lays his ghost to rest. The episode is introduced by Richard Beckett (David Buck), who, speaking directly to the viewer, claims that the Colonel was a friend of his father's, thus offering the aforementioned direct link between the viewer and the diegesis. The action in this episode fluctuates between the Mortimers' house (where the family gather around Roland's bedside) and the haunted ruins; both locations are clearly constructed in a studio and shot on video from a relatively limited number of perspectives. Indeed, the ruins setting appears all the more artificial because it is meant to be a rugged outdoor location; in actual fact, this 'wildness' is far more successfully represented through the layering of 'wild' sound effects (whistling wind, howling dogs, owls and birds, etc.) than in the rather flat and insubstantial-looking set. This 'wild sound' is used continuously during the episode, even when the action shifts back to the house, in order to create an atmosphere of dread/foreboding, with the wind whistling constantly until the ghost is laid to rest at the end of the episode.

Throughout 'The Open Door', Colonel Mortimer repeatedly returns to the ruins to seek out the source of the crying voice that has been haunting his son; these are the moments which can be most accurately described as utilising the techniques of the radio play to suggest, rather than reveal, the presence of the supernatural. For example, in the first of these sequences, when Mortimer explores the ruins with his friend, Corporal Jones, the scene opens on a medium shot of Jones looking around to the sound of wind whistling, a dog howling and the hoot of an owl, and continues with a series of similar medium close-ups and close-ups of the two men reacting to a number of diegetic but visually unlocated sounds. As the scene progresses, other supernatural sounds are heard (an amplified heartbeat, unearthly sobbing and groaning, an ethereal echoing voice which repeats the Colonel's calls of 'Who is there?'), as the men are shot from a variety of positions and distances looking around for the source of the sound, reacting to the cacophony of sounds around them. In doing so, Colonel Mortimer and Corporal Jones take on the role of a diegetic audience and, like the drama's viewer, are driven on by the desire to see the ghost and the continual denial of this desire. Their facial performances of stupefaction and Mortimer's imploring cries of 'Who is it?' are expressive of the position of the viewer, or, more precisely, the listener of the ghost play. This sequence in the ruin, and the later sequences in which the doubting doctor and the local priest are drawn into the search, can therefore be read as an enactment of the frustrations of Gothic television (the desire to see which must be constantly thwarted in order to maintain suspense/atmosphere). Indeed, when the camera briefly cuts away from these 'performances of listening' to look into the space of the ruins, it is almost lost for something to look at: it tracks aimlessly round the edge of a wall to find nothing on the other side and at the end of the scene (just before the cut to a commercial break), as the two men stalk past the camera, it remains focused for a good deal of time on an 'empty' shot of the ruin, as the howling wind grows louder and continues after the fade to black over the *Mystery and Imagination* title.

In these moments, the camera reinforces the relative unimportance of the visual image in establishing tension and mood by showing the viewer nothing; as with radio then, 'The Open Door' is reliant on sound rather than image to tell its story. Moreover, as in a radio play, sound is not only used to imply the presence of the supernatural, but is also utilised for more routine narrative purposes: to signify transition from day to night, when a static, 'empty' long shot of the old ruins is first shown accompanied by the sound of owls hooting and then by birds singing, for example, or to signify transition from one location to another (through the use of incidental orchestral music). Emphasising the importance of sound in this teleplay, the *TV Times* article accompanying 'The Open Door' unusually focused on the creation of sound effects for the episode (more usually with *Mystery and Imagination*, a full or half page article was given over to an interview with the actor in the central role of the week's episode). In this article, the weekly interview was given by the actress Amanda Walker, who played the ghost's voice. The interview begins with description from the script: 'Loud whimpering cry . . . shuddering moan . . . sobbing sigh . . . pitiful cry . . . Just a few of the sound effect instructions on the script of "The Open Door" ' (Davis, 1966: 8), instructions which clearly emphasise the inherent 'aurality' of the episode, and continues to detail the work involved in producing the audio effects of what Dr. Simpson describes in the teleplay as a 'phonetic disturbance'.

While this teleplay differed from other episodes of *Mystery and Imagination*, which can be described as inheriting the gross visuality of other contrasting traditions of the British Gothic (discussed in the next chapter), 'The Open Door' can be understood as belonging to a wider tradition of suggestive, restrained storytelling on television which also characterised other ghost story adaptations during this period and later. Of course, the nomination of 'restraint' as applied to this episode clearly refers to visual, not aural, restraint; indeed, a reviewer in *The Times* commented that '[t]he haunting voice in the ruins provided the most chilling experience the series has so far brought' (Haining, 1993: 239). However, the teleplay's refusal to visualise its ghost finds it in keeping with the suggestive tradition of Gothic storytelling that was also taken up by the BBC in the M.R. James adaptations which formed a large part of the channel's annual *Ghost Story for Christmas* series during the 1970s. In fact, the makers of *Mystery and Imagination* also produced a number of James adaptations during its first three seasons,[8] but it is this BBC series which is most frequently associated with the work of this ghost story writer on television.

M.R. James and the 'gentlemanly' restraint of the television ghost story

During the 1940s and 1950s, readings and dramatisations of several of James' ghost stories had been broadcast on BBC radio, on the Home Service, the Light Programme and *Children's Hour*;[9] it is therefore unsurprising that James' stories were again to prove popular with television's domestic audience. Perhaps partly as a response to ABC's success with the James adaptations on *Mystery and Imagination*, and also coming out of the BBC's focus on innovation and experimentation in the late 1960s, the corporation broadcast their own adaptation of M.R. James' 'Oh Whistle and I'll Come to You, My Lad' in May of 1968. 'Whistle and I'll Come to You' was adapted, directed and produced by Jonathan Miller, and starred Michael Hordern as the central protagonist, the bumbling Professor Parkin. Miller's adaptation was a product of BBC arts broadcasting (it was commissioned by the Arts Features Department as part of the *Omnibus* series) and was remarkable in its sparse, economical direction and Hordern's minimal performance. These styles of direction and performance built on those developed in Miller's adaptation of *Alice in Wonderland* for the BBC two years previously (1966). The BBC were thus quick to highlight Miller's involvement in 'Whistle and I'll Come to You' in the publicity material for this production. For example, the press release on the second broadcast of 'Whistle and I'll Come to You' (on 27 July 1969) calls the programme 'an unconventional adaptation' and states,

> Like all [Miller's] work, it is remarkable, both for its uncanny sense of period and atmosphere, and for the quality of the actors' performance. Most of the dialogue in this film was improvised, and when this film was first shown just over a year ago, most critics were agreed that Michael Hordern's performance as the temporarily deranged professor was a highly impressive tour de force. (BBC, 1969)

Miller therefore used James' ghost story to explore new ways of working, mainly through the improvisation of dialogue, as well as the possibilities offered by the lightweight Éclair camera used to capture the haunting location filming of the Norfolk coastline, producing one of the most affective instances of Gothic television to date.[10]

The programme's sense of experimentation, its 'artiness', was felt by some to be a kind of false lure, however, and drew direct, somewhat unfavourable comparisons between Miller's adaptation and *Mystery and Imagination*. In an article in the *Stage and Television Today*, Allan Prior questioned the marketing strategies of these two programmes:

> Anything on ITV inevitably gets a rather popular, somewhat patronising treatment in press write-ups . . . This may have something to do with the way it is presented to the press by the Press Offices of the ITV companies. Even if the piece is *art*, they would never dream of saying so in their 'hand-outs' because this is not the way they want it presented . . . The BBC do not push or popularise. Also they do not advertise . . . They are part of the literary and cultural establishment and all that. Ipso facto, they must put out the best programmes. Well they very often do. But . . . if this piece had been included in ABC's *Mystery and Imagination* series (and some very distinguished writers were) would it have got anything like the same attention? I fear not. I'm delighted for Dr. Miller's sake that his adaptation got written-up. Did it get watched much, nobody knows, probably half the audience of any *Mystery and Imagination* production. (1968: 55)[11]

This review clearly outlines a distinction between the BBC's and ITV's Gothic adaptations on television, particularly in relation to the ways they were marketed and received by television critics. Whereas *Mystery and Imagination* is identified as both quality *and* popular drama in Prior's write-up, Miller's adaptation was seen as 'high brow' television, assigned qualities of restraint and decorum even in the way in which it was marketed.

It is clear that 'Whistle and I'll Come to You' sought to uphold the aesthetic of restraint in Gothic fiction outlined as desirable by Basil Nicholls in the 1950s, a suggestiveness which is also readily associated with the stories of M.R. James. As Julia Briggs has noted,

> When it comes to describing the source of fear, the ghost story writer must tread delicately. A certain vagueness, an element of mystery is essential . . . [V]ague allusions help to prod the imagination into action. They are also part of a more general use of understatement that characterises James' style. Implicit in the restrained, gentlemanly, even scholarly tone is the suggestion that it would be distasteful to dwell on unpleasant details, and this consistent 'meiosis' serves to increase our apprehension. (J. Briggs, 1998: 105–6)

On television, this 'gentlemanly' restraint is transformed into the refusal to clearly visualise the ghostly figure in Miller's drama, and in a constant deferral of the revelation of the ghost which haunts Professor Parkin. The drama is characterised by a certain stillness of shooting style, both inside the guesthouse and on the beach, with shots which are static on the whole, aside from sparing camera movements which follow Parkin and the other guests around the desolate beaches and sand dunes of the north Norfolk location. Much of Dick Bush's still cinematography presents the viewer with beautiful but haunting images of a barren Norfolk coastline, the sheer emptiness of these shots suggesting that the sinister or supernatural may lurk invisibly either within or outside of the frame, thus translating the Jamesian sense of restraint to the screen successfully. There is also a certain reticence in the sound design and use of dialogue in 'Whistle and I'll Come to You', in keeping with the sense of restraint demanded by the Jamesian ghost story. Much of the drama is filmed in silence (bar the sound of the wind blowing on the beach and around the guest house), and Michael Hordern's delivery of improvised dialogue is, on the whole, the muttering of repeated words or phrases as the absent minded ramblings of a distracted old man.

The ghostly figure called up by Parkin blowing an Anglo-Saxon bone whistle found in a coastal graveyard remains, on the whole, indiscernible, portrayed by a series of glimpsed, dark or distant images. Contrary to the acceptance of the existence of ghosts in James' fiction, when we do see or hear evidence of the presence of the supernatural figure, Miller's direction leads the viewer to believe that this manifestation of evil may in fact be a figment of Parkin's imagination. This is achieved by presenting the ghostly manifestation in a series of highly subjective, 'psychical' point-of-view shots. The first time the ghost appears to Parkin (beyond a general sensation that he is being followed or watched) is during a dream sequence which occurs two nights after he has blown the bone whistle. In this powerful scene, cuts are made between extreme close-ups of Parkin's face as he falls in and out of sleep and the following shots: a static long shot on a foggy beach as Parkin runs towards and away from the camera; a slow motion shot at an oddly canted angle of Parkin climbing over the breakwater fences on the beach; a travelling shot running alongside Parkin, keeping whatever is chasing him just out of shot; and a medium close-up of Parkin hiding behind a breakwater, steeling himself to look up and over at what has been following him (see figure 1.1).

All of these shots on the beach are accompanied by the sound of an amplified heart beat and distorted snatches of horrified gasps and cries, until, in the final shot of the dream sequence, the viewer is rewarded with a very brief reverse shot of Parkin in front of, and running away from,

1.1 Anticipating the horror in 'Whistle and I'll Come to You',
Omnibus (BBC1, 1968).

1.2 Visualising the horror in 'Whistle and I'll Come to You',
Omnibus (BBC1, 1968).

an indiscernible figure on the beach, created by swathes of ragged silk
(see figure 1.2): it is still genuinely difficult to see how this effect was
achieved.

In this sequence, we are constantly reminded that we are seeing the
chase on the beach from Parkin's subjective point of view (through the
cuts back to extreme close-ups of Parkin in his bed), and Miller withholds the revelation of the ghost for as long as possible, building up a
sense of suspense by suggesting that whatever is chasing Parkin is *only*

1.3 Visualising the horror in 'Whistle and I'll Come to You',
Omnibus (BBC1, 1968).

just out of shot. When the 'ghost' is revealed in a shot lasting a considerable length of time (seventeen seconds), it remains in the back to mid-
ground of the shot, a swirling mass of material which only *refers to* the
presence of a human form: as a special effect, the shot is indistinct
enough to remain suggestive rather than revelatory. Again, when we see
the ghost for the second and final time of the drama, in Parkin's
bedroom at night, it is briefly glimpsed as an animated sheet (see figure
1.3) only after a long sequence of Parkin looking aghast and terrified
from various angles, and this revelation is further undercut by the
arrival of Colonel Wilson (Ambrose Coghill), a fellow guest, who enters
and turns on the light, seeing nothing untoward. This sense of under-
statement or restraint in Miller's drama can be seen as a direct transfer-
ence of James' desire to 'show less and suggest more': indeed, as
indicated above, if anything, Miller's adaptation is even more suggestive
than the original story, given that it offers the viewer the possibility of
reading the ghost as being 'all in the mind' of Professor Parkin.

The Audience Research Report compiled by the BBC after the first
broadcast of 'Whistle and I'll Come to You' suggests that among their
sample audience, the emphasis on the creation of atmosphere over the
development of action and dialogue, and the indistinct representation
of the supernatural was, to a certain extent, seen to be effective:

> For about half [of the viewers], it seemed, it was a most successful evo-
> cation of atmosphere, a fascinating interpretation of a basically simple
> story . . . The atmosphere of foreboding, of unspeakable unpleasantness

to come, was built up with telling effect . . . It provided a spine chilling essay in the macabre, one in which atmosphere was all and lack of conventional dialogue served only to heighten the effect. (BBC, 1968a)

While many of the negative responses were also levelled at the programme's suggestiveness ('It was like reading a book with the last page missing' (BBC, 1968a), claimed one viewer), it was the emphasis on actual physical sensation (spine chilling, hair raising, blood curdling), caused by a feeling of unease or terror, which was key to the responses to Miller's adaptation. In turn, this viewer response was encouraged, as opposed to extreme feelings of horror or revulsion, by what Julia Briggs describes as the 'gentlemanly restraint' of James' work and its adaptations.

Moving into the 1970s, the other key site of M.R. James' ghost stories on television during this period was the annual anthology series, *Ghost Story for Christmas*, shown some time between 22nd and 28th December each year between 1971 and 1978; this series also held its senior personnel from one year to the next (namely producer Rosemary Hill, director/producer Lawrence Gordon Clark and cameraman John McGlashan). The remit behind *Ghost Story for Christmas* was to produce a television version of classic ghost stories, referencing the tradition of oral ghost storytelling at Christmas, and from 1971 to 1975 these stories were the adapted work of M.R. James. The latter episodes in the series were an adaptation of Charles Dickens' 'The Signalman' (BBC1, 1976), also written to be read aloud, and two original teleplays, 'Stigma' (BBC1, 1977) and 'The Ice House' (BBC1, 1978). When scholar and provost at Eton and King's College, Cambridge, James had specialised in writing short ghost fiction to entertain a group of friends and students who would meet in his chambers every Christmas Eve, thus prefiguring the tradition of the Christmas ghost story for television. In a discussion of the 1975 episode of the series, 'The Ash Tree' (BBC1, 1975), the writer Angela Carter explored this penchant for fear at Christmas:

> The Christmas ghost-story, the Christmas spine-chiller, horror for Christmas – somehow it's become part and parcel of the whole Dickensy seasonal myth of snow and holly and church bells and groaning boards . . . Christmas Eve . . . by suggestive candlelight or flicker of flame, the family gathers round an open hearth on which roasting chestnuts fizz and sputter, to scare themselves silly with whispered talk of spooks and ghouls and supernatural things. Nowadays, of course, television provides us with most of our supply of traditional Christmas fear – a fear that might perhaps originate in some primeval memory of the fear of the death of the sun . . . The annual M.R. James adaptation is a

television tradition, now: a more than satisfactory replacement for tales whispered round the hearth. (1975: 111–12)

In a similar vein to Terence Feely's introduction of *Mystery and Imagination* (discussed above), Carter suggests that the *Ghost Story for Christmas* series somehow replaced earlier traditions of oral storytelling at Christmas, reflecting a broader change in home entertainment. In light of this, the family around the fire ostensibly becomes the family around the television set, and thus the Christmas ghost also transfers to this medium. However, this does not answer the question of why the ghost story should be told at Christmas *in the first place*. Carter's analysis suggests that the season's pagan origins, and the inherent fear that the sun would never return from the gloomy winter night, are what inspires these tales, and thus reveals a wider concern with the supernatural forces of good and evil, death and rebirth at Christmas. In terms of television production and scheduling however, the ghost story offers an entirely different incentive during the festive season, in that it is sold as 'special', season-specific programming, as part of the Christmas television package. The need to attract viewers at a time when ratings are at a peak, and families are presumed to be gathered in their living rooms watching the television together (as opposed to more atomised modes of family viewing), therefore called for the production of a programme that reproduced the seasonal genre of ghost story telling, within the genre of the 'quality' literary adaptation.

The 'quality ghost story' was brought starkly into focus by the BBC's recent revisitation of James' Christmas ghost stories at the turn of the twenty-first century, a revisitation which owed a great deal to the aforementioned series from the 1970s. In December 2000, the BBC broadcast *Christopher Lee's Ghost Stories for Christmas*, a series of barely dramatised adaptations of M.R. James' ghost stories which were framed by Lee, playing James, telling the stories in his rooms at King's College to a group of students. These half hour episodes focused on the creation of an atmosphere of intimacy and suspense, with the act of oral story-telling given narrative precedence over the occasional images of books/papers/illustration and isolated dramatised images from the stories, in keeping with the notion that James' stories were in fact written to be vocalised rather than visualised. At the beginning of each episode the story was framed by a sequence in which Lee as James is shown preparing his cosy, homely rooms at the college, intercut by shots of the students gathering together to visit James, thus directly reflecting on the Christmas-specific domestic reception context, with its open fire and romantic visions of the hearth. This rather clever opening sequence, depicting people gathering to listen to a ghost story around the fire, offers a visualisation of exactly what the producers were hoping viewers would do: continually turn up to watch and listen. It also demonstrates a clear nostalgia for Christmases past (as well as Christmas television of the past), a nostalgia which is enhanced by the warmly lit, soft-focus images of domestic storytelling. In many ways these more recent 'ghost stories for Christmas' offer a more successful 'aesthetic of restraint' than Miller's 'Whistle and I'll Come to You' or Lawrence Gordon Clark's adaptations of the 1970s; by focusing on the act of reading rather than on the visualisation of James' stories, *Christopher Lee's Ghost Stories for Christmas* remain truer to the stories' literary and radiophonic heritage. In order to support this contention however, it is necessary to elaborate further on the ways in which *Ghost Story for Christmas* negotiated the problems of 'doing the ghost story' on television.

'Lost Hearts'

As stated above, *Ghost Story for Christmas* can be located within a trad-ition of the quality literary adaptation. Unlike *Mystery and Imagination* and many of the other Gothic anthology dramas on British television in the 1960s and 1970s, the series was shot on film and on location, with much attention paid to minutiae of period detail; as such it might be seen to visually prefigure the filmic stylishness and traditions of 'quality' of later literary adaptations, such as *Brideshead Revisited* (Granada, 1982) and *Jewel in the Crown* (Granada, 1984). However, there are significant differences between these Gothic adaptations and the more usual heri-tage dramas, differences which call into question the validity of applying the 'heritage' label to *Ghost Story for Christmas*. Specifically, in offering a darker, more sinister version of the past (particularly the nineteenth century), the series might be seen as a cycle more correctly termed 'feel bad' heritage television drama. In his examination of the heritage impulse in film and television, Andrew Higson defines the heritage drama as a 'cycle of quality costume dramas' (1993: 109) but later goes on to reformulate that 'not all costume dramas are heritage films – which is to say that not all costume dramas have the same prestige cultural status, or the same engagement with conservative and elite heritage dis-courses' (Higson, 1996: 237). Higson therefore suggests that the heri-tage text is essentially a costume drama (and, more often than not, a literary adaptation) with high cultural capital, which engages with a bour-geois notion of heritage, representing a very specific version of a past which may be compared favourably to the present, a time when life was 'civilised' and national identity stable and unchanging. The heritage spectacle, in Higson's terms, is therefore inextricably linked to the project of making the British audience of the heritage text 'feel good' about their national past and their collective national identity, about belonging to a '*Great* Britain, a *United* Kingdom' (1993: 110):

> By turning their backs on the industrialised, chaotic present, [the heritage film makers] nostalgically reconstruct an imperialist and upper class Britain . . . The films thus offer apparently more settled and visually splendid manifestations of an essentially pastoral national identity and authentic culture . . . The films turn away from modernity toward a traditional conservative pastoral Englishness; they turn away, too, from the high-tech aesthetics of mainstream popular cinema. (1993: 110–13)

The key term in understanding the development and uses of the heritage film and television cycles then, at least as Higson sees them, is that of 'nostalgia', a keen sense of sentimental yearning for the past or a desire for what has been left behind or covered up by the passing of time. Higson describes a 'nostalgic gaze' inherent in the viewing of heritage film and/or television, which 'resists the ironies and social critiques so often suggested narratively by these films' in favour of a consumption of the past 'displayed as visually spectacular pastiche' (1993: 109). It is therefore suggested that through the nostalgic gaze, narrative criticism of the era or society represented within the heritage film or programme is negated, offering the viewer the more simple visual pleasures of the past and an overriding sense of nostalgia. Higson concludes that heritage film and television often presents a less than idyllic past, while visually representing the beauty and spectacle of a sanitised or 'cleaned up' bygone age, though it must be noted that Monk (1996) and others have subsequently called this conclusion into question. However, while it cannot be said that *Ghost Story for Christmas* offers a more *authentic* visualisation of the past, it can be seen as a very different kind of heritage text, which refuses the sanitation of nostalgia. Both this series, and indeed other Gothic dramas discussed in this book (such as the adaptations of female Gothic literature discussed in chapter three), offer the viewer narratives of fear and anxiety set in a past which is not only marked by a sense of decay or dilapidation, but which is also disturbed by uncanny happenings and supernatural events. The past of the Gothic adaptation on television, while similarly saturated in period detail and the minutiae of the English heritage aesthetic, is therefore less stable and pleasant than the past offered to the viewer in the more traditional heritage text. In essence, the Gothic literary adaptation removes the surety of the past as a haven or site of nostalgia. While this idea is explored at greater length later in this book (in relation to the adaptation of the female Gothic literature), it is important to note at this stage that *Ghost Story for Christmas* retained the production values of the heritage drama, but rejected its attitude towards the past as a desirable place and time.

These high production values and the associated cultural kudos of the literary text can be seen as being bound to the 'gentlemanly restraint' of *Ghost Story for Christmas*, to the eschewing of spectacular horror and to the desire to 'show less and suggest more'. In an interview to co-incide with the broadcast of his more recent horror anthology series, *Chiller* (Yorkshire, 1995), Lawrence Gordon Clark proposed that 'the unseen is much more frightening than the full-frontal Hollywood splat. M.R. James, who was the master of ghost story telling, allows the veil to be drawn apart for a second, so you can look into the abyss' (Williams, 1995: 17). In turn, Gordon Clark's interviewer also describes this need to 'show less, suggest more' in the television ghost story:

> Instead of graphic depiction, [the programmes] focus on suggestion. The aim, they say, is to chill rather than shock. Partly because television is not best suited to carrying off big screen pyrotechnics, but mainly because they want to keep faith with the notion of a ghost story in its literary rather than cinematic tradition. (Williams, 1995: 17)

To outline the ways in which the 'full-frontal Hollywood splat' and 'big screen pyrotechnics' were both rejected (and ultimately reverted to) by the makers of *Ghost Story for Christmas*, this discussion now turns to a closer analysis of a single episode from the 1970s series: 'Lost Hearts', broadcast at 11.35 p.m. on Christmas Day, 1973. This teleplay tells the story of Stephen (Simon Gipps-Kent), the orphaned nephew of Mr. Abney (Joseph Connor), with whom he is sent to stay. On arrival at Abney's stately home, Stephen discovers that the ghosts of two children who had previously been taken into the care of his uncle are haunting the house and grounds, attempting to warn Stephen that his uncle mur-dered them in order to remove their hearts and gain the secret of eternal life. On the eve of Stephen's own murder, the ghosts attack and kill Mr. Abney, thus freeing Stephen and themselves.

The beginning of 'Lost Hearts', as Stephen approaches his uncle's house in a carriage, poignantly introduces the viewer to the heritage setting as it is presented within the ghost story; this scene begins in a foggy country lane, where the first shot shows the carriage appearing out of the gloom, as if out of nowhere. As with other episodes of *Ghost Story for Christmas* (e.g. 'A Warning to the Curious' (BBC1, 1974), which owes a great deal to Miller's 'Whistle and I'll Come to You'), the tremulous sound of a wind instrument (a flute in this case) is used as a means of establishing the chilling mood of the drama. Throughout the episode music becomes a vital tool for the creation of an eerie atmosphere, and is constantly tied to the appearance of the supernatural. The carriage and the costume of Stephen are in keeping with the detail of the mid-Victorian era, with the profusion of dull colours (the browns and blacks of the interior of the carriage and Stephen's suit), giving the image the appearance of a sepia toned photograph, a faded or degraded pictorial version of 'past-ness' familiar to the viewer through this limited palette.

In this opening scene we are also introduced to the two ghost children (Christopher Davies and Michelle Foster) through two point-of-view shots from Stephen's perspective; again, we see here the television ghost story's desire to suggest rather than clearly delineate the presence of the supernatural, through the creation of an unreliable, subjective point of view (as in the 'ghost' sequences of 'Whistle and I'll Come to You' discussed above). Firstly, Stephen is shown looking out of the carriage (the 'point-glance' shot according to Branigan's (1984) taxonomy of the grammar of point of view), then a cut is made to a point-object shot of the two children standing in the opposite field, waving slowly. Their appearance is marked by a lack of colour, their skin sallow and shadowed, and their clothes brown and black: here, the lack of vibrancy suggests the degradation or decomposition of these figures that have appeared 'out of nowhere', from the past. After a series of rapid reverse shots (a close-up of the spooked horse whinnying, followed by a repeat of the point-glance shot of Stephen looking, followed by a low angle shot of the driver steadying the horse), a cut is made back to a repeat point-of-view shot of the field, this time empty and without the ghost children. The glimpsed figure or object (in this case the ghost children) is one of the key narrational devices whereby the television ghost story can achieve its primary goal: to suggest, rather than confirm, the presence of the supernatural on screen. In a sequence such as this where the supernatural figure appears only briefly, and neither the viewer nor the protagonist can feel sure of the presence of these figures, it is the 'blink and you'll miss it' edit which, playing on the impermanence of the television image, creates suspense successfully. By offering a dislocated 'replacement' shot (e.g. the same shot of the field, with and without the ghost children), an uncanny point-of-view shot is created, a shot which is familiar and yet different from the shot seen only moments ago. This replacement shot of the two ghost children is again utilised at the end of the drama at Abney's funeral, when a sequence of facial close-ups (first of Stephen looking, then of Mrs. Bunch (Susan Richards) looking in the same direction) is interspersed by a long shot of the grounds of Abney's house, first with the children present in the centre of the shot, and then, when Bunch looks, with no one in shot. In these brief moments of revelation, the 'just glimpsed' images of the ghost children do not dwell on what might be potentially unpleasant or 'improper' (the mutilated bodies of dead children) within the restrained, gentlemanly ghost story. To a certain extent, this 'just glimpsed' action, an essential element of the Gothic drama's restrained and gentlemanly aesthetic, also challenges the notion of the distracted viewer and the character-isation of television viewing as a glance, rather than a gaze, at the screen (see Ellis, 1982). The television ghost story demands concentrated, rather than distracted, viewing in order to make sense of a narrative in which moments of revelation are fleeting and key figures are glimpsed on screen for a matter of seconds.

As the carriage progresses towards its destination and the title credits continue to appear on screen, the viewer is offered several shots from Stephen's travelling point of view, of the countryside which surrounds the house. However, here we see a radically different version of pastoral England than that of other, more benign versions of the literary adapta-tion on television. Firstly, the pastoral idyll of the rolling English hills is replaced by the sinister gloom of a wooded landscape shrouded in mist and fog. Instead of the wide open spaces, rolling lawns and long shots of a stately home on a hill which are more usual in the heritage drama of the 1980s and 1990s, we are offered a landscape full of hidden spaces. Here, the shade of the trees provides a visual metaphor for the dreadful secret threatening Stephen throughout the rest of the teleplay. The woods might therefore be read as interstitial spaces, representing a sug-gestion of the 'unseeable' (the grotesque horror of slaughtered children in this case), rather than the visual splendour of the past.[12] The appar-ently empty shots of the countryside or the night sky, repeated through-out the drama, thus evoke the hidden secrets of Mr. Abney's house, locating threat beyond the margins of an apparently benign and *empty* pastoral image.

However, of all the *Ghost Story for Christmas* adaptations of M.R. James' stories, 'Lost Hearts' also most fully visualises the super-natural, in the form of the ghost children who appear throughout the narrative. While their appearances are brief, they are clearly identified both in flashback and in sequences of haunting, rather than merely sug-gested. The children are marked as ghostly in a rather theatrical way, through the use of costume and make-up and an almost pantomime zombie-like performance. Furthermore, the ghost children are far more present throughout this adaptation than they are in the original story, where the boy, Giovanni, only appears to Stephen once, in a dream, until their final appearance at the end of the story. The television adaptation therefore increases the presence of these characters at various points throughout the narrative in order to fulfil its status as a visual, rather than literary or non-visual, medium. It is the viewer's desire to view the ghostly or supernatural which seems to lie at the problematic crux of the television ghost story, and which constantly troubles the director's desire to be 'faithful' to James' story, to 'show less and suggest more'.

Ultimately, Gordon Clark's adaptation falls back on the desire to display the source of horror at the end of 'Lost Hearts', perhaps garnering the same sense of disappointment attached to the final cut of Jacques Tourneur's film adaptation of M.R. James' 'Casting the Runes', *Night of the Demon*.[13] It appears as if the 'gentlemanly restraint' of James' ghost story can only be taken so far on an audio-visual medium, and that ultimately, the viewer must be simultaneously 'rewarded' and disappointed by the presentation of the horrific moment, if not the spectacularly grotesque (as when the ghost boy, Giovanni, reveals his open, empty chest cavity as a warning to Stephen (see figure 1.4)).

It is never explicitly stated how Mr. Abney died at the end of James' 'Lost Hearts': 'It was the opinion of the coroner that Mr. Abney had met his death by the agency of some wild creature. But Stephen Elliott's study of the papers I have quoted led him to a very different conclusion' (James, 1992: 19). However, the sense of ambiguity offered here in the final paragraph of the story is not present in the televised version, which more fully represents the ensuing horror of Abney's death. A series of

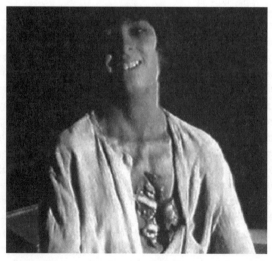

1.4 The moment of horror: 'Lost Hearts', *Ghost Story for Christmas* (BBC1, 1973).

shots of the ghost children descending on the old man are cross-cut with his terrified face, arm raised up above his head to protect himself, which is then followed by two shots of the children driving a sabre into their victim's chest. At this point in the teleplay, horror is clearly displayed and the narrative departs from that 'basic policy of ultimate good taste' which was seen as so central to the presentation of the Gothic in the early years of television drama production.

The other James adaptations in the series ('The Stalls of Barchester Cathedral' (BBC1, 1971), 'The Treasure of Abbot Thomas' (BBC1, 1972), 'A Warning to the Curious' and 'The Ash Tree') retained, to a great extent, a sense of the decorum and restraint in evidence in most of 'Lost Hearts', withholding the full revelation of the supernatural until the very last moment, and centring on the *suggestion* of a ghostly presence rather than the horror of visceral excess and abjection. The sixth episode in the series, an adaptation of Dickens' own 'ghost story for Christmas', 'The Signalman', signalled a stylistic break from Gordon Clark's James adaptations. Like Miller's 'Whistle and I'll Come to You', it attempted a more sparse style of performance and dialogue, with Denholm Elliot offering a chilling performance of suffocating dread. However, it was the first of the original teleplays in the series, and the final play to be directed by Gordon Clark, which indicated a new direction for the television Gothic. 'Stigma', written by Clive Exton and starring Peter Bowles and Kate Binchy as an affluent middle-class couple who move to the countryside, centres on the haunting of Katherine (Binchy) following the unearthing of a 'menhir' stone in the garden of their new home. In a nod towards the burgeoning trend for full-on body horror on television, and the abjection of everyday homes and families in the 1970s (discussed at length in the following chapter), 'Stigma' rejected an 'aesthetics of restraint' in favour of the near-hysterical depiction of Katherine's naked body bleeding profusely from ghostly wounds; it becomes apparent in the dénouement of the teleplay that her body is re-enacting the ritual murder of a 'witch' whose body is also found on the site of the house. Through the representation of a dysfunctional family suffering the horrors of a sinister past returning to haunt them, 'Stigma' in fact seemed more in step with Gothic horror television at the end of the decade than the 'gentlemanly', restrained adaptations of M.R. James' work earlier in the series, which looked back to the horror plays of the 1940s and 1950s. To this end, looking at the transformations of an annual series which ran across most of a decade of broadcasting tells us a great deal about the shifts in the Gothic paradigm on British television during the period, shifts charted in the next chapter.

Notes

1 This distinction, between Clayton's film and the films of the Hammer studios, was also outlined by Andrew Higson (1991).
2 'The Cask of Amontillado', 'Some Words with a Mummy' and 'Fall of the House of Usher' were all shown between 9.30 p.m. and 10.15 p.m. on 6 October 1949, adapted by Joan Maude and Michael Warre. These plays could therefore be seen as an early form of anthology drama.
3 Files at the BBC Written Archive centre (R73/136/1) suggest an organised letter-writing campaign, producing 187 complainants in the Sutton Coldfield area of the West Midlands alone.
4 Dyall also starred in his own radio series entitled *The Man in Black*, broadcast on the Light Programme between January and March 1949.
5 ABC's application in the 1967 franchise awards was not entirely successful. A reorganisation of the London contractors, and the formation of London Weekend Television [LWT], meant that ABC was forced into a merger with Rediffusion, the latter being the junior partner, to form Thames Television.
6 Blackwood, who had died a decade earlier, was immensely popular with both radio listeners and early television viewers on the BBC, where he read his own stories direct to camera under the titles *A Ghost Story* (1947) and *Saturday Night Stories* (1948–49). He was voted television personality of the year by the Television Society in 1947.
7 This character device had, however, been used in *Thriller* (NBC, 1960–62), an anthology series from the United States (see chapter four of this book for a brief discussion of early US anthology series).
8 These were 'The Traccate Middoth' (ABC [UK], 1966), 'Lost Hearts' (ABC [UK], 1966), 'Room 13' (ABC [UK], 1967) and 'Casting the Runes' (ABC [UK], 1968).
9 See the invaluable *Ghosts and Scholars Newsletter* website, a web based resource for the scholarship of M.R. James deriving from the journal *Ghosts and Scholars*, which holds an updated list of film, television and radio adaptations of James' stories (Pardoe, 2005).
10 The assumed 'quality' of this programme has retrospectively been made plain by the programme's 'afterlife': in 2001 'Whistle and I'll Come to You' was one of the first of the BFI's 'Archive Television' DVD releases, advertised as 'a series of releases from bfi Video Publishing aiming to provide access to key television programmes preserved in the National Film and Television Archive', and was also screened theatrically at the National Film Theatre in 2001 and Nottingham Broadway's *Out of Sight* film and television archive festival in 2000.
11 Original emphasis.
12 This depiction of pastoral space is similar to that of a much later example of Gothic television, *Twin Peaks* (Lynch-Frost Productions, 1990–91), as discussed in chapter five.
13 Hal E. Chester, executive producer of the film, decided that the film lacked commercial appeal, and overrode Tourneur's cut, insisting on the addition of a 'demon' very close to the beginning of the narrative.

Blood, guts and special effects: the heritage of horror on British television

2

'An equally respectable Gothic line . . .'

In the previous chapter, the history of the Gothic anthology drama on British television was understood as being founded upon a tradition of decorum and 'ultimate good taste', bearing a close relationship to the narrative forms of the literary ghost story and the radio play. In part, this restrained, 'gentlemanly' aesthetic was assigned to the policy making and protectionist sensibilities of a Reithian approach to public service broadcasting in the earlier years of British television. However, as was noted in the introduction to chapter one, these literary and radiophonic predecessors were not the only Gothic heritages referred to by the anthology drama of the 1960s and 1970s in Britain. Simultaneously, a mode of Gothic drama developed which clearly referenced the 'equally respectable Gothic line . . . which precisely depends upon the clear visual portrayal of every stage of action' (Pirie, 1973: 41), as defined by David Pirie in his seminal study of Gothic horror in the British cinema. This line, moving from the mad monks of M.G. Lewis to the horror 'classics' of Shelley and Stoker, and through *grand guignol* theatre to the 'blood and lust' spectaculars of the Hammer and Amicus studios in post-war British cinema, has as strong a presence in British Gothic television as its more refined counterpart, the televised ghost story. This chapter seeks to delineate this opposing tradition by looking at two strands of anthologised Gothic drama. Firstly, we will begin by examining the effects-laden anthologies of the 1960s and 1970s which, in their heyday, offered original and adapted teleplays that pushed the boundaries of television production through the visualisation of the supernatural and the grotesque. Secondly, we will turn towards the moment in which *grand guignol* Gothic was no longer confined to a dim and distant past but was brought up to date, with a shift towards a more quotidian kind of horror.

Beginning with the former cycle, many of these anthologised dramas, which might more correctly be defined as horror plays than the ghost stories discussed previously, demonstrated a strong link between technological innovation in television drama production and the presentation of Gothic horror. The producers of Gothic horror drama sought to 'show off' the possibilities of television as a dramatic medium with a full array of gory or supernatural special effects, shunning the restraint and decorum of the adapted ghost story. Returning to *Mystery and Imagination* for example, 'The Open Door' (ABC [UK], 1966), discussed in the previous chapter, was in fact an uncharacteristic episode of this series, which far more frequently featured spectacular Gothic adaptations, especially in the latter seasons produced by Thames Television. While it was suggested previously that this series answered the demands of competition with a sense of respectability and 'literariness', it simultaneously created what might be termed a 'television of attractions', with diverse innovative visual styles forming a large part of the series' allure for potential audiences. It will therefore be argued that theatrical, cinematic and ultimately *televisual* styles were referenced and developed by the makers of the British Gothic anthology series during the period at hand.

The word 'televisual' is used specifically here to refer to the mode outlined by John Thornton Caldwell as television which seeks to 'flaunt and display style' (1995: 5) and those programmes which 'battle for identifiable style markers and distinct looks in order to gain audience share within the competitive broadcast flow' (1995: 5). For example, Caldwell identifies television which exploits a cinematic visual style as 'televisual', thus departing from the use of the term 'televisual' to delineate the medium specific.[1] Caldwell's analysis of televisual television is mainly confined to a time of intensified broadcasting competition in the US in the 1980s and 1990s, but his definition of televisuality can equally be applied to the output of series like *Mystery and Imagination* (ABC [UK]/Thames, 1966–70), *Late Night Horror* (BBC2, 1968) and *Supernatural* (BBC1, 1977) in the 1960s and 1970s, also a time of intense competition within British television broadcasting. Caldwell's terminology can therefore be seen as far more flexible and more broadly applicable than it might, at first, appear to be. Responding to an increased sense of competition (brought about, in part, by the expansion of broadcasting hours, as well as the expansion of the service from two channels to three, and heading towards a fourth), these decades in British broadcasting can be seen as a moment in which significant production innovations were being made and showcased in order to gain audience share, beginning in a decade which saw the birth of the term 'ratings war' in the UK.

As discussed in the introduction to this book, S.S. Prawer has argued that the Gothic anthology series of this period, made under 'the restraints of money, location and shooting time', was prompted to develop 'flexible, sophisticated technical equipment, specially adapted to the lower definition of the TV screen . . . to disguise this' (1980: 20). Subsequently, Prawer argues, the production of the Gothic anthology series on television led to 'the rediscovery of avant-garde devices – violently clashing images, unusual angles of vision, frozen frames, shooting through gauze, negative prints, etc.' (1980: 21). This description of television's formal experimentation *despite* technological and budgetary restrictions precisely describes the case of *Mystery and Imagination*, as well as other later Gothic anthology drama series such as the BBC's *Supernatural* or the one-off adaptation, *Count Dracula* (BBC2, 1977), directed by Phillip Saville and featuring Louis Jourdan in the title role. The terms of this experimentation and innovation will be delineated below.

In their analysis of the development of television drama, Carl Gardner and John Wyver discuss the theatrical heritage of the early teleplay, arguing that the dramatic output of the BBC consisted of 'televised stage plays, "faithfully" and tediously broadcast from the theatre, or reconstructed in the studio, even down to intervals, prosceniums and curtains' (1983: 115). They go on to argue that this theatricality precluded any sense of innovation in the production of television drama in the 1950s. While Gardner and Wyver's approach to the single play has been successfully contested, particularly in the work of Jason Jacobs (2000), their history of the single play offers a clear indication of the ways in which television's relationship with theatre has been viewed: theatre, in their analysis, is seen as a negative influence which prevented television from 'moving on' to discover its own, medium-specific dramatic forms. However, by looking towards *Mystery and Imagination* as an anthology series which quite obviously referenced theatrical style in its performances and its production design, we can begin to see the ways in which Gothic theatre was alluded to as a significant point of generic heritage within individual episodes, without confining the entire series to the presentation of 'boringly theatrical' forms of television drama.

An adaptation of Bram Stoker's 'Dracula' (ABC [UK], 1968), from the first season of *Mystery and Imagination* produced by Thames, scripted by Charles Graham and directed by Patrick Dromgoole, demonstrates a clear debt to Gothic theatre, particularly in the style of performance employed by its key actors. The episode, a very liberal adaptation of the novel,[2] introduces Dracula (Denholm Elliott) from the outset, and figures him not as an insubstantial shadow or suggested presence, but as a rather 'hip' looking individual with a trim goatee and square shades.[3]

Elliott as Dracula offers a performance here which plays on the 'close-ness' of television, drawing on the intimate connection between viewer and screen through the constant narrowing of his eyes and arching of eyebrows in close-up. However, his performance also exploits several of the conceits of Gothic stage acting which defy television drama's tendency towards naturalism, seen in expansive arm gestures and typi-cally 'vampirous' body movements, whereby the actor's body becomes entirely gestural (see figure 2.1). While this style of performance can also be traced through contemporaneous Gothic cinema (particularly those films produced by the Hammer and Amicus studios), its roots are to be found in the London patent theatres of the eighteenth and nineteenth centuries (see Ranger, 1991).

At the time of broadcast, Elliott stated in an interview with the *TV Times* that 'you can't overdo playing Dracula . . . the fatal thing is to try to be subtle' (Anon., 1968a: 9); in 'Dracula', this lack of subtlety is care-fully wrought. For example, a gestural performance to a static camera often replaces dialogue in this teleplay, allowing the actor's body and facial expression to do the work of storytelling. In the final confronta-tion between Dr. Seward (James Maxwell), Van Helsing (Bernard Archard) and Dracula (depicted in figure 2.1), all conflict and emotion is represented by a synthesised, harpsichord-sounding soundtrack and the facial and bodily performance of Maxwell, Archard and Elliott, as the actors strike poses towards one another rather than engaging in con-frontational dialogue. In a wide-ranging discussion of performance styles on television, Karen Lury has suggested that the theatrical actor

2.1 Denholm Elliott's gestural performance as Dracula: 'Dracula', *Mystery and Imagination* (Thames, 1968).

(such as Elliott as Dracula) brings a certain 'expressiveness' to television performance, and Lury argues that theatrical performance on television is most accurately characterised by the fact that 'the theatrical performer can be seen to *be* acting' (1995: 123). In the aforementioned instance, these moments from 'Dracula' precisely demonstrate this mode of self-conscious acting, in which the very activity of performance is placed on show.

However, it is not enough to simply define all exaggerated or gestural performance in *Mystery and Imagination* as 'theatrical': this nomination does not take into account the range and specificity of different types of theatrical Gothic performance which are replicated in the series. For example, 'Uncle Silas' (Thames, 1968) references the Victorian melodrama's modes of Gothic performance. This episode, adapted from Joseph Sheridan Le Fanu's novel and broadcast in the same season of *Mystery and Imagination* as 'Dracula', centres on Maud Ruthyn (Lucy Fleming), a young woman left in the care of her wicked and drug-addled uncle, Silas Ruthyn (Robert Eddison) when her father dies. This narrative is thus typical of the female Gothic cycle, as the story of a young girl trapped in a menacing stately home who is abused by an older man (see chapter three of this book for a discussion of the female Gothic cycle). As such, 'Uncle Silas' presents an opportunity for the exaggerated performances of victimhood and villainy typical of Victorian melodrama. The eponymous villain of the teleplay can be seen as the epitome of the villain on the Victorian stage: beyond the fact that his appearance fits this type (dusty, black, ill-fitting suits, long straggly grey hair and a heavily shadowed, gaunt face), his gesture and intonation reflect the villainous performances of late nineteenth century melodrama. Furthermore, the camera angles and shot compositions frequently employed to frame this performance (such as the use of the low angle close-up and mid-close-up) accentuate these theatrical gestures; for example, on Ruthyn's introduction into the narrative at the end of the first part of the teleplay, the glowering menace of the villain looking down on his potential victim for the first time is intensified by the low angle of the shot (see figure 2.2), and left to linger as a pre-advertisement cliff-hanger.

Another accentuation of the melodramatic style of performance is also made possible through the 'look' of the camera, whereby the facial close-up is used to highlight the theatrical 'aside' typical of Victorian melodrama. As Silas Ruthyn discovers the dead body of his cohort, Madame de la Rougiere (Patience Collier), he turns to the camera, acknowledging its presence and by extension the presence of the viewer, as he hisses 'Then the brat is still alive!' This speech direct to camera/viewer is atypical of

2.2 The melodramatic villain: 'Uncle Silas', *Mystery and Imagination* (Thames, 1968).

performance in television drama in the 1960s, but is typical of the relationship between performer and audience in nineteenth century theatrical melodrama. The figure of Madame de la Rougiere, the governess to Ruthyn's niece and his covert partner in crime, also presents a theatrical characterisation, based on a 'Madame Guillotine' or *tricoteuse* character. As Madame de la Rougiere, Patience Collier pantomimes this grotesque character in a series of cackling appearances throughout the episode; the *tricoteuse* is particularly identified by her heavy black costume, make-up and wig, which she removes to terrify her young charge with her grotesque bald head, in a moment reminiscent of the burgeoning body-horror of Parisian *grand guignol* theatre. She often self-consciously performs to both the camera and to Maud as her diegetic audience, as in the scene where she offers a rendition of the trance-like intonations of the phantasmagoria showman (a moment which has little impact on furthering the narrative). Standing by the door to a crypt in the grounds of Ruthyn's home, she announces 'Come meet my friends, Monsieur Cadaver and Monsieur Skeleton. See me die here today a little time and be among them', as Maud screams and runs. Here, Collier's exaggerated facial expression and arm movements, the flourishes of an organ on the episode's extra-diegetic soundtrack and her positioning against a suitably Gothic setting (the arched door to a crypt), all identify her performance as melodramatically theatrical. As Anthony Lejeune argued two years later, *Mystery and Imagination* was 'the nearest modern equivalent of Victorian melodrama' (1970: 13).

Such is the extent of *Mystery and Imagination*'s theatricality that both the structure and the mise-en-scène of each episode also reflect the representational heritage of Gothic drama on the stage. For example, each advert break in the latter two seasons was framed by overlaid titles announcing the beginning or end of each 'act', rather than the segmentation of the narrative into 'parts', as was more usual for television drama at the time. Visual references to theatrical space are also contained within the mise-en-scène of these Gothic teleplays: for example, the sinister mansion of 'Uncle Silas' features a proliferation of archways in the Gothic architectural style which also act as a kind of proscenium arch, framing the theatrical performances of Eddison, Collier and Fleming. While the narrative is not confined to the presentation of action within these frames, at key moments within the drama a sense of theatrical performativity is heightened by the presence of a diegetic proscenium frame (as in the moment where Maud explores her uncle's house for the first time).

Indeed, set designers on many of the teleplays in this anthology series negotiated the problem of low budget production by producing two-dimensional sets which did not attempt to replicate locations realistically, but rather utilised theatrical conventions of set design. For example, the opening shots of the 1970 episode, 'Sweeney Todd' (Thames, 1970), one of three *Mystery and Imagination* episodes shot in colour, reveal a 'flattened' street scene as the central location of the episode. Here, the rest of London is referred to by a one-dimensional painted backdrop featuring an image of the dome of St. Paul's cathedral, very much in keeping with theatrical conceits of stage setting and design (see figure 2.3).

Subsequently the limitations of studio production are bypassed by designer Fred Pusey: no attempt is made to recreate a naturalistic setting within the confines of the studio, but rather a space is created for the drama which draws attention to the fact that *Mystery and Imagination* forms part of a wider theatrical tradition of Gothic presentation. Minimal location filming had been available to the producers of *Mystery and Imagination* episodes at Thames (as seen in all the episodes in the previous season), but here it was either consciously eschewed or the option had been withdrawn (due to the switch to colour). Either way, while Gardner and Wyver (1983) might see these blatant references to the theatre as backward-looking, evidencing television's own lack of medium-specific stylistic traditions, it might be more appropriate to read these references to theatre in the late 1960s and early 1970s as the self-conscious referencing of a number of established Gothic theatrical traditions. Thus these episodes of *Mystery and Imagination* are rendered complex networks of allusions to earlier dramatic presentations of the Gothic, allusions which,

2.3 Theatrical set design: 'Sweeney Todd', *Mystery and Imagination* (Thames, 1970).

it will be argued below, are not confined to theatre but which draw on theatrical drama as much as they do cinematic traditions of the Gothic.

Mystery and Imagination did not simply turn towards theatre to produce a more spectacular version of Gothic horror for television, however. Even more vividly, the series drew on cinematic versions of the Gothic genre, referencing diverse filmic traditions, from the mise-en-scène of German Expressionism to the dilapidated excess of the British Hammer horror films, to produce a distinctive visual style for individual episodes. The adaptation of Poe's 'The Fall of the House of Usher' (ABC [UK], 1966), transmitted the week before 'The Open Door' which remained so faithfully 'anti-spectacular' (as discussed in chapter one of this book), clearly acknowledges this cinematic Gothic heritage, in the form of a homage to German Expressionist cinema within its opening sequence. Beginning unusually without the presence of the storyteller, Richard Beckett (David Buck), the episode opens after the credits on a three shot sequence which clearly evokes the striking images of Gothic horror in German Expressionist cinema, such as the coffin of the sleep-walking Cesare in *Das Kabinett des Doktor Caligari* (Germany, 1920) or the splintered coffin which reveals Max Schreck's grotesque face in *Nosferatu, eine Symphonie des Grauens* (Germany, 1922). The first shot of this sequence is a medium close-up of two two-dimensional candles, accompanied by a fanfare of trumpets and kettle-drums, from which the camera tracks past the candles to a high angle shot of the top of a coffin (surrounded by four more two-dimensional candles), and then slowly zooms in to the lid of the coffin. Following this shot, a cut is made to a low angle, dimly lit shot of a pair of hands scratching frantically at the inside of the coffin lid, as blood drips down the fingers. From here, a further cut is made to a medium tracking shot towards the coffin, past the two-dimensional candles, and on to the lid of the coffin as it is pushed through from the inside and the bloody hands break out. As the camera tracks into the hands, a dissolve is made into the black surface of a pool. During this short sequence, which sets the tone and mood for the rest of the episode, the lack of dialogue, the extra-diegetic score dominated by the pounding of kettle drums, the two-dimensional props and minimalist set, and the isolated images of the scrabbling hands and the coffin, all mark this introduction as a moment of heightened expressionism. The sequence exists outside of the flow of narrative information (the main thrust of the narrative following Richard Beckett's developing relationship with the Ushers and their inevitable downfall), to express the more abstract concerns of the episode (darkness and illumination, the insufferable claustrophobia of domestic space, and ultimately the dread and horror of being buried alive). This thematic exposition is achieved through a short series of interconnected images rather than through dialogue, just as the symbolic empty shots of the night sky which punctuate this episode reflect on the fear of supernatural power and otherworldly forces. The sequence is therefore in keeping with S.S. Prawer's notion that the makers of series like *Mystery and Imagination* negotiated the aesthetic limitations of the medium creatively, and in doing so produced a sense of experimentation within the production of Gothic drama for television. Working within the constraints of television drama production at the time then, *Mystery and Imagination*'s version of 'The Fall of the House of Usher' emphasises the symbolism of Poe's story, drawing on an earlier art cinema tradition of Gothic representation (German Expressionism) to produce a visually distinctive teleplay. It is notable that this episode, which features such a striking instance of experimentation with Expressionist form for television, was produced less than two years after Troy Kennedy Martin's prediction that there was an 'interest in moving away from naturalism [in television drama] . . . towards a kind of expressionism' (Kennedy Martin et al., 1964: 47). Kennedy Martin, writing a response to the critics of his seminal article 'Nats go home' (1964), conceded that as an alternative to naturalism,

> expressionism pre-supposes the existence of the television studio at the beginning of the show. In this way it does not lie to its audience, pretending that it is a slice of 'real life' . . . Once having shown the studio, the expressionist director brings together actors, scenic form, sound and light and builds up a dramatic structure within it. (Kennedy Martin et al., 1964: 47–8)

In 'The Fall of the House of Usher', we see this acknowledgement of studio space in this expressionist sequence at the beginning of the programme, precisely as Kennedy Martin describes it. As such, it both acknowledges the space of the television studio as a 'performative space' (to borrow John Caughie's term (2000: 77)), while at the same time acknowledging the genre's cinematic heritage of Gothic horror.

However, the cinematic style most obviously referenced by many *Mystery and Imagination* episodes is that of the British horror film (predominantly produced by the Hammer and Amicus studios), which enjoyed a heyday before, during and after the production of this anthology series. This heyday began in the late 1950s with the production of the Hammer/Terence Fisher adaptations *The Curse of Frankenstein* (UK, 1957) and *Dracula* (UK, 1958), and ran well into the 1970s with Amicus portmanteau films such as *The House that Dripped Blood* (UK, 1970) and *Asylum* (UK, 1972). The Amicus films also remind us that the relationship between British Gothic cinema and television is not necessarily one-sided, with television 'feeding off' cinematic versions of the Gothic. The proliferation of the portmanteau format from this studio in the late 1960s and early 1970s, whereby three or four short stories were grouped together within a single film, framed by frequently implausible devices for storytelling established at the start of each film, might in fact be seen as British horror cinema referencing television's anthology format. Peter Hutchings (2002b) offers a thorough account of the origins of the portmanteau format within the output of the Amicus studios and, while Hutchings does not directly make the link between anthology television and the portmanteau film, he draws attention to the fact that studio heads, Max J. Rosenberg and Milton Subotsky, had come to Amicus from television in the US. Amicus portmanteau films also frequently featured adaptations of stories from writers such as Robert Bloch and Richard Matheson in their films (whose work had previously been popular in the television anthology series in the US[4]). Thus, a more symbiotic relationship between these two Gothic horror industries might be supposed.

Returning to Graham and Dromgoole's adaptation of Bram Stoker's *Dracula* for *Mystery and Imagination*, this teleplay draws heavily on the style of contemporaneous British horror cinema (particularly Hammer horror), in both the dilapidated Gothic décor of its set design (recreated in the studio for the Westons' house and shot on location in Dracula's mansion), and in the representation of the female vampires and victims who appear during the episode. The heavily sexualised threat which the female vampire poses in this episode clearly references Hammer films such as *Kiss of the Vampire* (UK, 1964) or *Dracula, Prince of Darkness* (UK, 1965), released only a few years before the production of this *Mystery and Imagination* adaptation. For example, one of the filmed inserts in 'Dracula' (a flashback sequence in which Jonathan Harker (Corin Redgrave) recalls the events which ensued in the Count's castle) demonstrates a number of striking similarities to the Hammer *oeuvre*. When the scene is introduced by a long tracking shot of Dracula's stately hall, taking in all the usual trappings of Gothic architecture and mise-en-scène (heavily ornate archways and staircases, dripping candelabras, cobwebs, etc.), we see an overt visual referencing of British horror cinema. The fact that this is one of only two short sequences in the episode which are shot on film rather than video, and on location rather than in the studio, perhaps also directly marks this moment as distinctly 'cinematic', referencing the stock 'look' of Hammer horror in the 1960s. After the camera tracks with Harker around this space, a cut is made to his point of view, looking up in medium-long shot at a group of female vampires at the top of a dark staircase. Although these figures are presented as grotesque, dressed in rags with blackened teeth, they are also simultaneously sexualised, striking erotic poses and displaying an excessive sexual desire towards Harker and each other for the camera. As each shot draws closer, the horror of their gaping, blackened mouths and the extreme carnality of their lascivious tongues are brought into increasingly stark relief, until Harker is stalked up the stairs by the vampires. The dramatic, sporadic score of the sequence, representing Harker's simultaneously horrified and desiring memory (the melodramatic music of whining strings and music box chimes), is also in keeping with the sound design of Fisher's *Dracula* cycle for Hammer.

Later in this episode, the supernatural possession of Lucy (Susan George) by Count Dracula back in London (and back in the studio) is also represented by a similar performance of excessive sexual desire. As Lucy lies on her bed, struck down by the vampire, the camera tracks in to her writhing body, her performance of possession resembling a state of orgasmic rapture. Throughout the drama, Lucy's interest in Dracula is represented as sexual, her desiring gaze on him often accompanied by the sound of tremulous violin strings, and this suggestion of desire is finally realised in this highly sexualised performance on her death-bed. After she has been bitten, in a series of shots which recall the Hammer horror film's excessive representation of sexuality, Lucy's performance of orgasmic rapture is rendered through a series of extreme facial close-ups, her burgeoning desire literally filling the screen. As with the female vampires in the flashback, a subtext of lesbian desire is also traced through the relationship between the dying and dead Lucy and her cousin, Mina (Suzanne

Neve). As has been noted by Molly Haskell (1987), Andrea Weiss (1993), Barbara Creed (1993) and others, the horror films of the Hammer studio were particularly notorious for this convergence of excessive lesbian desire and vampirism, and thus we again see the cinematic influence in this episode of *Mystery and Imagination*. For example, a scene in the garden in which Mina meets Lucy after her death draws on the association made between lesbian eroticism and vampirism. This overt display of their desire for each other (close-ups of grabbing hands and ecstatic faces) was daring for a television drama which started prior to the nine o'clock watershed (the episode ran from 8.30 p.m. to 10.00 p.m.), and could suggest a certain increased permissiveness in television scheduling in 1968. In light of this, it is clear that *Mystery and Imagination* not only showcased the supernatural and grotesque (rather than hiding it in suggestion and restraint), but also challenged television taboos around eroticism and homosexual desire by placing sexuality firmly on display at the same time.

While this discussion of Gothic television's relationship to Gothic theatre and horror cinema has focused on set design, performance and the risqué subject matter handled in *Mystery and Imagination*, a further examination of the series' visual style finds evidence of the development of more television-specific production technologies utilised in the representation of the supernatural, rejecting the decorum and restraint of Gothic television discussed at length in the previous chapter. Just as digital production technologies would later be showcased in Gothic serial drama in the US in the 1990s (see chapter five of this book for a discussion of this moment), innovative video shooting and editing techniques were showcased in the Gothic anthology series of the 1960s and 1970s, particularly at the service of visualising the monstrous and the uncanny. Whereas Denholm Elliott's performance as Dracula is substantially theatrical, when the vampire is portrayed as insubstantial in 'Dracula' (i.e. the moments in which he is supernaturally 'transported' through solid pieces of set, or materialises or decomposes mid-shot), the episode makes full use of, and in fact 'shows off', the possibilities of video production technology. The final scene of 'Dracula', in which the vampire is reduced to a pile of ashes, is a model of the way in which television-specific production techniques were utilised to excessively display the grotesque within the Gothic anthology series. After being struck down by the brandished crucifix of Van Helsing (a moment in which the force of Dracula's loss of power is rendered through white flashes in the image produced by dramatically manipulating the contrast of the video tape), Dracula's degeneration is shown through a series of close-ups on his face and

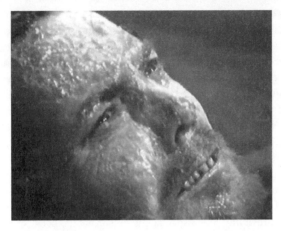

2.4 Grotesque effects: 'Dracula', *Mystery and Imagination*
(Thames, 1968).

2.5 Grotesque effects: 'Dracula', *Mystery and Imagination*
(Thames, 1968).

hands. In this moment, Dracula's face biodegrades on screen, an effect
which seems to have been achieved by overlaying an image of melting
ice on to the face of the vampire (see figure 2.4).

Following this, the image very slowly dissolves to an identical shot of
a wax model of Dracula's head, slowly melting off its skull (see figure 2.5).
As the skull begins to degenerate, and the flesh/wax also melts off a
skeletal hand, cuts are made between these grotesque images and the
horrified reaction shots of Van Helsing, Dr. Seward, Mina and Jonathan,

in a sequence which Peter Haining has described as 'a display of special effects unlike anything previously seen on television' (1993: 292). The combination of slowly dissolved images of melting prosthetics (a low-budget special effect) coupled with the extreme processing of the video image (switching to high contrast) which marks the move into this climactic sequence, can be seen as an overtly *televisual* display of the supernatural/grotesque, with the cuts to the onlooking characters diegetically representing the position of the awe-struck viewer. Indeed, the fact that there is no dialogue in this ninety second sequence privileges the televisual representation of the Gothic. While the impact of this effect lies, to a very great extent, in it being seen in the context of other television dramas of the late 1960s, it may be presumed that the shock of these images of the decomposing body of Dracula for a contemporary audience was pronounced.

In light of the decomposition sequence discussed above, truly *televisual* Gothic drama of the 1960s and 1970s was that which placed emphasis on the overt visual display of the supernatural, as opposed to the suggestive, restrained version of Gothic television drama discussed in the previous chapter. If, as John Thornton Caldwell (1995) argues, televisual television is self-consciously visual, exhibitionist and excessive, then by producing this kind of Gothic adaptation, the programme makers of *Mystery and Imagination* deliberately showcased the medium's possibilities during a period of experimentation, producing truly exhibitionist television drama which utilised a number of striking visual styles and effects as marks of distinction. Several other examples of the showcasing of visual effects and creative vision mixing can be seen in the surviving episodes of *Mystery and Imagination*: the 1968 adaptation of 'Frankenstein' used split screen techniques to show Viktor Frankenstein and his monster (both played by Ian Holm) confronting one another in the same shot, thereby utilising the special effect to fully display the uncanny image of the doppelganger on screen. These moments of technical exhibitionism within the Gothic anthology series all run contra to the notions of decorum and restraint emphasised by script editor Terence Feely at the beginning of the series' broadcast (see the introduction to *Mystery and Imagination* in the previous chapter for a discussion of Feely's comments). However, this perhaps highlights the ultimate paradox of Gothic television: by moving towards a more visually excessive style, owing much to theatrical and cinematic traditions of Gothic representation, the anthology series also moved away from the narrative preoccupation with the domestic and domestic storytelling, a preoccupation which was to dominate Gothic fiction on television in the following decades.

'We're in the horror business . . .'

Throughout the 1970s, Gothic horror flourished on British television and also infiltrated other genres and series, most notably science fiction and telefantasy. From *The Quatermass Experiment* (BBC, 1953) onwards, there has been a close link between telefantasy and Gothic horror in the UK, but in this decade a preoccupation with the Gothic genre was writ large across a number of series. This generic hybridity can be seen most clearly in the cult telefantasy series *Sapphire and Steele* (ATV, 1979–82), which featured, for example, a narrative based around a disused railway station where the dead wait for a train that never comes, or another story arc in which a shapeless being moves between time-zones via photographs and has the ability to imprison or release people from them, thus drawing on the uncanny and blurring the lines between representation and reality. Gothic horror was also a key element of the long-running series, *Dr Who*, particularly the era produced by Philip Hinchcliffe (between 1975 and 1977). The Hinchcliffe/Tom Baker years on *Dr Who* clearly saw a number of visual and narrative references being made to the Gothic, in story arcs such as 'Pyramids of Mars' (BBC1, 1975), which transported the Doctor back to an old priory in the year 1911, where the owner, Marcus Scarman, had become possessed by the spirit of Sutekh, bringer of 'the gift of death to all mankind' while excavating Egyptian tombs. A plethora of literary Gothic references were also woven into 'The Talons of Weng Chiang' (BBC1, 1977), a six-part story arc set in Victorian London, inspired by *The Phantom of the Opera* and Sax Rohmer's tales of Fu Manchu, alongside references to Jack the Ripper, *Dracula* and *Sherlock Holmes*. Prompted by the revival of the series in 2005, Matthew Sweet discussed *Dr Who's* penchant for Gothic horror in the 1970s on BBC2's arts magazine programme, *The Culture Show* (BBC2, 2004–).[5] In this feature, Sweet argued that *Dr Who* created the affect of the 'uncanny' ('the juxtaposition of the cosily familiar and the totally weird') and that *Dr Who* in the 1970s 'made you feel unsafe in your own home and on the street where you live'. Questioning whether this penchant for the Gothic uncanny was still relevant in today's television landscape, he pointed towards episodes in the new series such as 'The Unquiet Dead' (BBC1, 2005), which embraced this Gothic ancestry, set in Victorian Cardiff and starring Simon Callow as Charles Dickens, featuring a race of aliens that live by reanimating dead bodies.

Also shifting from a sci-fi focus towards Gothic horror in the 1970s was the anthology series, *Out of the Unknown* (BBC2, 1965–71), which, after switching from original producer, Irene Shubik to Alan Bromly in its fourth season, concentrated on tales of Gothic horror and suspense.

In the *Radio Times*, Bromly cited shifts in expectations of television drama, as well as shifts in the credulity of the audience, as reasons for the demise of science fiction and the popularity of 'tales of mystery and imagination':

> To do [science fiction] really successfully must involve you in spending an enormous amount of money on special effects which the cinema can for an epic like *2001 – a Space Odyssey*, but which is beyond the reach of television. The other problem for the science fiction enthusiast is simple reality. When everyone has seen men walking on the moon and sat through a real cliff-hanger about getting them back alive, then just setting a story somewhere in space is not, you can see, the automatic thrill it once was. (Fiddick, 1971: 4)

The brand of Gothic horror produced by Bromly's series was, in contrast to the other-wordly science fiction described by Bromly above, set in the present day, taking place in more everyday locations (homes, offices, etc.), and prefiguring the domestic horrors discussed at the end of this chapter. For example, the most notorious of these teleplays, 'To Lay a Ghost' (BBC2, 1971), starred Lesley Anne Down as Diana Carver, a young woman traumatised by rape as a teenager in the 1960s, who is visited by the ghost of an eighteenth century rapist in her new marital home. In this episode then, the monstrous villain of earlier Gothic horror horrifyingly enters television's modern day, domestic spaces. While viewers wrote in to the *Radio Times* complaining about this generic shift in the series,[6] Bromly defended *Out of the Unknown*'s 'change in tastes' by arguing that the change had taken place under the direction of the Plays department (possibly responding to the success of programmes like *Mystery and Imagination* on the commercial channel), and that the plays had, in actual fact, proved to be attracting larger ratings than their sci-fi predecessors. It is this sense of commercial populism however with which readers of the *Radio Times* really took issue. Writing in June 1971, viewer Peter A. Fryer complained that,

> The popular science fiction series *Star Trek* ended recently, leaving a sizable sf vacuum which is not filled by the current *Out of the Unknown* ghost and psychological – that is, horror – series . . . The current series may be popular but it appeals to a *different audience* [original emphasis]. Indeed I and most of my friends no longer watch it . . . ratings alone are not everything and the BBC enjoys a reputation for educating taste and catering for minorities – unlike other networks. (Fryer, 1971: 5)

Gothic horror television in the UK really reached its zenith in 1977, with the BBC producing a prestigious adaptation of *Dracula* entitled

Count Dracula, directed by Phillip Saville and starring Louis Jourdan in the title role. This adaptation relied heavily on those special video effects first introduced in *Mystery and Imagination* a decade earlier in its representation of the supernatural. Also in the same year the BBC produced its own Gothic anthology series, *Supernatural*, produced by Pieter Rogers, mainly written by Robert Muller, and featuring eight original Gothic teleplays about ghosts, doppelgangers, werewolves, supernaturally animated dolls and marionettes, and vampires. The series, based around the conceit of a Victorian storytelling club, 'The Club of the Damned', framed each of the stories with a diegetic audience who also, at the end of each episode, acted as diegetic critics, commenting on the quality and validity of each tale. Like *Mystery and Imagination*, *Supernatural* utilised a number of innovative filming and editing techniques, drawing on the possibilities of vision mixing technology in portraying supernatural figures and uncanny events. Following the lead of the earlier series, shots and scenes were often switched to negative or black and white to demarcate a supernatural presence, images from several different shots were overlaid or juxtaposed in the same frame to create an 'uncanny' image, and montages of still photographs and drawings were, on occasion, inserted into the narrative to suggest a sense of haunting or a kind of supernatural link with the past. For example, in an episode entitled 'Mr. Nightingale', written by Muller and directed by Alan Cooke, a number of these techniques are employed to represent the ensuing madness of the eponymous character (played by Jeremy Brett) who is brought face to face with his own doppelganger. Following the opening sequence of the teleplay, in which the storyteller performs for the Club of the Damned as a cackling madman (another exaggerated performance of a Gothic stereotype), a slow track towards the flames of an open fire dissolves to an overlaid montage of photographs and paintings of Hamburg. Here the still, pictorial image is used to both establish a sense of time and place, and to create a feeling of unease around the representation of a European past (notably, many of the teleplays in this series were based in an often loosely identified European country, rather than in the UK). However, this episode employed innovative vision mixing to its fullest effect in the representation of paranoia and madness. Throughout the teleplay, even relatively routine edits, such as the moment where Mr. Nightingale goes upstairs for the night, are made strange through the use of a diagonal wipe, drawing attention to the vision mixing technology employed in the production of the drama. Once upstairs, Mr. Nightingale's experience of uncanny paranoia (the feeling that he is being followed by a doppelganger) is represented in a montage of images linked together by ostentatious mixes: a point-of-view shot out of his bedroom window, of two identical paintings of Germanic architecture overlaid on top of one another, is repeatedly spun 360°, followed by a point-glance of Nightingale's face overlaid with an image of a seagull, which is then switched to an iris (an edit more usually seen in early cinema) which in turn 'irises out' to a woman standing outside his room in the corridor. In moments such as these we see a truly *televisual* aesthetic within the Gothic teleplay, marking a shift beyond the naturalist paradigm towards something closer to impressionism.[7]

Reviews of the series were mixed, as were the BBC's Audience Research Reports, with both again suggesting that television was simply incapable of creating a suitably eerie Gothic 'atmosphere'. One reviewer from the *Glasgow Herald* wrote that '*Supernatural* . . . put out in the most expensive looking way with special music, big names and cartloads of frenzied Gothic, proves all over again that television simply tramps the occult into the ground' (Anon., 1977: 25). Here, as with many of the series' reviews, it is the privileging of style over content which was seen as its ultimate downfall; to quote the opening monologue of the series, delivered by the chairman of the Club of the Damned, 'You must tell a true story of supernatural terror. If you succeed in chilling our blood, you will be permitted to join [our club]. But if, in the opinion of only one of us, you fail, the penalty is death.' In the opening lines of *Supernatural*, Robert Muller pre-empted the critical response to his teleplays, offering a telling nod to the role of television reviewer in the life of a television series.

Even prior to *Supernatural*'s production, however, the BBC had used the Gothic anthology series to showcase a technological development in the medium that was to have a wide-ranging impact on television drama as a whole: the introduction of colour. In 1967, coinciding with the introduction of colour to BBC2 transmissions, the corporation started a practical training experiment to familiarise its staff with the use of the new equipment for the service. As a result of this training, *Late Night Horror* was commissioned, a six-part series which again focused on the literary adaptation (this time adapting short stories by Roald Dahl, Arthur Conan Doyle and some lesser known horror writers). The programme drew on the Gothic, and in particular the profusion of blood and gore required by *grand guignol* Gothic horror, to experiment with the possibilities of the medium, just as the phantasmagoria showmen of the eighteenth and nineteenth centuries had used images of supernatural beings to demonstrate the potential of their early projection equipment (see Mannoni (2000) for a discussion of this phenomenon). The producer of the series, Harry Moore, was very much aware that *Late Night Horror* was to be seen as a showcase for colour 35mm film production on television, as was Gerald Savory (Head of Drama), who referred to the series as 'six experiments' in a memo to the controller of BBC2 about the scheduling of *Late Night Horror* (Savory, 1967a), outlining the need for the series to 'headline' the evening's drama output: it was eventually broadcast at 11.50 p.m. on Friday nights, a slot which perhaps reflects the fact that the experiment wasn't seen as being entirely successful as well as the gruesome subject matter of its teleplays. Moore delineated precisely what he wanted from the series in a memo to his directors, who had been sent on a 'colour course' to learn the possibilities and limits of the new equipment prior to the beginning of production. These directors, Rudolph Cartier, Naomi Capon, Paddy Russell and Richard Martin, were told:

> *Late Night Horror* will be the first drama series to be recorded in colour. We may not be the first to be transmitted, but all the more reason for us to do all we can to ensure that we create a standard which the other drama people have to follow . . . I would like to stress that we must do everything we can in our shows from the very beginning to stimulate suspense, tension, atmosphere, potential horror and HORROR! As I suggested before, use music, if there is blood, let's see the blood. If somebody is nasty, let's make them 'real nasty' . . . We're in the horror business and this series will stand or fall on the enthusiasm and delight we show in our approach to it. So blood, guts, thunder, lightning, eyeballs, dark corners, cobwebs, close-ups, faces, faces, faces, and above all EXCITEMENT! Let's tease our audience and get them to love it. (Moore, 1967a)

The sense of innovation and experimentation in Moore's instruction is very clearly coupled with the explicit portrayal of gory horror in *Late Night Horror*, emphasising both the need to display the possibilities of the new technology and the desire to place blood and gore on show in close-up. An example from the series, such as the removal of Diane Cilento's lower lip in the episode 'The Kiss of Blood', directed by Richard Martin, is telling of just how graphic these six 'experiments' were, although the gimmicky nature of the series was not easily missed in the press. A report on the episode from the *Sunday Telegraph* states that '*Late Night Horror* culminated in another easily bought thrill, the particularly revolting mutilation of Diane Cilento . . . The reaction was a very loud ugh, but . . . you felt the story existed only to make its effects, and when these were expended the whole thing shrivelled away' (Anon., 1968b: 35).

Although the series strove for technical innovation and the showcasing of new technology, the production teams working on *Late Night Horror* were disappointed by the limitations of the new equipment, which was heavy and difficult to manoeuvre, and worried that the majority of the audience still watching in black and white would find the camera work dated and unimaginative. On this subject, producer Harry Moore wrote the following:

> If we want to sell the excitement of colour we're not going to do it by restricting our shooting capacity. We have a good standard now, but as most viewers will be watching in black and white we'll be giving them 'old hat' production standards. They are not going to be excited about having a colour television if it doesn't look as good as the old black and white. (Moore, 1967b)

Gerald Savory also added to this in his report on the filming of *Late Night Horror*: '[It] is proving exceedingly slow with the result that only the most primitive camera techniques can be employed. The most serious result of this can be seen in the inadequacy of the lighting . . . Unfortunately it is really very far below the standard we expect' (Savory, 1967b).

It appears that in privileging the representation of blood in colour above all else, other production values in this series suffered, and what started out as an experimentation in the depiction of horror in all its gory glory ended up as a rather disappointing and pedestrian teleplay. While the Audience Research Report on the *Late Night Horror* episode 'The Kiss of Blood' reports that '[a student] was one of two or three viewers who saw the transmission in colour, and, for his part, it seems that the "blood" flowing from Lady Sannox' excised lower lip, "looking exactly like the real thing", was an impressive and terrible sight' (BBC, 1968b); the report also acknowledges that the series, 'intended to give "a real fright" to those who relish a lurid tale, has not always met expectations of passing an agreeably blood-curdling time' (BBC, 1968b). Writing of this moment in television history, Andrew Crisell states:

> The obvious effect of colour was to make the medium of television immensely more vivid and picturesque: costume dramas and natural history programmes were only two of its more obvious beneficiaries. But there were also negative implications. Those who worried about effects and influences of television were not slow to point out that in its representation of violence . . . the blood would now run red. (1997: 116)

As a self-confessed horror programme, *Late Night Horror* really encapsulated the morally ambiguous effects of colour television as expressed by Crisell, while at the same time showcasing new production technologies.

Narratively, *Late Night Horror* was in fact closer to later Gothic anthology series on British television than it was to series such as *Mystery and Imagination* and those episodes of *Ghost Story for Christmas* discussed above, with their emphasis on the adaptation of literary horrors set in the past. While these series featured literary ghosts and monsters dislocated from the present day to another time and place, *Late Night Horror*'s episodes mainly took place within a contemporary, domestic setting. As such, they represent a mimetic tradition within Gothic cinema and television drama, like those films made by the Amicus studio in contemporaneous British cinema (see Hutchings, 2002b). Series such as *Haunted* (ABC [UK], 1967–68), *Journey to the Unknown* (ATV, 1968–70), *Dead of Night* (BBC2, 1972), *Thriller* (ATV, 1973–76) and *Hammer House of Horror* (Cinema Arts International, 1980), beginning in the late 1960s but becoming increasingly prevalent throughout the following decade, all situated themselves within this 'mimetic tradition', featuring narratives which emphasised the everydayness of television horror. In these series, hauntings and possessions mostly took place within the domestic locale, explicitly playing on the fears around the home and family which had become prevalent during the decades in question.

The house that bled to death: the emergence of domestic horror

As discussed in the introduction to this book, Gregory A. Waller makes reference to a connection between the domestic subject matter of the made-for-television horror film and the domestic viewing context of television. According to Waller, these programmes are 'focused on the personal and the intimate, and are particularly given to narratives that feature an isolated victim . . . endangered young wife, or threatened middle-class family' (1987b: 145), going on to state that in these programmes 'horror comes from outside the house and the family, infiltrating normality just as effortlessly and invisibly as the television programmes that appear in our living rooms' (1987b: 159). Similarly, the final part of this chapter on Gothic horror on British television finds the family and domesticity at the centre of a number of Gothic anthology series, though Waller's observation that 'horror comes from *outside* the home and family' may be less appropriate in this context. While the series discussed previously in this chapter offered distinctly televisual adaptations of classic Gothic literature, set in the distant past (decaying mansions, vaguely defined European cities), horror television in the late 1960s and 1970s was to take a simultaneous potentially terrifying turn towards the domestic, with the Gothic anthology relocating from the past to the present day. Series such as *Out of the Unknown*, *Haunted*, *Dead of Night* and *Thriller* brought horror back into the home in no uncertain terms, transposing tales of haunting, possession, witchcraft and devil worship to suburban semis, and depicting the nuclear family as an institution simultaneously threatening and under threat. In *Dead of Night* for example, teleplays such as 'The

Exorcism' centred on a dinner party ruined by wine glasses full of blood and the possession of the hostess, and the final episode of this series, 'A Woman Sobbing', told the story of a neurotic, unhappy housewife who is driven to commit suicide by the sound of a ghostly woman sobbing in the attic of her suburban home. While the formal experimentation of series such as *Mystery and Imagination* and *Supernatural* marked them as distinctively *televisual*, flaunting the possibilities of video production in creating affective Gothic horror, the anthology series in this cycle were more formally conventional, referring to the visual styles, and the ordinary spaces and situations, of television drama, only to turn this milieu on its head. In essence, the turn towards everyday horror in these series is more 'televisual' in the traditional sense of the word, meaning medium specific rather than stylistically distinctive. While many of these series were shot on film and prepared simultaneously for domestic viewers and an export market (of which, more below), they also drew on British television's recognisable narratives and image repertoire, from the hapless family of the domestic sitcom to the homes and work spaces of the social realist soap, producing a series of horrific narratives out of the everyday fare of television drama. The final part of this chapter on the British horror anthology series will therefore examine the quotidian turn in Gothic television, focusing on *Hammer House of Horror*, produced by Cinema Arts International (under the name of Hammer Films) for the Incorporated Television Company (ITC) in 1980, in which the cycle reached its zenith. In fact, this was Hammer's second foray into television, following another anthology series, *Journey into the Unknown*, an ITC/Hammer/20th Century Fox co-production made between 1968 and 1970, a series of taut psychological thrillers which prefigured *Hammer House of Horror* in their contemporary, domestic settings. *Hammer House of Horror* was also followed by the less successful *Hammer House of Mystery and Suspense* (Hammer Film Productions Ltd, 1984) which, under the direction of its US co-producer, Twentieth Century Fox, watered down the full-blown horror of the former series. However, it is in *Hammer House of Horror* that we find the most complete anthology of the typical settings and narrative concerns of domestic, quotidian horror.

In 1979, at the end of Hammer Films' life as a film producing studio, Brian Lawrence and Roy Skeggs, who had recently formed their own company, Cinema Arts International, bought the rights to the Hammer name from the official receivers. Lawrence, who had been at Hammer since 1945 and became a director of the company, and Skeggs, who arrived in 1963 as production accountant, later rising to production supervisor, had proposed an idea for a television series in 1976, in an attempt to counter some of Hammer's financial difficulties. However, it was not until heading up their own production company in 1978 that these plans were put into action. Once the series had been commissioned by Lew Grade's ITC (ATV's programme making division), Lawrence and Skeggs brought in experienced television producer, director, writer and script editor Anthony Read[8] in April 1980 as script editor on *Hammer House of Horror*, ostensibly to advise them on the specifics of creating horror drama for television. Renting country manor Hampden House in Buckinghamshire as their production base (which would also appear as a location in several of the episodes), the series was shot entirely on film and on location in the surrounding area as the most economically viable option at the time. The series featured work by, among others, directors Peter Sasdy ('The Thirteenth Reunion', 'Rude Awakening', 'Visitor from the Grave'), Alan Gibson ('The Silent Scream', 'The Two Faces of Evil') and Don Leaver ('The Mark of Satan', 'Witching Time', 'The Thirteenth Reunion') and writers David Lloyd ('The House that Bled to Death'), Don Shaw ('The Mark of Satan') and Gerald Savory ('Rude Awakening').

Like many of the programmes discussed in this book and, particularly, many of the other series in this cycle, *Hammer House of Horror* traded on a certain congruence between the situations and spaces of horror on screen, and the lives and homes of the viewers who watched the series. Introducing the series in the *TV Times* listings guide, Tony Whitehead set out to explore the attraction of the genre for the domestic viewer, offering a pseudo-psychoanalytic analysis of typical horror narratives: 'Some people risk their lives to feel fear but most welcome the sensation if it can be engendered without hazard. The feeling causes changes in the body which excite . . . Horror films allow us to experience these emotions vicariously by what we see on screen' (Whitehead, 1980: 20–1). While Whitehead's analysis of horror speaks about the *general* attractions of the genre, it is the specific nature of horror at home which, we might argue, amplifies these sensations of vicarious endangerment, particularly if the narratives viewed on screen reflect this viewing context in some way.

It has been argued elsewhere that homes and families became the standard fare of horror narratives beyond the medium of television during the 1970s, and that this preoccupation was not limited to the UK. For example, examining the cycle of American horror films which includes films such as *Night of the Living Dead* (US, 1968), *Rosemary's Baby* (US, 1968), *The Exorcist* (US, 1973), *It's Alive* (US, 1973), *The Last House on the Left* (US, 1972), *The Texas Chainsaw Massacre* (US, 1974), *The Omen* (US, 1976) and *The Hills Have Eyes* (US, 1977), Robin Wood has argued that 'the process whereby horror becomes associated with its true milieu, the family, is reflected in its steady geographical progress toward

America' (1986: 85). Combining Marxist and Freudian approaches, Wood analyses the horrific representation of families in these films in relation to the notions of basic and surplus repression:

> Basic repression is universal, necessary and inescapable . . . Surplus repression, on the other hand, is specific to a particular culture and is the process whereby people are conditioned from earliest infancy to take on predetermined roles within that culture . . . *Basic* repression makes us distinctively human, capable of directing our own lives and co-existing with others; *surplus* repression makes us into monogamous heterosexual bourgeois capitalists. (Wood, 1986: 70–1)[9]

Therefore, according to Wood (and others, such as Williams (1996)), in the American family horror film of the 1970s, it is the return of these surplus repressions, in the form of monstrous family or family members, which characterises the genre in this period, producing non-normative representations of familial, social and sexual relationships. It is worthy of note that in his discussion of these films, Tony Williams argues that these family horror films are contrapuntal to depictions of the family on television. He argues that 'all these depictions contradict normal idealized family images in mainstream American film and television. They disrupt the ideological norms of family sitcoms such as *Father Knows Best, I Love Lucy, Ozzie and Harriet* . . . and *Leave it to Beaver*' (1996: 13). It is striking, however, that all of Williams' examples of the family sitcom are taken from a much earlier broadcasting era, the 1950s, and that perhaps it might be more pertinent to ask what images of domestic life were being offered by American television contemporaneously (see chapter four of this book for a discussion of Gothic television in the US during this period).

In the United Kingdom during the same period, horror cinema was taking a similar turn towards the home and family. In his extensive history of the British horror film, Peter Hutchings has argued that the 'marginalisation of both Count Dracula and Baron Frankenstein in British horror cinema of the 1970s was only one part of a much wider rejection and casting out of those male authority figures who had been so important in earlier Hammer horrors' (1993: 159). Carefully situating his analyses within their social contexts, Hutchings argues that films such as *Blood from the Mummy's Tomb* (1971) or *And Now The Screaming Starts* (1973), reflected era-specific concerns surrounding issues of masculinity, authority and, particularly, crises within the family:

> Throughout the late 1960s and early 1970s, 'family' became an increasingly contested term. For the Women's Movement, it was the prime

institution of patriarchal repression of women . . . For psychiatrists R.D. Laing and David Cooper, it employed a more general repressiveness . . . For the various conservative moral movements of the time, however, it was the beleaguered repository of religious and moral value, that which bound modern society together and which had to be protected. (1993: 166)

Employing psychoanalytic theory to unpack the representations of 'horror families' in these films, Hutchings argues that continuing to set British Gothic films in the past during this period allowed for an exploration of the 'psychological effects of the family structure' (1993: 167), away from the familiarity of the more recognisable modern family, as found in the contemporaneous American horrors.

On the one hand, this work on the horror film simply suggests that the turn towards more domestic horrors on British television was part of a broader cultural trend, and that it was therefore not specific to the medium, beyond the certain congruence between the homes and families on screen and the domestic context of viewing, discussed above. According to Hutchings' analysis, fears about the family as either repressive institution or as an essential, but threatened, part of modern society underscored horror narratives in the 1970s, whether disguised in a Gothic past (in the UK) or relocated to homes of contemporary America (in the US). However, what distinguishes the Gothic horror anthology series on British television during this period is the very ordinariness of the homes and families on screen. In a rather self-referential move, 'Witching Time', the first episode of *Hammer House of Horror* (written by script editor Anthony Read), plays on this difference between the Gothic horror of British cinema and the anthology series for television, by centring its narrative on the haunting of a composer of cinematic horror soundtracks (David Winter, played by horror stalwart Jon Finch). While the pre-credit sequence depicts an attack on a seventeenth century heroine in a typical wood-panelled stately home, the shot which immediately follows the credits reveals this teaser sequence being played on a monitor in the home of David Winter as he composes the score for the 'film within the programme'. Here a gap is created between the filmic representation of horror safely placed within a Gothic past and the 'real', contemporary horror of Gothic television, suggesting that the latter is far more threatening to the television viewer than the former. Filmic horror is depicted as fake, a mere representation, at the beginning of this episode; the trappings of its production are exposed by the depiction of soundtrack composition to create maximum horror 'affect'. By comparison television horror is authenticated through its representation of the everyday life of the composer within a recognisable domestic space (a space which is nevertheless invaded by the arrival of a seventeenth century ghost later in the episode).

In *Hammer House of Horror* therefore, a tension is quickly established which might be best described by the phrase 'nothing is what it seems': episodes from the series constantly remind their viewers that the horrific and the banal are coexistent, that children who appear sweet and innocent may in fact be murderous and sadistic, and that the most unassuming-looking family home might house any number of grisly Gothic secrets. In short, the Gothic television of the 1970s and early 1980s embraced the dualism of the family described by Hutchings above, building its narratives around the notion that horror exists 'all around us'. Typically, the sense that the family is a simultaneously threatened and threatening institution is manifest in a number of recurring images and motifs in *Hammer House of Horror*. The house is repeatedly depicted as a space of haunting ('The House that Bled to Death', 'Witching Time', 'Visitor from the Grave'), imprisonment ('The House that Bled to Death', 'The Silent Scream', 'Children of the Full Moon', 'The Mask of Satan'), paranoia ('Rude Awakening', 'The Mask of Satan') and monstrous invasion ('The Two Faces of Evil', 'Visitors from the Grave'). Recurring characters including the wife or mother who is disbelieved by her husband and/or another figure of patriarchal authority ('Children of the Full Moon', 'The House that Bled to Death', 'Two Faces of Evil', 'The Silent Scream', 'Visitors from the Grave'), and the seemingly innocent but murderous child ('Children of the Full Moon', 'Growing Pains', 'The House that Bled to Death', 'The Two Faces of Evil'), also speak to the quotidian nature of the series' particular brand of horror.

Turning to a single episode from *Hammer House of Horror* to illustrate this approach to family horror for television, 'The House that Bled to Death' (Cinema Arts International, 1980)[10] encapsulates many of the recurring themes, motifs and images from the series, and is the episode which most obviously engages with both its Gothic heritage and the specificities of made-for-television horror. The narrative, which bears a striking resemblance to the film *The Amityville Horror* (US, 1979), centres on the story of William (Nicholas Ball), Emma (Rachel Davies) and their daughter, Sophie (Emma Ridley), a young family who move into an unoccupied house that had previously been the scene of a grisly murder. Once they arrive at the house it appears that they are being haunted by the old man who murdered his wife in their kitchen and a number of gruesome incidents take place which terrify their neighbours and drive the family out of the house. However, in an unexpected twist at the end of the episode it is revealed that the haunted couple, who are now living in luxury in the United States, were not in fact married and had faked the haunting (at the behest of a 'real horror' writer) in order to make money out of selling their story. However, when Emma's daughter Sophie discovers this fact she stabs her mother's lover to death in the episode's final moments.

With most of the episode taking place inside an ordinary-looking sub-urban semi (see figure 2.6), which we presume to be haunted by its previous occupants until the *dénouement* of the episode, 'The House that Bled to Death' transports the traditional Gothic haunted house narrative into the domestic milieu of television drama. Here the very 'everyday-ness' of this location serves to emphasise the connection between the homes and families under threat within the narrative and the homes in which the television drama is viewed.

The opening shot of the episode encapsulates the coexistence of the horrific and the everyday. The shot, which begins on a close-up of two old fashioned china cups and a tin of Cadbury's cocoa powder, bringing to mind both the role of advertising within the television text as well as the viewing rituals of the audience at home (settling down in front of the tele-vision with a 'nice cup of cocoa'), is swiftly revealed as the setting up of a murder, with the old man preparing the drinks tipping a pack of poison into one of the cups. This sinister beginning, a flashback to the murder which precipitates the 'hauntings' in the episode, is therefore structured around the disruption of the everyday; as the camera tracks away from the old man preparing the drinks and around the homely-looking kitchen, it settles on his wife, who sits at the table knitting, not paying much atten-tion to her husband, actions which suggest habit and routine. As she

2.6 The location of everyday horror: 'The House that Bled to Death', *Hammer House of Horror* (Cinema Arts International, 1980).

looks up, a cut is made to a pan of milk boiling over (the proverbial 'spilt milk', a visual metaphor which is repeated later in the episode), as an inherently domestic image which nonetheless forewarns the viewer of the old woman's impending doom, all the while staying within the image repertoire of home and family. In fact, the episode only begins to transform into a more recognisable horror narrative when the old woman takes a drink of her cocoa, prompting tremulous extra-diegetic music to begin. Once his wife has fallen to the floor, the old man takes a pair of decorative knives from the wall and begins to sharpen them menacingly. Again, it is telling that these knives are an integral part of the home décor of this old couple, emphasising the fine line between domesticity and horror. The threat to the home and family is therefore established from the outset as essentially horror *from within*, rather than something 'alien' which infiltrates the domestic space from beyond its boundaries.

After the credit sequence, the episode proper begins, as the family is shown round the semi-detached, pebble-dashed house at 42, Colman Road by a man who appears to be an estate agent (it is later revealed that he is the writer who set up the haunting scam). In these establishing moments, and throughout the majority of the episode, it is the ordinariness of the family which is emphasised: they dress in contemporary fashions, work in 'ordinary' jobs (as a hospital porter and a housewife) and socialise with their similarly ordinary neighbours. Furthermore, it is the 'ordinary' moments of their everyday lives which are constantly disrupted by horrific and gory moments of 'haunting'. Unpacking is disrupted by bleeding walls in Sophie's bedroom, housework is disrupted by the gory discovery of the family cat, garrotted and bleeding on the window ledge, the preparation of cornflakes is halted by the appearance of a severed hand in the fridge, and an extended montage of children eating at Sophie's birthday party is suddenly and spectacularly interrupted by jets of 'blood' spilling out over the dinner table (and the children) from above. It is also significant that it is the return of everyday objects from the pre-credit sequence (the ornamental knives which hung on the wall, and the old woman's knitting and false teeth) which mark the moments of haunting in the episode, reminding the viewer once more that horror here is found, not in the unknown, but in the known and the familiar. Even in the conclusion of the episode, when the couple's deceit is revealed, Sophie's slaughter of her stepfather suggests to the viewer that corruption and horror are created within, not outside of, the nuclear family. As the final shot of the episode freezes on Emma's blood-splattered face, the viewer is left with the possibility that the horror of living in the 'haunted house' has produced a new monster from within in the form of a nine year old girl.

Like many of the episodes in *Hammer House of Horror* then, 'The House that Bled to Death' begins *in media res* and ends without a clear sense of absolute conclusion; we might therefore understand these narrative devices as specific to the episodic television narrative, inviting a textual overlap with the programmes which precede and follow each episode and suggesting that horror exists within the context of the everyday. By utilising these opening and closing devices, episodes of *Hammer House of Horror* were meaningfully inserted into the flow of the broadcast text and the flow of the viewer's everyday life. This suggestion runs counter to Gregory A. Waller's proposal that in the made-for-television horror film, the flow of the broadcast text dissipates any sense of horror; as Waller argues, 'the happy reconciliatory, restorative endings of virtually all the tele-films' mean that 'having been to hell and back the viewer can also proceed with life as usual, staying tuned for the 11 o'clock news' (1987b: 159). In the case of the anthologised horror of series such as *Hammer House of Horror*, the sense that episodes begin and end in the middle of the action undercuts this restorative sense of closure.

Throughout the series, casting was also used to emphasise this congruence of the everyday and *grand guignol* horror: for example, in the episode 'The Silent Scream', Peter Cushing is revealed, not in the high collared shirt and waistcoat of the Gothic anti-hero/mad scientist, but in the brown overalls of the small-time pet shop keeper, as a further reminder that 'nothing is what it seems' in television horror. While prior knowledge of Cushing's association with the genre leads us to believe that he will play the part of sinister antagonist in the episode, his initial entrance into the narrative 'against type' leads us to believe otherwise (even though it is later discovered that Cushing is playing exactly *to type* as a German ex-Nazi and mad scientist). The appearance of Diana Dors as a matronly foster mother in the episode 'Children of the Full Moon' also creates a similar effect, playing against expectations of the actress as star and stressing the 'ordinariness' of her non-glamorous character. With a wig of greying hair pulled into an untidy bun and dowdy, motherly clothes, the appearance of this character sets out to belie her position as unconventional *'femme fatale'* in the episode.

While it has been argued above that *Hammer House of Horror* played on its status as television, drawing on medium-specific representations of home and family to create potential frisson within the domestic viewing context, this use of actors from British cinema, and particularly the horror genre, denotes a close link between the series and its filmic ancestry. As discussed previously, Lawrence and Skeggs were experienced producers of horror *films*, and their series certainly drew on this experience, producing an aesthetic which simultaneously referenced the familiarity of television drama and the seedy glamour of the low budget horror film. Like Cinema Arts International's next television series, *Hammer House of Mystery and Suspense*, *Hammer House of Horror* was shot on 35mm film, and consequently looked very much like the British horror cinema of the preceding decade. However, unlike the former series, *Hammer House of Horror* was made with a mainly British audience in mind, and retained a style and a mode of address specific to the late night anthology series on British television. *Hammer House of Mystery and Suspense*, which was partly funded by Twentieth Century Fox in the US and would air on American television as *Fox Mystery Theatre*, toned down the horror and supernatural effects of *Hammer House of Horror* in order to placate the US censors; the spectacular gore of episodes like 'The House that Bled to Death' would be untenable on primetime network television in the US. Fox also dictated a new running time of 90 minutes for this series, so that the anthologised teleplays could be sold to the American audience as 'features'. The impact of US co-production was seen elsewhere in relation to the Gothic/horror anthology series: for example, *Thriller*, another ATV co-production with US television network ABC Television, was produced using a number of US actors and storylines incorporating visiting Americans, in order to bridge the gap between domestic, British television and its viewers and an international audience.

Aside from the minimal output of the ex-Hammer production team from Cinema Arts International, the Gothic anthology eventually dwindled in popularity during the 1980s. With a few notable exceptions it would appear that quotidian horror had become deeply unfashionable in a decade where television drama was dominated by nostalgic, big-budget classic drama series which were less problematic for an export market, and socio-politically aware serial drama which had an inherent 'seriousness' at polar opposite to the Gothic anthology series. The main exceptions to this were to be found in children's drama, an area which receives scant attention in this study of Gothic television, but which produced a number of haunting Gothic serials during the late 1970s and 1980s. This trend was initiated by a cycle of dramas produced for the Welsh company HTV, under the direction of Patrick Dromgoole (who had earlier directed *Mystery and Imagination*'s 'Dracula' episode for ABC). Produced by Leonard White, who also partly directed the latter serial, programmes such as *The Georgian House* (HTV, 1976) and *The Clifton House Mystery* (HTV, 1978) found children at the centre of Gothic narratives in which figures from the past returned to haunt them, channelled in both cases by a sinister haunted house. Similarly, in the 1980s Paul Stone produced a number of Gothic literary adaptations for children's television on the BBC, where again the child protagonist was transported through a haunted house or garden into a sinister past. The first two of these, *The Children of Green Knowe* (BBC1, 1986) and *Moondial* (1988) were directed by Colin Cant; *Tom's Midnight Garden* (BBC1, 1989) saw Stone collaborating with Christine Slocombe. All were permeated with an eerie atmosphere and a sense of unease, though *Moondial* was particularly dark, a chilling struggle between good and evil which was hauntingly shot in and around Belton House in Lincolnshire by Trevor Wimlett. The Gothicism of these serials was, at the time, highly unusual for children's drama, and there is certainly scope for further research to be conducted into their production and reception.[11] For example, to a certain extent they can be seen as part of the continuing cycle of Gothic or 'feel bad' heritage texts discussed in this book. However, there is not space in this chapter to discuss their significance any further.

Another striking exception to this downward trend in quotidian horror was the BBC's spoof documentary, 'Ghostwatch' (BBC1, 1992), an episode of the *Screen One* series which caused outraged reactions from viewers and the press when TV presenters Sarah Greene and Craig Charles, playing themselves, ostensibly reported from a family home which was possessed by an evil spirit. When the children of the family began speaking in tongues, Greene was killed during the Outside Broadcast and Michael Parkinson, as studio anchor, became possessed by the spirit under investigation, a number of people rang the BBC and ITC to complain, suggesting that the closeness between horror and the familiar could in fact be taken too far for some viewers. Of course, the 1980s was also the decade which saw the introduction of home video, and the domestic reception of extreme horror became more commonplace thanks to this development in film exhibition and distribution. Perhaps, as a result of this, television horror, and Gothic television in particular, may have seemed rather tame by comparison.

More recently, the Gothic anthology format has been evoked on British television in a number of ways, from straight revisitations of the genre (with *Chiller* (Yorkshire, 1995), *Ghosts* (BBC2, 1995) and *Urban Gothic* (Channel 5, 2000–1) all providing anthology dramas of the supernatural) to satirical parodies of the British television Gothic. Series such as *Dr Terrible's House of Horrible* (BBC2, 2001) and *Garth Merenghi's Darkplace* (Channel 4, 2004) make explicit visual and narrative reference to many of the anthology series discussed above, lampooning the televisual display of the supernatural in programmes like *Mystery and Imagination* and *Dr Who*. *The League of Gentlemen* (BBC2, 1999–2002) also wove a

plethora of references to earlier British Gothic films and television programmes into a dark situation comedy about the fictional town of Royston
Vasey, offering the dedicated fan-viewer the opportunity to recognise a
series of allusions to the genre. This series celebrated a rich heritage of
British Gothic fiction in all media, and explicitly utilised the anthology/
portmanteau format in its 1999 Christmas episode to underline its debt
to the genre. In all of these programmes, the memory of watching Gothic
television is placed in the foreground, both through visual style and by
narrative allusion, suggesting that programmes from this genre remain
somehow indelibly marked on the viewer's psyche. Even while programmes such as *Dr Terrible's House of Horrible* and *The League of
Gentlemen* satirise the clichés and effects of Gothic television of the
1960s, 1970s and 1980s, they acknowledge that domestic viewing of the
horror genre produced a lasting effect on its audience, whereby the child
crouching behind the sofa, transfixed by late-night horror television,
becomes the knowing, adult producer and viewer twenty or thirty years
later.

Notes

1 A more comprehensive assessment of 'televisuality' and the impact of Caldwell's
   work is offered in chapter five of this book, in relation to Gothic television from
   the US in the 1990s and beyond.
2 Liberal in the sense that the character Renfield is replaced in this version by an
   insane Jonathan Harker, and all of the action takes place in London, ostensibly
   after Harker and Count Dracula have returned from Transylvania, aside from an
   extended flashback.
3 Elliott's appearance is quite similar, in fact, to the appearance of Gary Oldman as
   the Count in Francis Ford Coppola's more recent adaptation, *Bram Stoker's
   Dracula* (US, 1992).
4 For example, both Bloch's and Matheson's work featured heavily in the NBC
   anthology series from the early 1960s, *Thriller*, hosted by Boris Karloff (see
   chapter five for a further description of this series).
5 Episode broadcast on 17 March 2005.
6 These responses are collected on the excellent *Mausoleum Club* website, a site dedicated to the appreciation of classic British television: http://www.the-mausoleum-
   club.org.uk/Out_Of_The_Unknown/out_of_the_unknown_appendix. htm.
7 See Wheatley (2006) for a further exploration of the impressionist style in anthology drama.
8 Read had had a long career in television as producer (e.g. *The Troubleshooters*
   (BBC1, 1966–72)), director (e.g. *Sapphire and Steel*), script editor (e.g. *Dr Who*) and
   writer (e.g. *The Professionals* (LWT, 1977–83)).
9 Original emphasis.
10 Written by David Lloyd and directed by Tom Clegg.
11 My thanks go to Dr. David Butler at the University of Manchester for reminding me about the phenomenon of children's Gothic television drama in the

1980s; perversely, given the lack of space given in this book to a discussion of this programming, I believe these programmes may have initially whetted my appetite for the Gothic. Dr. Butler also pointed out to me that the cycle of Sherlock Holmes adaptations produced by Granada in the 1980s and early 1990s, beginning with *The Adventures of Sherlock Holmes* (Granada, 1984–85), demonstrated many of the tropes of Gothic television outlined in this book, particularly the mini-serial *The Eligible Bachelor* (Granada, 1993), directed by Peter Hammond and adapted by T. R. Bowen.

The female Gothic: women, domesticity and the Gothic adaptation

3

The female Gothic continuum

The following chapter brings together many of the central concerns of this book, particularly the question of the Gothic drama's awareness of its domestic viewing context and domestic viewer, and the centrality of domestic space within the image repertoire of Gothic television. It does this in relation to the female Gothic television adaptation. Adaptation of female Gothic literature, a term which encompasses a broad range of sources from Daphne du Maurier's *Rebecca* to the work of Joseph Sheridan Le Fanu, Wilkie Collins and others, has always been popular on British television. Adaptations of this material frequently featured in the anthology drama series of the 1950s and 1960s, such as *Hour of Mystery* (ABC [UK], 1957) and *Mystery and Imagination* (ABC [UK]/Thames, 1966–70) in the UK, and the sub-genre recently enjoyed a renaissance in the form of the two-part Sunday night 'feature' drama on both the BBC and ITV in Britain. The texts discussed in this chapter, both drama serials and one-off dramas, were all broadcast in the UK between the late 1970s and the turn of the century: *Rebecca* (BBC1, 1979); *Woman in White* (BBC2, 1982); *Northanger Abbey* (BBC2, 1987); *Rebecca* (Carlton, 1997); *The Woman in White* (BBC1, 1997); *The Haunting of Helen Walker* (aka *Turn of the Screw*) (Rosemont Productions Ltd, 1997); *The Turn of the Screw* (United Film and Television Productions, 1999); and *The Wyvern Mystery* (BBC1, 2000).[1] Several of these stories were also adapted during the formative years of British television production,[2] and the very proliferation of these adaptations may attest to the fact that television has been seen as inherently suited to their presentation, as well as affirming their continual popularity with an easily identifiable, and targetable, audience. This chapter will explore these dramas in an attempt to define the particular ways in which narratives of domestic fear and entrapment appear on television.

Made as lavish co-productions with North American television companies, or sometimes with smaller independent domestic producers,
these recent adaptations were clearly attractive to schedulers in that
they offer a well-defined group of dedicated viewers. While it would be
inaccurate to suggest that the female Gothic drama has no male
viewing contingent, or that there are not equally complex and interesting viewing pleasures for the male viewer, it is the case that television
takes on traditions of distributing and consuming the female Gothic
text which pre-date the last century, and which include a clear characterisation of a certain kind of female reader. This chapter explores
the placement of female Gothic television adaptations within this
continuum.

Like the preceding analyses, although arguably more explicitly, this
chapter seeks to define a textually inscribed viewer, to theorise her relationship to the Gothic text, and to analyse the modes of address within
the female Gothic adaptation which speak directly to this viewer.
Umberto Eco's notion of the model reader is useful in introducing this
approach. In his *Six Walks in the Fictional Woods* (1994), building on
work first presented in *The Role of the Reader* (Eco, 1979), Eco discusses
the ways in which the model reader is created by the author through
certain textual processes, and examines how these processes incite the
reader to explore a fictional work from a particular perspective. He
acknowledges that, 'in a story there is always a reader, and this reader is
a fundamental ingredient not only of the process of storytelling but also
of the tale itself' (1994: 1). Eco thus distinguishes an understanding of
the model reader from an exploration of the empirical reader,[3] arguing
that the reader can be located within, as well as outside of, the literary
text. In the following exploration of the female Gothic television adaptation, it will be proposed that we might also locate a *model viewer* by
looking at a number of textual strategies which work towards addressing an assumed female viewer, drawing them into the text of the television drama. As discussed in the introduction to this book, there have
been a number of illuminating empirical studies of the domestic viewer
and the domestic viewing space of television which have brought to light
and challenged some of the key assumptions about the ways in which
we watch television (e.g. Morley, 1986; Gray, 1992; Gauntlett and Hill,
1999; Tufte, 2000; Wood, 2001). However, in the context of the following analysis it will be argued that it is equally possible to make supposi-
tions about who might be watching a drama on television (and indeed,
where and how that act of viewing might be taking place) by looking to
television itself, and by seeking out textual evidence, supported by
archival research, for the ways in which television drama addresses a

domestic viewer. Situating this textual analysis in the context of research into the production and broadcast of these programmes is at odds with Eco's notion of the model reader, since Eco's work holds no interest in the empirical author (and therefore no interest in the moment of production per se). However, throughout this analysis of the female Gothic television adaptation, an understanding of intended address to the model viewer as delineated by those producing the dramas (through marketing material, press interviews, tie-in publications and other intertexts of the adaptations in hand) will be intertwined with a textual exploration of viewership.

To begin this exploration, it may be pertinent to evoke existing discussions and definitions of the particularities of this sub-genre of the Gothic, in both its literary and cinematic forms. A great deal of critical work has been done on the female Gothic novel, a sub-genre of Gothic fiction which is described in broad terms by Robert Miles as featuring narratives of 'a heroine caught between a pastoral haven and a threatening castle, sometimes in flight from a sinister patriarchal figure, sometimes in search of an absent mother, and often both together' (1994: 1). There is some disagreement within the academy as to whether the 'female Gothic' refers to texts written by authors of both genders; nevertheless, Miles' necessarily general description outlines the overarching structure of the female Gothic novel as a narrative featuring a female protagonist caught up in a matrix of domestic paranoia, trapped within a decaying home by a suspicious, and/or murderous, husband. More often than not, these narratives also centre around the heroine's departure from an idealised family home to the threatening marital home, and her eventual escape to independence in a home of her own.

Diverse critical positions (psychoanalytic, Marxist, feminist) clearly highlight different elements of these narratives. Psychoanalytic readings of the genre, such as Claire Kahane's essay 'The Gothic Mirror' (1985) or Tania Modleski's work on popular female Gothic novels (1982a), explore the female Gothic as female Oedipal narrative, mapping the progress of the novel as a *bildungsroman* whereby the psychic individuation of the heroine may be achieved. Other work on the female Gothic (Fleenor, 1993; Milbank, 1992) has explored these novels as subversive/resistant texts or, alternately, as writing with a conservative ideological function, reading the Gothic heroine as a woman struggling through patriarchal oppression towards self-sufficiency. In addition, work on popular or 'pulp' female Gothic fictions of either the nineteenth (Howells, 1978; Ferguson-Ellis, 1989) or twentieth centuries (Russ, 1993; Modleski, 1982a) has combined these approaches to think about the ways in which the female Gothic novel of the popular presses centralises the domestic space as a site of anxiety, and has dealt with the act of reading as an act of catharsis, self-exploration or masochistic identification for the female reader (see also Massé, 1992). This focus on the text as a site in which domestic anxieties may be worked through or worried at very much informs the following discussion of the female Gothic adaptation on television.

A number of key analyses have also been written about cinematic versions of the female Gothic, particularly in relation to the woman's film of the 1940s[4] (e.g. Doane, 1987a; Waldman, 1983; Walker, 1990), those films based on the overarching structure defined by Helen Hanson as 'romance, suspicion, investigation/discovery, confrontation or confession, and resolution' (2000: 131), which closely mimic the traditional 'Bluebeard' narrative (a young woman investigates her new husband's past through an exploration of a hidden room in his castle, only to find evidence of murder or foul play). Most pertinent, in relation to this discussion of Gothic television, is their exploration of domestic space in the Gothic woman's film. The importance of the home in female Gothic films, in the form of the dilapidated Gothic mansion, is made most clear in Mary Ann Doane's extensive analysis of the Gothic woman's film of the 1940s, in which she categorises the representations of domestic space typical to this genre and period: 'The paradigmatic woman's space – the home – is yoked to dread, and to a crisis of vision. For violence is precisely what is hidden from sight . . . The home is not a homogenous space – it asserts divisions, gaps, and fields within its very structure. There are places which elude the eye' (1987a: 134). Doane's description addresses the representation of domestic space as the site of fear within these films, and she goes on to outline the specificities of this representation (in relation to the appearance of the hidden room, and the significance of the staircase and window, for example) in an extremely insightful analysis.

In addition, Doane makes the point that these films implicitly addressed an assumed female audience:

> In the first half of the [1940s], due to the war and the enlistment of large numbers of young men in the armed forces, film producers assumed that cinema audiences would be predominantly female . . . [T]here is an intensity and an aberrant quality to the 1940s films which is linked to the ideological upheaval signalled by a redefinition of sexual roles and the reorganisation of the family during the war years. (1987a: 4)

Doane therefore argues that not only were these films addressed to a female audience, but also that the Gothic woman's film of the 1940s was timely, working through or worrying at some of the crises and paranoia surrounding the family and domesticity in the early and mid-1940s. This argument is also prefigured by Tania Modleski's analysis of the

genre: '[these films] reflect women's fears about losing their unprecedented freedoms *and* being forced back into homes . . . In many of
these films, the house seems to be alive with menace' (1982a: 21–2).
However, what Doane does not take into account, and what Modleski
implicitly infers but does not explicitly address, is that the predominantly female, cinema-going audience *had* escaped the confines of this
dreadful place (the home) in order to attend the cinema. Arguably then,
a certain amount of the frisson built up around this paranoid depiction
of the home might thus be dispelled by its public viewing context, creating a dislocation between the domestic spaces on screen and the
domestic spaces of the (presumed female) audience. This point therefore provides a segue in to the crux of this analysis of the female Gothic
adaptation on television: by bringing the narrative of domestic fear and
paranoia back into the home from the late 1940s onwards, the closeness
between the threatened heroine and the viewer of the text is re-
established or intensified on television, as a domestic medium. Playing
on television's sense of intimacy, female Gothic fictions made for this
medium are re-domesticated, and consequently emphasise the dual
anxieties of the diegetic and extra-diegetic domestic spaces of television.
This analysis of female Gothic television in the late twentieth and early
twenty-first centuries seeks to outline the self-reflexivity of these texts,
looking at the ways in which these adaptations seem aware of both their
domestic viewing context and the female viewer. Unlike several of the
analyses of the woman's film of the 1940s discussed above, the question
of the timeliness of these dramas is not really the issue here, although
the discursive contexts of domestic violence in the home and spousal
abuse arguably became more visible at the turn of the twentieth century.
Fuelled by the campaigning of groups like *Justice for Women* (established
in 1991), the disclosure of domestic violence rose rapidly in the late
1990s. As an example, in an adjunct to the 1996 *British Crime Survey*,
the report *Domestic Violence: Findings from a New British Crime Survey
Self-completion Questionnaire*, published in January 1999, provided the
alarming statistic that twenty-three per cent of its female respondents
had reported being physically assaulted by a partner during their life-
time (Mirrlees-Black, 1999: vii), though they had not necessarily
reported this abuse to the police or, indeed, considered it a crime.[5] In
addition, many of the adaptations made in the 1990s may be seen to
reflect broader anxieties around women's independence inside and
outside of the home, a central concern of post-feminist readings of television drama in the 1990s and beyond (see Dow, 1996). The question
of the adaptations' timeliness in relation to the fears and anxieties surrounding domestic space will therefore remain an implicit considera-

tion in this chapter, while the questions of viewer identification and textual inscription lie at the forefront of the following analysis.

Finding the reader-viewer in the female Gothic

As suggested in the introduction to this chapter, television borrows from traditions of marketing/distributing the female Gothic text which pre-date the inception of audio-visual media and which characterise the reader-viewer in gender-specific ways. From the end of the eighteenth century onwards, popular, inexpensive outlets for the female Gothic nar-rative attracted the female reader, who was thought to avidly 'devour' the serialised fictions of domestic terror and the female victim-heroine. As Alison Milbank describes,

> Many Gothic tales first appeared in the pages of journals like *The Lady's Magazine*. Women's periodicals also encouraged submissions from their readers and in this way a reciprocity of female reading and writing of Gothic was established. Through the circulating libraries for the middle class, and the Gothic chapbooks of the lower classes, a new gen-eration of women readers was able to enjoy [female Gothic fictions]. (1998: 53–4)

Similarly, Kate Ferguson-Ellis suggests that the woman novel reader was at the epicentre of the boom in female Gothic literature, 'whose newly created leisure allowed her to make use of the circulating library and whose "placement" in the home made her a reader eagerly courted by publishers' (1989: x). Other research suggests that this characterisation of a predominantly female readership is, perhaps, spurious; as Alison Milbank points out, 'whether the description of the devourer of Minerva Press productions as female was accurate is debatable, as men were extensive novel readers' (1998: 54).[6] However, what is certain is that, rightly or wrongly, the reader of these Gothic fictions was conceptualised as female by those producing and marketing female Gothic novels, and that these female consumers have been assigned a certain 'voraciousness' by those commenting on the phenomenon, both at the time and since.

Joanna Russ' work on popular female Gothic fiction in the twentieth century places an emphasis on the ways in which the novels of publish-ing houses like Ace Books (producers of female Gothic 'pulp' fiction) are marketed and distributed:

> Anywhere paperback books are sold you will find volumes whose covers seem to have evolved from the same clone: the colour scheme is pre-dominantly blue or green, there is a frightened young woman in the

foreground, in the background there is a mansion, castle, or large house with one window lit, there is usually a moon, a storm, or both, and whatever is occurring is occurring at night. (1993: 31)

Russ then goes on to argue that this standardised Gothic image repertoire is directed precisely towards a specific middle-class, female readership, quoting Terry Carr, ex-editor of Ace Books: 'the basic appeal . . . is to women who marry guys and then begin to discover that their husbands are strangers' (1993: 32). Subsequently, Russ' essay explores the particular pleasures of the popular female Gothic novel for women who 'have a keen eye for food, clothes, interior décor, and middle-class hobbies (e.g. collecting sea shells, weaving, or collecting china)' (1993: 36), concluding that 'these novels are written for women who cook, who decorate their own houses, who shop for clothing for themselves and their children – in short, for housewives' (1993: 39). Russ is not alone in her delineation of this market: for example, in her exploration of mass produced literature for women, Tania Modleski (1982a) also characterises the reader of Ace and Fawcett novels (another producer of 'pulp' female Gothic fiction) as a married woman working through or worrying at the paranoia and anxiety of married life. Therefore, Milbank, Ferguson-Ellis, Russ and Modleski (as well as others, such as Coral Ann Howells (1978) and Tamar Heller (1992)) have gone some way towards delineating the target market for popular female Gothic fictions, critical contexts which become important in understanding the mode of address at play in the adaptations discussed in this chapter.

In the twentieth and twenty-first centuries, this avid readership has also extended to the (supposed) equally avid viewership of television, and the consumption of female Gothic narratives through journals, chapbooks and 'dime-store' novels can be understood as prefiguring the reception of this sub-genre on television in very specific ways. Like the journals and pulp fiction discussed above, television offers a domestic, rather than public, space for the reception of these narratives; also like the literature discussed above, television has provided a platform for the serialisation of female Gothic fictions. Just as the Minerva Press saw the Gothic as a viable, lucrative investment in the eighteenth and nineteenth centuries, so television companies in the latter part of the twentieth century turned to the genre, with its pre-sold audience, as a 'safe bet' for both domestic viewing figures and international sales.

We can look at the marketing of Carlton/Portman Production's *Rebecca* (1997) in order to understand the ways in which this genre has been addressed towards its target audience. This adaptation of Daphne du Maurier's novel was a lavish and expensive production, costing four million pounds to make, and was obviously seen by its production companies as a viable investment in a pre-sold property, based on the popularity of the novel, Hitchcock's film and the numerous earlier television adaptations outlined above. By portraying *Rebecca* as a two-part television 'event', Carlton attempted to capture dedicated viewers on consecutive nights, at the tail-end of the special Christmas schedule (it was shown in a primetime slot on the 5th and 6th of January). In a Carlton press release detailing the 'greatness' of *Rebecca*'s stars, locations and budgets, issued as early as June the previous year in order to pique viewer interest, the producers emphasised both the event status of the adaptation and its exportability, as well as the drama's inherent appeal to a continuum of avid reader-viewers: 'Portman Productions' executive producer Tim Buxton says: "The wealth of talent which is working together to bring this du Maurier classic to the screen is certain to create a television 'event' to be enjoyed by her fans, old and new, around the world" ' (Carlton Productions, 1996). Scheduled on consecutive nights against two of the BBC's most popular serial dramas (*Ballykissangel* (1996–2001) and *Eastenders* (1985–)), *Rebecca* received, on average, an impressive thirty-five per cent audience share,[7] an audience inevitably drawn by the drama's intensive advertising campaign (from the previous summer onwards), extensive coverage in the press (in particular the *TV Times* listings guide) and a tie-in book which accompanied the adaptation (Tiballs: 1996). This book offered a series of informative contexts, including information on du Maurier, profiles of members of the cast, location information, and an illustrated chapter, entitled 'Dressing for the Part', on the costumes used in the adaptation. With its emphasis on the details of dressing up and home furnishings, the tie-in book clearly appealed to the cultural competences of an assumed female audience. Indeed, the reader-viewer figure evoked in Carlton's press release is explicitly referred to as female within the tie-in book: for example, director Jim O'Brien states in an interview for the book, 'a lot of girls read the story and they can treat it as being entirely innocent if they want to, but older women can see what Du Maurier is getting at' (Tiballs, 1996: 54). Thus the female reader/viewer is addressed as a knowing figure, an avid fan of the genre, and a consumer of 'lifestyle' goods in Tiballs' book. In fact, the marketing campaign for *Rebecca* seems relatively low key compared with that of Wilkie Collins' novel *The Woman in White*, published in August 1860, which was accompanied by a whole range of tie-in goods:

> [*The Woman in White* marked] the marketplace's power to transform both text and author into a seemingly endless series of commodities . . . [Collins'] best-selling novel was reproduced as *Woman in White* perfume,

bonnets and quadrilles . . . It was, however, the novel's very status as commodity – not merely as a best seller but as a rage, a sensation, a stimulating food to be 'devoured' in one sitting – that contributed to its mixed reception as a work of art. (Heller, 1992: 3)

As with the 1997 television adaptation of *Rebecca*, the publishers of Collins' novel addressed the female reader/viewer as both an avid fan of the genre and as a consumer of 'lifestyle' goods.

This continual conflation of the female reader, viewer and consumer therefore brings us back to the question of television's suitability for the presentation of female Gothic narratives. As in the above instance, the programme makers clearly relied upon a continuum of female reader-ship/viewership, implicitly occurring within the domestic, rather than public, sphere, to sell their product. In the case of *Rebecca* (1997) at least, Carlton appealed to this female reader-viewer through the seductive discourse of 'lifestyle' (ideal homes, fantasy fashions, etc.), and it is perhaps no coincidence that many of these adaptations appeared on television at precisely the same time as an explosion in lifestyle programming and makeover shows (see Brunsdon et al. (2001)). The irony of this congruence is that *Rebecca*, along with many of the other female Gothic narratives, also implicitly critiqued the representation of the domestic space as ideal home, and expressed a certain anxiety about the image of the 'perfected' woman and/or wife. The following analysis seeks to explore these representations, outlining the tension created around conflicting images of 'home' and 'family' in these dramas.

Subverting perfection in the female Gothic adaptation: a topographical analysis

In order to provide the female Gothic drama on television with a keen sense of the tension found between idealised fantasies of heterosexual love/domestic bliss and the horrific realities of home life as experienced by the Gothic heroine, the visual tropes of the romance and the heritage drama, both genres of 'domestic perfection', are evoked at key moments in the female Gothic narrative, particularly in establishing sequences. Within the conventions of the female Gothic narrative, a sense of happiness or equilibrium must be established at the beginning of the drama, in order that the heroine's removal to her husband's/brother-in-law's/employer's Gothic pile be marked as a disruptive event in her life story. Therefore, before this removal can occur, an innocent, benign romance (not necessarily with the future suitor/captor) must take place, utilising the generic audio-visual tropes of the heterosexual romance. For example, in *Rebecca* this romance is between the young girl and Maxim de Winter, and in *The Woman in White* the innocent romance is begun (and subsequently thwarted until the conclusion of the drama) between Laura and her art tutor, Walter Hartright. These moments in the female Gothic narrative, utilising many of the stock visual tropes of the romance, are marked by the heavy use of soft lighting and soft focus, and by the repeated use of the courtship montage sequence, whereby the potential lovers are seen enjoying themselves together in a variety of locations and activities. In both the 1979 and 1997 adaptations of *Rebecca* for example, the courtship between the young girl (Joanna David (1979) and Emilia Fox (1997)) and Maxim de Winter (Jeremy Brett (1979) and Charles Dance (1997)) is represented by a single montage sequence, without diegetic sound but enhanced by a soaring orchestral score, dominated by violins, as the couple travel round Monte Carlo. During these sequences, the facial close-up conveys the intensity of their developing love for one another, coupled by long shots of the openness of the surrounding Monte Carlo countryside which offer a stark contrast to the confinement of the domestic space later in the drama. Indeed, both these adaptations explicitly address the heroine's own desire for this 'romantic montage' through a speech delivered by Maxim after his wedding proposal. For example, in *Rebecca* (1979), Maxim states

> Oh my poor darling, I'm sure this isn't your idea of a proposal. We should be in a conservatory, hmm? You in a white dress, with a flower in your hand and a violin playing a waltz in the distance. And I should make love to you under a palm tree, hmm? Never mind. I'll take you to Venice on honeymoon and we'll hold hands in a gondola.

Expressed in this sardonic speech is an awareness of the young girl's received ideas of 'the romantic', both in terms of the ideal locations of the montage sequence which Maxim depicts here, and in her need for a soaring soundtrack (the 'violin playing a waltz'). The female Gothic adaptation thus draws attention to this audio-visual rendering of 'perfect romance', only to undercut it with the heroine's contrasting experience of married life.

However, the female Gothic television adaptation plays on its identity as a heritage drama even more strikingly. In some senses these dramas are heritage texts, literary adaptations which pay a great deal of attention to creating an era-specific milieu in which the events of the drama will take place. However, as argued in chapter one of this book, the Gothic narrative provides heritage texts with a difference, which are pointedly anti-nostalgic. In relation to the female Gothic, the heritage drama's association with a female audience is significant. As Claire Monk and others have argued, the heritage text may be read as generically identified as 'feminine':

> If we take the 'woman's film' characteristics [the diegetic and spectatorial privileging of female point-of-view structures, and thematic concerns designated as 'feminine' within patriarchal culture] . . . as a starting point, and consider also the conventional cultural designation of talk, costume/fashion and the domestic sphere as areas of female competence, it is clear that a considerable number of the best-known heritage films [and television] qualify as 'feminine' texts on the thematic, diegetic and aesthetic levels. (Monk, 1996)

Monk's representation of the heritage text as feminine thus speaks to the fact that the cycle has a certain association with idealised notions of feminine self-presentation and domesticity, situated in a historical setting. One of the most popular and successful heritage dramas on television in the 1990s, *Pride and Prejudice* (BBC1, 1995), is a good example of the kind of text Monk describes here, particularly with regard to a display of the fine detail of heritage costume and location. The publicity surrounding this adaptation clearly took this configuration of the ideal home/woman to heart: weekly coverage of this adaptation in the *Radio Times* focused on these elements of the drama. For example, Kate Lock's article, 'Lifting the Skirts on *Pride and Prejudice*' (1995) included interviews with Dinah Collin, costume designer (along with reproduced costume notes and sketches) and Gerry Scott, production designer (with design sketches and swatches of wallpaper and fabric), as well as details of dance styles from the serial. The following week's *Radio Times* even offered instructions for the reader about how to throw a *Pride and Prejudice* dinner party, complete with menu guide and recipes (Dodd, 1995). These bold intertextual addresses to the viewer of the heritage drama through the *Radio Times* clearly place the appeal of the adaptation in the realm of the feminine cultural competences of fashion, cooking, decorating and entertaining.

However, although the female Gothic adaptations also construct 'heritage' spaces and characters through an attention to the detail of 'authentic' mise-en-scène which is as carefully wrought as that of *Pride and Prejudice*, female Gothic adaptations on television might be seen as a response to more benign, contemporaneous, forms of the heritage text, in that they expose a more sinister underside of domestic life in the past, rather than simply focusing on its glossy surfaces. Additionally, if one of the most relentless fictional and non-fictional narratives on television in the 1990s was that of home (and, implicitly, self) improvement (as argued in relation to 'lifestyle' programmes by Rachel Moseley (2000)), one could conclude that the female Gothic drama provides an antidote to the broader narrative of the 'ideal home' on television, and offers a starkly contrasting configuration of domestic space. This comparison of lifestyle programming, the traditional heritage drama and the female Gothic adaptation is similar to an argument made by Diane Waldman (1983: 36) in relation to the contrast between the representation of the home in female Gothic films of the 1940s and other contemporaneous 'family films', such as *Meet Me in St. Louis* (US, 1944) and *I Remember Mama* (US, 1948). Similarly Kate Ferguson-Ellis has suggested that, from the end of the eighteenth century onwards, a preoccupation with the 'ideal home' gave rise to the female Gothic novel (1989: ix). Heritage texts on television, such as *Pride and Prejudice*, clearly provide a striking counterpoint to the female Gothic adaptation when it comes to the representation of domestic space: indeed, one could argue that this intervention is an essential part of the 'working through' (Ellis, 2000: 78–9) of women's domestic life on television. As I have argued elsewhere, television drama has an important role to play in the process of 'worrying at' women's position in the home and, more generally, their position in society (see Wheatley, 2005), and we see this in all elements of the television text, from storyline and dialogue to set dressing and performance style.

Not only can the traditional heritage drama be seen to prompt the very existence of the female Gothic adaptation on television, but it also lends its particular narrative tropes and image repertoire to these dramas, in order that they may be transformed or subverted in some way. Taking the exterior long shot of the key heritage location (the stately home) as a striking instance of this textual borrowing, we can observe the ways in which a characteristic shot of the heritage drama is utilised by the female Gothic drama on television, with a number of key differences. It may be useful here to offer the approach to Netherfield Hall in *Pride and Prejudice* as an example of the traditional handling of this space within the heritage drama. In the opening of *Pride and Prejudice*, this extreme long shot of the hall, which is taken from behind Mr. Bingley (Crispin Bonham-Carter) and Mr. Darcy (Colin Firth) as they survey the house before Mr. Bingley decides to rent it, can be seen as both an encapsulation of the splendour of upper-class living and an idyllic image of potential domestic bliss (achieved in the conclusion of the serial through the Bennett sisters' marriages). The qualities of sunny light and soft focus here serve to frame the house's appearance as a space of hope, and express the possibility of the Bennetts' social climbing. In contrast, in the 1997 version of *The Woman in White* a similar shot of the stately home is also employed as Marian (Tara Fitzgerald) approaches Glyde for the first time, and is taken from the heroine's point of view as she contemplates her future. However, in this sequence, explicitly taken from Marian's subjective position, an accompanying voice-over is given as the camera remains in tight close-up on her face which expresses the fear and dread attached to the house. Her mind's voice states: 'I begged Laura to forget all my doubts. It had been agreed I would join her as soon as the honeymoon was over and how strange it seems now to think that I travelled that long road in hope.' During this dialogue, a cut is made on the words 'the honeymoon was over' to an extreme long shot of the house, thus bringing the house into view in relation to a clichéd metaphor for the end of initial happiness ('the honeymoon is over'). This dialogue, along with an ominous extra-diegetic soundtrack of strings and French horns, thus undercuts the sunny exterior shot of the house and, implicitly, Marian's belief that she is travelling towards hope, significantly altering the shot as it would have been presented in the non-Gothic heritage text.

The Wyvern Mystery also alters the generic approach to the heritage location to express the distinct uneasiness attached to domestic spaces within the female Gothic narrative. Here the approach sequence introduces the audience to a degraded version of the heritage location, and thus demarcates the space as one of potential collapse or degradation for Alice (Naomi Watts), rather than for potential self-improvement. Carwell, the house in question, looms into long shot, not surrounded by the sunlit, polished grandeur of Netherfield (*Pride and Prejudice*), but rather covered in dead vines and approached by a muddy, weed-ridden track; once again, this establishing shot is cross-cut with a close-up of the heroine's face, thus strengthening the visual link between the protagonist and this location. Once inside the house, long shots, tracks, pans and zooms serve only to emphasise the degraded emptiness of the house, rather than to allow an elaborate display of heritage detail more usual in the heritage adaptation (as argued by Higson (1993)). As Alice and her new husband, Charlie (Iain Glen) enter their new home in *The Wyvern Mystery*, a canted, static long shot of them climbing the stairs is accompanied by their housekeeper's (Ellie Haddington's) statement, 'I've made a list of the contents of the house Ma'am – there's not so much I'm afraid', emphasising the emptiness and distinct lack of decoration within this particular stately home. Whereas Andrew Higson has argued that camera movement in the traditional heritage drama places the ornamented domestic space on display, fetishising the mise-en-scène of the heritage domestic space (1993: 112–13), this interior shot in Carwell shows only the bad fortune attached to homes and families within the Gothic adaptation. In the female Gothic adaptation then, the overarching narrative structure of all of these dramas is found in the heroine's removal from a place of safety to the threatening location of her husband's/employer's familial mansion, with many of the narratives finding resolution in her removal from this dangerous domestic space and subsequent move into her own home (with the exception of *Rebecca*, where the young Mrs. de Winter moves into a new house *with* her husband, albeit in an incapacitated state). In relation to this narrative structure, these dramas 'play upon' certain anxieties focused on and experienced by women in the marital home through an investigation of the threatening, cage-like, labyrinthine and, ultimately, 'un-homely' domestic spaces of these adaptations. An exploration of the representation of domestic space in the female Gothic television drama will illustrate this tendency.

As a contrast to the abject domestic spaces which dominate these dramas, the female Gothic narrative frequently begins with a representation of idealised, pastoral domesticity. This configuration of the house, often the parental home, presents a stark contrast to the house which the heroine will eventually move into: her second home is often far more grand and imposing, but lacking in a sense of homely security. To offer a specific example, the opening of *The Wyvern Mystery* finds the young Alice ensconced in her father's house, a modest image of domestic bliss (it is safe, warm and lit with mellow light), reading from a book of fairy stories. During this sequence of idyllic tranquillity, Alice's adult voice-over states, 'When I was very young, my father held me tightly and told me of witches and goblins; if only I had known how close they were'. Aside from the significance of positing Alice as a diegetic consumer of Gothic fictions (discussed at greater length below), this sequence sets up a certain tension by offering an image of domestic perfection, and implicitly addressing its impossibility through Alice's suggestion that threat and terror were always close at hand. Within this sequence, initially shot in soft focus and lit brightly to evoke feelings of warmth and safety, the mobile camera visually prefigures Alice's impending entrapment (first in Wyvern Hall, the home of her benefactor, and later in Carwell, the home of her husband) by constantly reframing her through a number of diegetic frames or bars (the backs of chairs, the square panes of the window, etc.) (see figure 3.1).

However, as the opening sequence progresses, Alice's father's death is graphically portrayed through the image of his clammy, blood-spattered face (he dies of consumption), and the warm glow of the family home is replaced by the stark blue light of winter, at the moment in which Alice is removed from the house by her benefactor and enters Wyvern Hall. Even within this short opening sequence then, anxiety is built around leaving the security of home through voice-over dialogue, diegetic framing and a change in lighting.

3.1 Prefiguring entrapment: *The Wyvern Mystery* (BBC1, 2000).

Contrary to the representation of idyllic homes, the central homes in the female Gothic narrative visually represent a keen sense of domestic anxiety. As the Gothic victim heroine moves into her new abode (Laura and Marian to Glyde in *The Woman in White*, Miss/Helen Walker to her employer's house in *The Haunting of Helen Walker/The Turn of the Screw*, the new Mrs. de Winter to Manderley in *Rebecca*, Alice to Wyvern and then to Carwell in *The Wyvern Mystery*), it is immediately implied that she is more a newly interred prisoner than the 'lady of the house'. Indeed, domestic space is rarely spoken of as house or home from the moment of the young woman's arrival, but rather as a space of entrapment or confinement: in *The Woman in White* (1982), Marian (Diana Quick) asks her sister's husband 'I am to assume that your wife's room is a prison?' and later Sir Percival (John Shrapnel) leaves Glyde, bellowing 'I am not spending another minute in this dungeon'. This sentiment is exemplified in an impassioned speech by Marian in *The Woman in White* (1982), who, as a counterpoint to her sister's compliance in the state of marriage as imprisonment, acts as a stridently feminist voice of resistance throughout the narrative: '*Men* – they're enemies of our peace and innocence. They take us to their body and soul, and fasten us helpless to their lives like dogs in kennels.' This dialogue, implying forced rather than protective enclosure within the home, is also reflected in the mise-en-scène of these dramas, which explicitly reiterates the imagery of the cage/prison within the domestic locale. For example, in *The Woman in White* (1997), the space surrounding Laura is almost always depicted as cage-like, even before she enters her husband's Gothic pile. When she is shown for the first time in her uncle's home, she appears at a window against and behind a number of objects which reflect the cage/bar motif (the panelling, chair back, window panes and easel in figure 3.2), as she stands in front of an ornate birdcage, an object which symbolises her position as a potential prisoner in her own house.

This visual symbolism of Laura's eventual predicament anticipates her future and, indeed, the image of bars against Laura's body will eventually be repeated at the end of the drama when she is rediscovered, imprisoned in an asylum in the place of her half sister, Anne Catherick. The use of bar shadows is a recurring visual motif in the female Gothic and is repeated elsewhere in the cycle (as in the medium-long shots of Alice lying alone in her marital bed at Carwell in *The Wyvern Mystery*). Thus we begin to identify a recognisable image repertoire of the female Gothic on television which acknowledges the imprisoning nature of domestic space in these dramas.

In her analysis of female Gothic cinema, Mary Ann Doane isolates the window as an important space within the mise-en-scène of the Gothic home: 'The window has special import in terms of the social and symbolic positioning of the woman – the window is the interface between inside and outside, the feminine space of the family and reproduction and the masculine space of production (Doane, 1987b: 288). Doane's delineation of the window is also pertinent to these adaptations of the female Gothic on television, particularly in its ambivalent position

3.2 Prefiguring entrapment: *The Woman in White* (BBC1, 1997).

as an interstice, a liminal space between the house and the outside world, which may be read as either benign (providing access for the entrapped heroine to the outside world) or malignant (withholding her from that world, or somehow representing her anxiety about entering the outside world).[8] In both television versions of *Rebecca* discussed here, for example, it is the window within Rebecca's room which acts as a space of crisis for the new Mrs. de Winter: it draws her towards an exploration of the 'other side' of the house, and is ultimately the space where Mrs. Danvers is most threatening, goading the young woman to jump out of the window and kill herself.

One could perhaps view this analogy of the window as fearful interstice between the domestic space and the outside world as an extension of a broader metaphor relating to the television screen, and those critical configurations of the medium as a 'window to the world'. By bringing the potential dangers of home and matrimony into the domestic viewing context, the programme makers of the female Gothic drama allow the viewer a particularly fearful view of another domestic space, thus affording the television screen both the properties of the window (a view of 'outside' the viewing space/home) and the mirror (a reflection of the viewing space/home). This uncanny 'doubling' of domestic space is also reflected in the presence of a number of objects representing houses within the diegetic domestic space of these narratives (dolls' houses, ornaments, paintings, etc.). However, this reading of television as simultaneous window and mirror must be taken with caution as it clearly relies on a metaphorical reading of television broadcast and reception. As Jostein Gripsrud notes, 'while a metaphor is rarely entirely false, it does give prominence to some features of the phenomenon in question, and leaves others in the shade. This is why all metaphors [in television studies] should be regarded with a degree of suspicion' (1998: 17).

In addition to reading the window as an interstitial and dangerous space, the garden of the threatened/threatening home is also a significant but ambivalent space within the female Gothic adaptation. The grounds of the house are the location in which the heroines of these dramas struggle for their freedom from the tyrannies of marriage: in the garden Marian and Laura attempt (unsuccessfully) to break through the wooded boundaries of Glyde Hall to reach the comparative safety of the outside world (*The Woman in White*), Alice runs from the advances of her lecherous benefactor, only to run into the equally dangerous arms of her future husband (*The Wyvern Mystery*), and the young governess struggles with the sexually threatening ghosts of her new home (*The Turn of the Screw* and *The Haunting of Helen Walker*). Again, the ambivalence of this

interstitial space is found in the close proximity of protection and entrapment in these dramas. At key moments of conflict, as in the moment
when Marian discovers part of Percival's (James Wilby's) and Fosco's
(Simon Callow's) plot to do away with the two sisters in *The Woman in
White* (1997), the heroine is positioned in the garden and on the balcony,
on the very boundaries of the house, in a position of acute danger.
Similarly, in *The Wyvern Mystery* Alice is positioned on the balcony (a
simultaneously interior and exterior space) when she overhears parts of
a conspiracy between her husband and his brother. Therefore, as the
grounds of the home are neither inside nor outside the bounds of the
domestic space, they provide no real sense of safety or escape: they merely
re-emphasise the borders that the wife/domestic prisoner may not cross.

The prison-like qualities of domestic space within the female Gothic
adaptation are also reflected in costuming in *The Woman in White*
(1997); here an overarching analogy between body, home and entrapment is reiterated precisely at the moment in which Laura becomes a
'domestic prisoner' (i.e. on her wedding day). The notion of marriage as
imprisonment resonates in the sequence in which Laura is tied into her
cage-like wedding dress by a bevy of housemaids, a sequence which
departs from the more usual wedding day montage primarily through
the lack of dialogue, the use of mournful, foreboding music on the extra-
diegetic soundtrack, and the low-key lighting which casts dark shadows
across the bride's face. During this sequence, a series of near-static,
dialogue-less shots darkly lit by dusty light, Laura is completely, unnat-
urally still and unsmiling, almost mannequin-like as the maids work
around her to tie her into her dress. This sequence prefigures Laura's
impending fate immediately following her wedding, whereby she is
imprisoned in her new marital home through the collusion of the
female housekeeper and her serving girls. Analyses of female Gothic literary fiction, most notably Elaine Showalter's discussion of *Jane Eyre* in
her wide-ranging study of British women's writing (1977: 33), have
drawn close parallels between the heroine's body and domestic space;
thus, the representation of Laura's body becoming cage-like (surrounded by the stiff, corseted wedding dress) is in keeping with this tradition. As her body becomes stiffened and encased in the swathes of
material which make up her wedding dress, a visual/spatial analogy is
made between the 'trappings' of the wedding and the entrapment of the
marital home.

Domestic space is not only configured as a prison within the female
Gothic narrative, however; the family secrets which prefigure the
heroine's imprisonment are also writ large upon the domestic space itself
throughout many of these dramas. As suggested in the introduction to

this chapter, the female Gothic narrative often centres on a hidden family secret which necessitates the heroine's position in her new home; these secrets make up the back-story of the drama and the heroine's need to uncover them propels the narrative. In the narratives in question, covered-up murders/deaths (*Rebecca, The Woman in White, The Wyvern Mystery, Turn of the Screw*), the unknown substitution of two characters (Laura and Anne in *The Woman in White*, the two babies in *The Wyvern Mystery*) or a previous failed/unhappy marriage (*Rebecca, The Wyvern Mystery*) provide the central narrative enigmas which must be explored and understood by the central female protagonist. The most potent image portraying these destructive secrets within the houses of the female Gothic drama on television is that of the shrouded room. This space, symbolic of the hidden past of the Gothic household, is a room in which all furniture and ornamentation has been covered with dust cloths, ostensibly to protect these objects from the neglect of the previous owner's prolonged absence. In *Rebecca* (1979), the new Mrs. de Winter discovers a series of shrouded rooms as she explores the west wing for the first time, the space in the house which is marked as 'belonging to' the previous Mrs. de Winter. Here the dust-sheets not only provide a visual metaphor for her husband's unknown past, but they also tellingly cover Rebecca's comparative panache for home-décor, which, the viewer is later informed, was a 'cover' for her lack of love/desire for her husband. Both the 1982 and 1997 television adaptations of *The Woman in White* also feature a scene which takes place in a shrouded room, shortly after the newly married couple return to Glyde. In the 1997 version, for example, Marian confronts her brother-in-law about her sister's strange, withdrawn behaviour in a shrouded room (see figure 3.3).

3.3 The shrouded room: *The Woman in White* (BBC1, 1997).

As Marian enters through a dark doorway, the camera pans left to follow her movement towards Sir Percival, revealing a large room full of furniture and paintings covered in dust-sheets. Surrounded by concealed tables and chairs, and underneath a covered portrait, Sir Percival is seen in the extreme background of the shot (it is subsequently revealed that Sir Percival is in this room looking through legal documents, signifying his drive to gain control of Laura's money at all costs). It is entirely apt that Marian's confrontation of her brother-in-law occurs within this setting, as the surrounding mise-en-scène eloquently communicates the dangerous secrets inferred within the scene: Percival's abuse of Laura, and his plot to render his new wife powerless, will eventually lead to Laura's false imprisonment and the death of Anne Catherick (Susan Vidler). The covered furniture and family portraits thus metaphorically represents the hidden secrets contained within the domestic space. In relation to the female Gothic adaptation's hybrid generic identity, the image of the shrouded room has further impact, in that it also denies one of the central pleasures of the heritage text. By covering the furnishings and décor of the central heritage location (the stately, ancestral home), the female Gothic drama denies the pleasure produced by the viewer's gaze on the detail of heritage set dressing. In such sequences, the surface glamour or allure of the domestic space is hidden at precisely the moment in which the question of idyllic domesticity is challenged. Instead, what the viewer is shown are traces or blank spaces where these markers of the heritage 'ideal home' would have appeared, visualising a lack rather than a sense of opulence within the mise-en-scène.

The ultimate family secret present in the female Gothic adaptation is that of domestic violence. The discovery of child abuse and/or spousal brutality is the subtext of many of these female Gothic adaptations, particularly those made since the mid 1990s. Through the representation of domestic violence, glimpses are offered into the underside of family life in the eighteenth and nineteenth centuries. While the introduction to this chapter stated that this analysis would not seek to dwell on the question of the female Gothic adaptation's timeliness, it does appear as if these texts 'worry at' some of the current fears surrounding the high media profile of issues such as domestic violence and retrospective investigations into child abuse in the 1990s. Tania Modleski has argued that the female Gothic novel allows for a displacement of contemporary fears surrounding the home on to a fictional text, a text which must necessarily be set in a distant place and time:

> Because [female Gothic] novels so radically displace reality by putting the action into distant times and strange and ghostly lands, they are uniquely equipped to become a site for the displacement of repressed wishes and

fears. In other words, Gothics can present us with the frighteningly familiar precisely because they make the familiar strange . . . Thus set in a remote place, in a faraway time, the female Gothic . . . expresses women's most intimate fears, or, more precisely, their fears about intimacy – about the exceedingly private, even claustrophobic nature of their existence. (1982a: 20)

The argument that the female Gothic narrative set in the past provides a 'safe', displaced space for the exploration of the repressed fears of women offers some explanation for the presence of these narratives on television in the 1990s, in relation to the aforementioned discursive contexts of domestic violence and child abuse. However, an alternate approach to the presence of domestic violence within the heritage text sees this narrative as far more disruptive than Modleski's account would suggest. In *The Woman in White* (1997), the reference to domestic violence is writ large across the drama during a sequence in which Laura's bruises from her husband's violent abuse are revealed to her sister, Marian. The close-up shots which show Laura peeling back the shoulder of her lacy gown contain added 'shock value' when exposing dark welts set against the lace of eighteenth century period costume, within the heritage setting. Contrary to Modleski's argument, and in line with the previous discussion of the ways in which the female Gothic adaptation undermines the visual pleasure of the heritage text in this chapter, the combination of period costume with the marks of abuse creates a disruptive frisson within this hybrid television genre, marking a moment in which the safety of the past is challenged. Rather than reading the female Gothic narrative as a safe, displaced venue for the exploration of contemporary fears then, one could in fact argue that contemporary fears explode into the space of the heritage text at moments such as this, again refuting a depiction of the past as a place of domestic harmony, free from the threat of violence.

Points of conjunction: subjective narration and the diegetic reader/viewer

This chapter has thus far outlined the ways in which the heroine negotiates her position within the domestic space of the Gothic narrative; as such, it has focused on a topographical analysis of the mise-en-scène of female Gothic fiction on television (the house and its particular elements), and has perhaps taken for granted the connection between text and domestic viewer. The questions of exactly how the model viewer enters, or is implicated in, the spaces of this mise-en-scène must now be addressed: from which, or rather, whose, position are the exploratory tracks, pans and zooms around this milieu taken? The latter part of this analysis of the female Gothic television adaptation will therefore explore the uses of subjective narration in these dramas, as the connection between heroine and model viewer is delineated, and will focus on the notion of identification. Jackie Stacey offers a useful set of definitions of the term 'identification' as it is applied in screen theory:

> Identification has often loosely meant sympathising or engaging with a character. It has also been understood to suggest something analogous to the idea of 'point of view', watching and following the film from a character's point of view. This involves not only visual point of view, constructed by a type of shot, editing sequences and so on, but also narrative point of view, produced through the sharing of knowledge, sympathy, or moral values with the protagonist. Identification has thus been used as a kind of common sense term within some film and literary studies, referring to a set of cultural processes which describe different kinds of connections between spectators/readers and fictional others. (1994: 130)

In the following discussion of the female Gothic adaptation, identification will be understood in relation to all of the above definitions: as a narrative/narrational position, as a position of sympathy and engagement, and as a 'set of cultural processes' connecting 'spectators/readers and fictional others'.

It is, perhaps, unsurprising that the female Gothic television drama centres on the point of view of the central female protagonist. This shared subjective position implies both optical and aural point of view (through the predominance of subjective camerawork and character-specific sound perspective), and narrative point of view (the viewer shares the protagonist's basic knowledge of 'what's going on' throughout the drama, and, it is expected, is sympathetic towards the heroine's predicament). This conjoined position, between the heroine and the model viewer, has a great impact on the way in which the plot is perceived and organised; for example, once inside the generic 'dreadful house', much of the audiovisual perspective, which the viewer implicitly shares with the heroine, is taken from an obscured position (cracks through doors, wind-whipped balconies, a shadowy window, etc.). Tania Modleski notes the importance of this shared position of uncertainty in relation to literary versions of this genre, stating that 'the reader shares some of the heroine's uncertainty about what is going on and what the lover/husband is up to. The reader is nearly as powerless in her understanding as the heroine' (1982a: 60). In the television adaptation, the viewer, like the heroine, does not hear or see all they need to make sense of the plot from the outset, but rather is privy to snatches of dialogue and glimpses of visual clues to the central enigma of the drama (the secret which must be uncovered in order to achieve narrative resolution). This depiction of subjectivity on the verges of the domestic space very much reflects the wife's position within the nineteenth century home in general, and marks an exclusion from the understanding of events which comes from her husband's ability to move between the public and domestic worlds.

In *The Woman in White* (1997), for example, Marian is barred from consulting the solicitor who arrives to discuss her sister and brother-in-law's financial position; this exclusion is marked by an obscuring of vision and sound, which also clearly withholds the discussion between Sir Percival and the solicitor from the viewer. An overhead shot, taken from the landing above the two men, is viewed from Marian's optical position: as the men walk past, she (and the viewer) hears a snatch of their conversation ('Matters have reached a head and the situation may have become serious . . .'). At this point, a hand-held camera tracks up from this point-of-view shot to a close-up of Marian's face as she listens, looking down in the direction of the two men; as their conversation continues ('We must address ourselves to . . .') the sound again trails out, prompting Marian to move stealthily down the stairs, tilting her head to listen to the conversation ('If I can obtain a signature to the papers . . .', 'That will resolve the . . .'). As she turns her head towards the men on a lower flight of stairs, another cut is made to a wobbly, hand-held point-of-view shot, which tracks past an ornamental banister carving in the foreground of the shot (a raven) and settles on a shot through a doorway into another room which the two men pass through; again, the sound of their conversation returns briefly as we hear the solicitor say 'We can then proceed to clear the outstanding bills as they become due'. As a pronounced moment of subjective camerawork and sound recording taken from Marian's point of view, vital plot information is withheld from the central female protagonist and the viewer. This is achieved through the constant loss of sound (via subjective sound perspective) and image, as elements of mise-en-scène continually obscure parts of the frame (the ornate banister carving of the raven, the doorway and walls of the room which the men pass into). The motif of obscured sound is subsequently repeated in the following scene; as Marian lies in bed at night, the camera slowly tracks into a facial close-up as an indecipherable argument and faint cries are heard in another room of the house. Marian's reactions to this noise express the fear and confusion felt in relation to her position within the domestic space (the noise is presumably the sound of her sister's new husband bullying and abusing her), a confusion which is also shared by the viewer. Importantly, no cut away is made to the source of the argument, thus providing the viewer with more information than Marian is privy to, but rather a sense of narrative suspense is retained. This shared perspective is crucial to the narrative structure of the female Gothic genre, where the viewer's shared position with the heroine means that ambiguity and uncertainty are maintained throughout the course of the drama.

Other striking moments of marked subjectivity frequently evoked in the female Gothic television adaptation are fantasy or dream flashbacks, often shown as an impressionistic montage of images from the past, present, and future of the drama. These psychical point-of-view sequences, occurring at moments of crisis for the heroine, build up an impression of the narrative in non-linear or non-chronological order, suggesting the significance of certain images, sounds and events without fully elucidating the drama's central enigma. In these sequences, sounds and images from other moments in the drama (and, occasionally, sounds and images from the back-story which are not shown elsewhere in the adaptation) are edited together in order to represent the protagonist's inability to make sense of her situation and the central enigma which must be uncovered in order to resolve the narrative. For example, as Mrs. Danvers goads the young Mrs. de Winter to kill herself by jumping through Rebecca's bedroom window (in *Rebecca* (1979)), a series of images are dissolved together which convey the young woman's troubled relationship to her domestic space and her dead predecessor. Following an initial shot of Mrs. Danvers' face which rapidly disappears into a fog, dissolves are made to the following shots: Rebecca's hand sticking out of the sea; a close-up of Mrs. Danvers' face; the front page of Rebecca's poetry book, burning (the new Mrs. de Winter threw it on to the fire in the first episode of the serial); a travelling shot of the trees on the drive of Manderley (from the newly married couple's return home); a medium long shot of a little girl standing at the gatehouse on the couple's arrival; a tracking shot (from Mrs. de Winter's point of view) of the line of house servants; an extreme close-up zoom into a rhododendron flower; the fog; a repeated close-up of Mrs. Danvers' face; an extreme long shot of the misty bay; a high angle close-up of Maxim's face saying 'Don't be afraid. Jump!'; and a tilted point-of-view shot looking down from the window to the courtyard below. This sequence of 'recovered memory', accompanied by a Debussy-inspired piece of piano music, utilises montage editing techniques to piece together a series of seemingly unrelated images as clues to the secret which threatens the young heroine (Maxim's murder of Rebecca and the inherent threat of Manderley), as well as offering a flashback which expresses the anxiety attached to the young Mrs. de Winter's position in her home. As her life is threatened and she feels the paranoia of her husband wishing her dead, she 'revisits' shots from her arrival at Manderley (the rhododendron, the little girl, the avenue of trees) in a sequence which builds up an image of domestic paranoia in a non-linear fashion until it begins to make sense.

The frequent use of subjective camerawork and sound perspective does not only hold the model (female) viewer in a position of victim-hood in the female Gothic adaptation, however. On another level, the extent of subjective narration within the female Gothic television drama may be read as evidence of female empowerment and agency. One of the most striking changes made in David Pirie's adaptation of *The Woman in White* (1997) is the reassignment of the narrator's voice from the beginning of the drama. Whereas the 1982 BBC adaptation of *The Woman in White* tells the story from the perspective of Laura and Marian's art teacher, Walter Hartright, and the opening monologue/flashback is taken from his perspective, Pirie's adaptation of the text begins in Limmeridge graveyard with a tracking shot over the gravestones accompanied by Marian's voice-over. The subsequent flashback following this voice-over is therefore taken from the central female protagonist's perspective, and her explanatory voice-over continues over the introduction of Mr. Hartright at the train station (an event which this character does not witness). This significant revision thus inscribes female subjectivity as important from the start, and frames the rest of the narrative as Marian's memory/flashback, marking the entire drama as univocal, originating from Marian's perspective. This narrational strategy is also strikingly different from the original narration in Collins' novel, in which the story is told from a variety of perspectives, and this unusual instance of female narrational omniscience is restated whenever expository voice-over is used throughout the adaptation, always spoken in Marian's voice. Therefore, female subjectivity is assigned an unanticipated strength within the female Gothic narrative, even though it also marks the heroine and model viewer's sense of isolation or exclusion at various points in the narrative. This reading of the flashback/interior point-of-view sequence as a sign of strength and resistance is in keeping with Susan Hayward's notion that 'the flashback . . . can be a moment when the psyche has control of its unconscious. So flashbacks of whatever gender should represent an ideal moment of empowerment' (1996: 86). Hayward goes on to state, however, that many female flashbacks in classical narrative cinema are mediated by a male 'expert' protagonist (analyst, detective, etc.), thus disavowing it as a moment of empowerment.[9] However, in the case of the female Gothic adaptation for television, the mediation of memory and imagination is almost always associated solely with the female heroine.

It has been argued that television offers a greater potential for identification through the essential 'closeness' of the medium to the viewer. For example, Lynne Joyrich discusses the potentially over-involved female viewer in an analysis of television melodrama: 'In the popular imagination . . . the woman's relationship to the screen is an overly close one – she is so bound to the drama, so susceptible to the image, that it can even evoke a physical reaction in her tearful response' (1992: 241). Joyrich subsequently goes on to argue that tropes of proximity (the female viewer's closeness to the screen) have been particularly prevalent in discussions of television viewing, and she outlines the ways that those over-arching structures of viewing which have come to be seen as the 'facts' of television reception (intimacy, immediacy, closeness, and so on), have been gendered in relation to the television audiences. In the case of the female Gothic adaptation, television's 'closeness', its proximity to its viewer, is rather obviously played upon by the programme makers. The most frequently used technique to denote this closeness is the facial close-up, whereby the heroine's face is writ large upon the screen, implying shared knowledge between the protagonist and the viewer. This close-up is also utilised at moments in which something has been left unsaid by the heroine but which, it is assumed, the viewer implicitly understands (often the expression of uncanny sensation/déjà vu, or a realisation related to the secret/enigma).[10] In a *Radio Times* interview given to co-incide with the broadcast of *The Wyvern Mystery*, director Alex Pillai emphasised the necessity of this closeness: 'we tried to express the world as [Alice] experiences it. The main thing for us was to use camera and lighting to get inside her head' (Griffiths, 2000: 20). This desire to create points of conjunction between heroine and viewer is taken here as one of the defining characteristics of the recent female Gothic adaptation. Indeed, as the writer David Pirie notes later in the same article, when he comments on the difference between the literary and television versions of *The Wyvern Mystery*, 'the whole point of dramatic narrative is to narrow the perspective, to keep the story taut and to make the audience sympathetic to the main protagonist' (Griffiths, 2000: 18).

In *The Woman in White* (1997), the use of racking focus, whereby the heroine's face is brought into focus in the foreground of a shot, excluding the figures and objects around her, is deployed to imply a moment of shared awareness between protagonist and viewer. As Walter Hartwright (Andrew Lincoln) paints Marian's sister in the garden of their family home, thus highlighting the striking resemblance between her and Anne Catherick (their illegitimate sister who has been sexually abused by Laura's husband-to-be), the camera pans left slightly and refocuses, obscuring all else but Marian's troubled face. While Marian cannot actually *know* any of the information implied by this link between Laura and Anne at this point in the narrative, the heroine's close-up acts as a recognition of her closeness to the viewer, as they both move closer to the disclosure of this association. This emphasis on the facial close-up in the female Gothic adaptation has been seen as replacing the more usual slow tracks and pans of the heritage drama. Gareth Neane, producer of *The Woman in White* (1997), has argued that the predominance of the facial close-up is what marks his production out from other literary adaptations on television. He describes the visual style of the adaptation as 'not sitting back in wide shot looking at costumes. There are big close-ups, shots tight on eyeline, and a camera that moves around with a slight untidiness that you don't normally see in period drama' (Ellis, 1997: 22). Therefore, Neane clearly understands his adaptation as being aimed towards the translation of subjectivity and identification, rather than the more usual drive towards spectatorship and a detached sense of visual pleasure found in the classical heritage text. Subsequently, the centrality of the domestic heroine offers the viewer something other than costumes/home furnishings to look at.

The protagonist of the female Gothic drama is further linked to the model viewer by undertaking the act of reading and/or viewing during the narrative; as a diegetic consumer of female Gothic fictions, the central female protagonist of these dramas is directly equated with the female viewer. The heroine of the female Gothic television adaptation is often shown reading Gothic novels (and their literary predecessor, the fairy tale) during the course of the drama, an activity which frequently occurs or is referred to at the beginning of the female Gothic adaptation. Through this seemingly innocuous introduction of the heroine's reading matter from the very outset of the dramas, the mechanisms of identification outlined in the preceding analysis are made more explicit. An example of this intertextual consumption of Gothic fictions is found at the beginning of *The Woman in White* (1997), when Marian announces her interest in the female Gothic narrative: 'I am sorry if you caught me observing your arrival. My sister and I are so fond of Gothic novels that we sometimes act as if we were in them', to which Walter replies, 'You would certainly seem to have the perfect setting for your pretence'. This self-referential exchange clearly draws a parallel between the female protagonist as diegetic consumer of the female Gothic narrative and the female viewer as extra-diegetic consumer of the same. Similarly, at the beginning of *The Wyvern Mystery* (discussed above), an establishing shot of the infant Alice (Tamara Harvey) shows her reading a fairy story, a 'junior' version of the female Gothic narrative which centres upon 'the transferral from one [house] to the other . . . as it in turn constituted the most crucial event in women's lives' (Warner, 1993: 30). In this establishing sequence, a certain closeness between the little girl and the female Gothic text is identified by her physical interaction with the book, as she traces the illustrations with

3.4 Illustration from the Gothic fairy story: *The Wyvern Mystery* (BBC1, 2000).

her fingers. Following this, a close-up point-of-view shot shows an illustration of a girl running in the woods (see figure 3.4), placing the eyes of the model viewer in conjunction with the young protagonist (here a confessional voice-over further establishes a sense of intimacy or shared experience). At this moment, the shared experience of domestic anxiety (shared between the protagonist and the model viewer) is reaffirmed through the shared experience of consuming female Gothic fictions, and the intimacy of the television drama ensures that the viewer is co-present or written into the female Gothic narrative.

By gazing at this image, the young Alice is not only depicted as diegetic reader, but also a viewer; furthermore, this image has added significance

3.5 Re-enacting the Gothic fairy story: *The Wyvern Mystery* (BBC1, 2000).

in that it will be repeated 'for real' later in the drama as the adult Alice runs through the woods of Wyvern, away from the advances of Squire Fairfield (Derek Jacobi), her lecherous benefactor (see figure 3.5). Here the direct match on image, the similarities in costume and composition, and the analogous patterns of light and dark within each frame configure Alice as a diegetic reader-viewer within her own text and as the diegetic consumer of her own Gothic narrative.

Ultimately, it is the desire to *view* or *consume* her own Gothic narrative that drives the female protagonist on throughout the drama, towards the revelation of her worst fears and her ensuing escape. It is this 'will to view', exemplified by Alice's adamant statement at the edges of her predecessor's room in *The Wyvern Mystery* ('No, I *want* to see'), which aligns the female Gothic heroine with the television viewer in no uncertain terms. The drama which perhaps most clearly represents this conflation of reading and viewing through the depiction of the central female protagonist as diegetic consumer of Gothic fictions is the BBC's 1987 adaptation of Jane Austen's *Northanger Abbey*. The original novel, a satire on the female Gothic novel, places this doubling of readership at the centre of its narrative: the heroine of the book, Cathy, is obsessed with reading Gothic 'pot-boilers', so much so that when she finds herself in her suitor's eponymously titled Gothic pile, her reading matter appears to be repeating itself in 'real life'.

The television adaptation of *Northanger Abbey* plays upon the representation of Cathy (Katherine Schlesinger) as a diegetic stand-in for the female Gothic reader-viewer by fully visualising extracts from her reading matter through imagined point-of-view sequences at key moments in the narrative. Much of the criticism of this adaptation in the press focused on these moments. For example, Peter Kemp of *The Independent* argued the following:

> Maggie Wadey's appalling adaptation and Giles Foster's vulgar production vandalised this ironic tale. Catherine's Gothic day-dreams got bloated into Hammer Horror sequences of blood-bespattered virgins and fiends with blue-lit faces. Jane Austen's scenes of crisp wit made way for mush of Wadey's own concoction. (Kemp, 1987: 11)

The *Daily Telegraph*'s review was more complimentary: '[Female Gothics à la Ann Radcliffe] live on in the conventions of the horror movie genre. It therefore seemed entirely justifiable that the director . . . chose to render the lovely Catherine's fantasies in a cod Hammer style, dripping with blood and hymeneal symbolism' (Anon., 1987: 13). Katherine Schlesinger was in fact cast in the role of Catherine with the express purpose of emphasising the possibilities of viewer-heroine identification.

Director Giles Foster commented on the importance of 'everywoman' casting and its potential to 'open up' possible points of identification between viewer and text in an interview for the *Observer* magazine. As David Lewin writes,

> For Giles Foster, the director of *Northanger Abbey*, the challenge was to find an actress with whom people could identify: 'A young actress whom could be both sophisticated and naïve, self contained and romantic and with a big dose of common sense: to be both the imperfect heroine and the desirable one.' (Lewin, 1987: 30)

Here Foster not only highlights the usual conflation of character and actress when discussing the decisions made in the casting process, but also states that the actress's accessibility to the viewer was a deciding factor in casting her.

The opening sequence of the adaptation begins with the act of reading as Cathy is shown engrossed in a Gothic novel (Ann Radcliffe's *The Mysteries of Udolpho*), her voice-over reading aloud from this founding Gothic text and thus immediately engendering a sense of closeness between protagonist and model viewer. From this image, a cut is made to a close-up of an illustration from the novel (see figure 3.6), and then an extreme close-up of the same, which is subsequently dissolved to the first shot of Cathy's fantasy world, an exact match on image which marks the transfer from the illustration in the 'found text' to Cathy's imagined point of view (see figure 3.7).

The following sequence features a Hammer-esque combination of gory, soft focus images of the victim-heroine (played by Cathy) being preyed upon by a dastardly male figure (in the shape of her future father-in-law (Robert Hardy)) and a loud, synthesised soundtrack. In this dissolve, and in the rest of this sequence, the notion of viewer-heroine identification is dramatised: here, Cathy is the diegetic representation of an over-involved reader/viewer who puts herself in the place of the victim-heroine through a subjective, imagined point-of-view sequence. As a dissolve is made from the protagonist's face as the victim-heroine of her novel to the protagonist's face as herself, the act of the viewer-heroine identification is intertextually portrayed. This visualisation of Cathy's Gothic day dreams may therefore be read as an amalgamation of the mechanisms of identification essential to the televisation of the female Gothic narrative. This is achieved through the doubling of domestic space (the house within the text and the house in which the text is viewed), the emphasis on subjective narration, and the configuration of the heroine as a diegetic 'stand in' for the female consumer of Gothic fictions.

3.6 Illustration from the Gothic novel:
Northanger Abbey (BBC2, 1987).

In conclusion, as in the resolution of the 1997 version of *The Woman in White* (which centres on the recovery of the feminine text (Anne's diary), and therefore on the possibility of two equally victimised women making contact with each other through the act of reading), perhaps the female Gothic television drama may be seen as potentially transgressive. Lynne Joyrich, referencing an argument made by Laura Mulvey (1986), has argued that the sense of resistance or subversion often associated with cinematic melodrama is impossible within the realms of the television drama: 'as TV brought popular entertainment into the home, national consensus triumphed over potentially oppositional melodrama'

3.7 Dreaming the Gothic novel: *Northanger Abbey* (BBC2, 1987).

(1992: 228). This analysis of the female Gothic adaptation, itself a form of television melodrama, refutes Joyrich's claim to a certain extent. Hopefully, it has become clear during the course of this discussion that the domestic viewing context brings the female viewer's fears about her home and domestic relationships into stark relief, offering a textual space in which these anxieties may be worked through, or rather 'worried at', if not necessarily resolved. In this sense, while it might be unwise to view these Gothic dramas as wholly radical, it is possible to argue that they offer sites for the recognition of domestic anxiety for a model viewer who is 'recorded into' the female Gothic television adaptation.

Notes

1 *Rebecca* (1979) and *Woman in White* (1982) are available to view at the National Film and Television Archive, British Film Institute. *Northanger Abbey*, *Rebecca* (1997), *The Woman in White* (1997), *The Haunting of Helen Walker*, *The Turn of the Screw* and *The Wyvern Mystery* are all commercially available on video and DVD.

2 For example, *Rebecca* (BBC, 1947), *Rebecca* (BBC, 1954), *Woman in White* (episode of *Hour of Mystery*) (ABC [UK], 1957), *Woman in White* (BBC1, 1966).

3 Eco defines empirical readers thus: 'empirical readers can read in many ways, and there is no law that tells them how to read, because they often use the text as a container for their own passions, which may come from outside the text or which the text may arouse by chance' (1994: 8).

4 For example, *Rebecca*, *Dragonwyck* (US, 1947), *Gaslight* (US, 1944) and *The Two Mrs. Carrolls* (US, 1947).

5 This increased visibility of the issue of domestic violence in Britain is further evidenced in the flurry of governmental activity which followed the publication of this report. *Living Without Fear*, a Home Office publication that outlined the Government's strategy for tackling domestic violence, was produced in June 1999 (see http://www.womenandequalityunit.gov.uk/archive/living_without_fear/index.htm). This set out to tackle the issue of domestic violence, and was accompanied by the Home Office conference, *Violence Against Women*, organised by the Special Conferences Unit at Shrigley Hall Hotel, near Macclesfield, 24–25 November 1999.

6 Milbank turns to Peacock's *Nightmare Abbey*, published in 1818, the same year as Jane Austen's satire on Gothic novel reading, *Northanger Abbey*, drawing on the character of Scythrop who reads *Horrid Mysteries* as an example of such an avid male fan of the genre.

7 Based on AGB Programme Ratings (week ending 5/1/97, p. 20, and week ending 12/1/97, p. 2).

8 This idea is also explored in Julianne Pidduck's discussion of Jane Austen adaptations (1998), though not in relation to the Gothic genre specifically.

9 For example, Mildred/Joan Crawford's narration in *Mildred Pierce* (US, 1945).

10 More recently this technique has been frequently used in the US series *Desperate Housewives* (ABC [US], 2004–), which might be seen as a modern reworking of the female Gothic narrative.

Keeping it in the family: American Gothic television in the 1960s

American Gothic and the family narrative

The concluding chapters of this book discuss Gothic television in the US context, exploring the notion that home and family are perhaps even more central in the American Gothic narrative than they are in the programmes discussed previously. By arguing that the Gothic genre on television transcends both historical eras and national boundaries, the usefulness of this generic category is revealed, as is the extent of the Gothic's popularity on television. This chapter centres on a discussion of two hybrid forms of Gothic drama in the 1960s, firstly the Gothic family sitcoms *The Munsters* (Kayro-Vue Productions, 1964–66) and *The Addams Family* (Filmways, 1964–66), and secondly the Gothic soap opera *Dark Shadows* (Dan Curtis Productions Inc., 1966–71). Focusing on the representation of the home and extended family in these programmes, an analysis of the ways in which these texts expose prevalent anxieties in the 1960s around the instability of the familial unit and normative gender identities will be offered. The previous chapter, examining the female Gothic narrative on British television, discussed the congruence between the domestic spaces represented on screen and the intended viewing contexts of television, noting the formal and narrative techniques deployed to emphasise the symmetries between these two spaces. In the following chapter, this relationship between text and context will be read in the light of the American Gothic as a nationally specific narrative, on television and beyond. In order to embark upon such an analysis however, it is first necessary to outline the divergent descriptions of the American Gothic as they stand within Gothic scholarship.

It is widely agreed, in those accounts which offer a genealogy of the Gothic in North America, that while related in a structural sense, the American Gothic is distinguishable from its European counterpart, preoccupied with different concerns. As Teresa A. Goddu notes, the transferral of a European Gothic tradition into the 'New World' led to a transformation of the genre: 'the American Gothic consists of a less coherent set of conventions [than the European Gothic]. Its more flexible form challenges the critically unified Gothic genre and demands a reassessment of the Gothic's parameters' (1997: 4). The precise nature of this change is what American Gothic scholarship continues to contest, however. Many understand American Gothic conventions by reading the American Gothic as a postcolonial genre, for example. As Jeanette Idiart and Jennifer Schulz explain,

> American Gothic literature reflects the 'haunted consciousness' of the nation: the awareness that at the heart of its governing text [the US constitution] are contradictions that threaten to unveil American democracy as a fiction. These texts bring to the surface the knowledge that the founding value of the Constitution, equality, is predicated on the exclusion of selected populations on the basis of race, gender and property. (1999: 127)

Here the political identity of the United States, questions of national guilt and conspiracy, the treatment of Native American communities, the legacy of slavery and, more latterly, American foreign policy, dominate our understanding of the American Gothic.

However, while this depiction of the American Gothic is compelling, there are others who see the national Gothic narrative as more quotidian than its European predecessor, with the American Gothic being firmly centred around images of the family and familial trauma. Henry James proclaimed in 1865 that American Gothic literature was 'connected at a hundred points with the common objects of life' (Davenport-Hines, 1998: 267), and contemporary critics have also recently taken up James' stance. Fred Botting, for example, characterises the early American Gothic as a 'domestication' of the European Gothic:

> the bourgeois family is the scene of ghostly return, where guilty secrets of past transgression and uncertain class origins are the sources of anxiety . . . Though the grand gloom of European Gothic was inappropriate, the commonplace of American culture was full of little mysteries and guilty secrets from communal and family pasts. (1996: 114–15)

Botting details the fact that the canonical texts of the American Gothic, such as Charles Brockden Brown's *Wieland* (1798), Nathaniel Hawthorne's *The House of the Seven Gables* (1851) and Edgar Allen Poe's 'The Fall of the House of Usher' (1834), all focus on familial psychodramas, with each of these key texts taking the ancestral home as their setting in narratives that focus on the resurfacing of family guilt. Richard Davenport-Hines also argues that in comparison to the

European Gothic, Gothic narratives in the United States became far more family centred, in response to the nation's more idealised depictions of family life:

> as Americans adopted a specialised, even extremist veneration of family, some of their writers adapted Gothic imagery to exemplify the destructive power of families. Gothic excess was deployed to represent domesticity's extreme horrors . . . In American Gothic the 'isolated puritan country household' . . . replaced Europe's 'brawling and childish and quite deadly mud castle household in a miasmic and spirit-ridden forest' as the locus of horror. (1998: 267)

In Davenport-Hines' terms, this extreme veneration of the American family created an inevitable fictional response, in the exposure of the American family's underside. In concurrence with this approach, Karen Halttunen has noted, in her wide-ranging study of North American murder narratives, that in the eighteenth century, 'certain categories of story-line lent themselves particularly well to Gothic narration. Tales of domestic murder evoked a powerful sense of horror over the crime's shocking violation of the new sentimental domesticity' (1998: 5). Halttunen suggests that, '[n]arratives of domestic homicide routinely invoked the sentimental view of the family as that "sacred, social institution, ordained by Heaven, to be productive of the greatest happiness to mankind," in order to emphasise the particular abomination of murder within its precincts' (1998: 144): this narrative strategy of systematically sentimentalising the American family has been particularly echoed in contemporary American Gothic serial dramas (as discussed in the final chapter of this book). All this is not to suggest, however, that images of home and family are unimportant to European versions of the Gothic narrative: this book has indeed argued that this is not the case. However, perhaps the most striking characteristic of the American Gothic version of the domestic narrative is its relationship to the quotidian. These are not the stately, ancestral homes or dynasties of well-to-do families of the European Gothic but haunted houses and troubled families of a more ordinary kind.

American Gothic television: origins

An examination of the formation of Gothic television in the US shows that, as with early British television drama, the Gothic anthology series on American television was prefigured by the genre's popularity on the radio, again highlighting the relationship between the domestic reception context and the Gothic text. Indeed, several shows which first appeared on the radio made a successful transition to television, such as the anthology drama series, *Suspense* (CBS, 1949–64). *Suspense* featured the adaptation of classic supernatural literature (Edgar Allen Poe, H.P. Lovecraft) and the more contemporary work of John Dickson-Carr, and was particularly noted for its outstanding casts, some of whom (Boris Karloff, Peter Lorre, etc.) were already associated with filmic horror. Shortly after *Suspense* was produced in the United States, NBC introduced their own version of the Gothic-horror anthology series, *Lights Out* (1949–52), again adapted from a successful radio series which began in 1934, on the back of four well-received television 'specials' of the same name which had been produced by Fred Coe three years earlier. This series was presented by a host, Jack La Rue, and featured both adapted literary ghostly classics and some specially commissioned ghost stories. The makers of *Lights Out* enriched the presentation of the Gothic narrative with a particularly creative approach to using sound to enhance the eerie mood of the drama (an aptitude which may have come, in part, from the series' radio ancestry):

> Each episode began with a close-up of a pair of eyes, followed by a bloody hand reaching out to turn off the lights. An eerie laugh would follow and a sonorous voice intoned, 'Lights out, everybody' . . . The transmissions were also enhanced by the special eerie musical effects of Arlo Hults on an organ and Doris Johnson on a harp. (Haining, 1993: 50)

Lights Out thus sought to terrify viewers through the deployment of low budget sound effects and minimal orchestration, which both betrayed a radiophonic background and which would also become specific to Gothic television (the sepulchral tonal quality of the narrator's voice, the combination of resonant musical instruments to create eerie sound effects, and so on).

During the 1950s, non-generic anthology series often adapted Gothic classics and produced ghost stories: NBC's *Matinee Theater* (1955–58), for example, produced adaptations of 'The Fall of the House of Usher' (NBC, 1956), 'Dracula' (NBC, 1956) and 'Frankenstein' (NBC, 1957), among others, and *Broadway Television Theatre* (WOR-TV, 1952–54) produced theatrical ghost plays like 'The Enchanted Cottage' (WOR-TV, 1952) and 'The Gramercy Ghost' (WOR-TV, 1954). However, the science-fiction anthology series would soon be set to surpass its Gothic counterpart in popularity in the United States in the 1950s, even though the Gothic literary adaptation would still appear from time to time within the bounds of the science-fiction anthology series (as in ABC [US] TV's *Tales of Tomorrow* (1951–53) series, where Lon Chaney Jnr. appeared in the title role of the 1952 episode 'Frankenstein' (ABC [US], 1952)). Indeed, stylistic similarities between the two genres are clear and a comparable penchant for the macabre and the horrific is discernible in later science-fiction series such as Rod Serling's *Twilight Zone* (CBS, 1959–65).

Supernatural anthology series were however broadcast in the US throughout the 1960s and 1970s, producing a broad range of Gothic teleplays which cannot be dealt with at any great length here. These series included *One Step Beyond* (ABC [US], 1959–61), based on supposedly 'real' instances of the paranormal; *Thriller* (NBC, 1960–62), a series hosted by Boris Karloff which moved further into the realm of the supernatural Gothic in its latter seasons; and Serling's post-*Twilight Zone* series, *Night Gallery* (Universal TV, 1970–73), which allowed Serling to explore Gothic horror more fully than his earlier creation had done (in an anthology series where each week's episode was based on the uncanny device of a painting found in an old museum). As in the UK, it is evident that the anthology form was well suited to the industrial and economic structures of programme making in the US during its formative period. There is clearly more work to be done here in uncovering the predominant styles and preoccupations of the US Gothic anthology series, charting its development and decline, and exploring the relationship between television horror and its cinematic counterpart in the US (comparable to the analysis offered in chapters one and two of this book, in the British context). However, we will now turn instead to look at some instances of a more hybrid form of Gothic television produced in the United States during the 1960s, which raise important questions about the domestic reception of the Gothic genre.

The neighbours from hell: the Gothic sitcom

The advent of the Gothic family sitcom in the mid-1960s perhaps indicates the extent to which the Gothic genre had become 'at home' on US television by its second decade of broadcasting. Subverting the traditional family sitcom of the 1950s, *The Addams Family* and *The Munsters* presented staple Gothic characters as 'just plain folks', taking the American Gothic's family-centric narrative and image repertoire into the suburban world of the white picket fence and the Ladies' League. In a striking example of television's generic hybridity, these shows fused the situation comedy with the horror drama (with heavy visual reference to Universal's filmic horror of the 1930s and 1940s), combining two highly popular genres and tapping into a broadcasting trend for what has become known as the 'magicom' or the 'fantastic family sitcom' in the mid-1960s. These programmes are interesting beyond the fact of their unusual generic hybridity, however: like other examples of Gothic television discussed in this book, close analyses of these programmes reveal a deeper concern with the instability of the family and the construction of normative gender identities, within the specific context of post-war America. In a sense, both *The Addams Family* and *The Munsters* 'worried at' the home lives of their viewers, albeit in a humorous way, thus acting as classic American Gothic texts as delineated in the introduction to this chapter. I use the term 'worried at' rather deliberately to suggest that these programmes were part of a much broader set of cultural anxieties which extended beyond these texts. As I have argued elsewhere (see Wheatley, 2005), I find the term 'worrying at' rather more appropriate than John Ellis' notion of 'working through', given that 'working through' suggests a sense of conclusion or 'exhaustion' (Ellis, 2000: 79) which does not seem apposite in this context.

The Addams Family first appeared in print rather than on television, in *The New Yorker* in 1932. Drawn by cartoonist Charles Addams, arguably one of the key figures in the history of American Gothic art, these single-cell cartoons created a dark, sometimes surreal, vision of American family life, based around the exploits of a ghoulish family. The family was nameless in the original drawings, but for TV they became the vampish Morticia Addams (Carolyn Jones) and her husband Gomez (John Astin), their son Pugsley (Ken Weatherwax) and dead-pan daughter Wednesday (Lisa Loring), the ghoul-like Uncle Fester (Jackie Coogan), Grandma Addams, a witch (Blossom Rock) and their butler, Lurch (Ted Cassidy), bearing more than a passing resemblance to Frankenstein's monster. Born on 7 January 1912, Charles Addams grew up in Westfield, New Jersey, an area populated by Victorian mansions and archaic graveyards; this backdrop was to provoke an obsession with the Gothic from adolescence onward. Importantly, given that Addams was surrounded by Gothic architecture and imagery from an early age, he saw no disconnection between the images and narratives of the Gothic and the scenes and spaces of everyday life in North America. As Robert T. Garcia has argued, 'Addams fathered a revolution in macabre art, melding the Gothic with modern day terrors. His ghastly Victorian houses were located across the street from suburban ranches. His strange creatures drove modern highways . . . No longer were monsters confined to the past' (1991a: 36). With this emphasis on the everydayness of the Gothic in its various forms, the cartoon might have been seen as eminently suited to television adaptation, given that Gothic television has continually drawn parallels between the horrific or the macabre and everyday life.

The television show was conceived by independent producer David Levy, a former programming executive at NBC specialising in family entertainment and variety shows, who struck a deal with Addams for the adaptation of his cartoon for television. Commissioning Ed James and Seaman Jacobs to write a pilot, Levy took the series concept to Martin Ranshoff and Al Simon at Filmways, who in turn took Levy's proposition to CBS. However, as CBS had chosen to develop Universal's rival show, *The Munsters*, it was turned down, and *The Addams Family* was also rejected by NBC, CBS' main rival. ABC, operating as the 'third network' at the time, was more interested in the programme, however, as part of its attempt to build a larger market share with what ABC Development Executive Harve Bennett called 'wild-ass programming' (Garcia, 1991b: 43). Alongside programmes like *Bewitched* (ABC [US], 1964–72), and later *Batman* (ABC [US], 1966–68) and *Dark Shadows*, *The Addams Family* would seem daring and outrageous, thus building the distinctive 'edge' ABC were looking for.

According to the production histories of both programmes, it was entirely coincidental that, at the same time as *The Addams Family* went into production, *The Munsters* was created by Universal's television company (also responsible for popular programmes such as *Alfred Hitchcock Presents* (CBS, 1955–65) and *Wagon Train* (NBC/ABC [US], 1957–65)). As Universal's early horror films from the 1930s were endlessly recycled on television and proved very popular with young audiences, the company wanted to build a show on the back of this popularity. They also wanted to make use of the rights they owned on the Boris Karloff 'Frankenstein's monster' image (from *Frankenstein* (US, 1931)) by designing the father of the family, Herman Munster (Fred Gwynne), along the same lines. Like the Addams clan, the Munsters live in an extended family unit: Herman, his wife Lily (Yvonne de Carlo) (a vamp in the same vein as Morticia Addams), his vampire father-in-law, Grandpa (Al Lewis), their wolverine son, Eddie (Butch Patrick) and their disappointingly 'normal' niece, Marilyn (Beverly Owen/Pat Priest). Irving Paley acted as executive producer on the programme; the original format for *The Munsters* was written by Allan Burns and Chris Hayward, and the show was produced and scripted by Joe Connolly and Bob Mosher, the creators of *Leave it to Beaver* (CBS/ABC [US], 1957–63). Connolly and Mosher's link to this earlier family sitcom is particularly significant, in that it suggests a direct continuum from the earlier, 'straight' incarnations of the genre to these Gothic family sitcoms: the relationship between these two sitcom cycles will be explored at greater length below. Indeed, on numerous occasions throughout *The Munsters'* two year run, Herman Munster, a big fan of television, makes reference to the family

sitcom and often quotes *Leave it to Beaver*. This not only serves to ironically underscore the very 'everydayness' of these monsters ('they watch
TV too!'), but also knowingly acknowledges their TV ancestry.

While the claims of coincidence in the development and commissioning of *The Addams Family* and *The Munsters* may not be entirely
believable, their appearance at the exact same time, and the fact that they
were cancelled within weeks of each other two years later, might suggest
that they tapped into the *zeitgeist* of the mid-1960s in a particular way,
or that they similarly articulated current cultural trends or anxieties.
Certainly, both programmes shared a significant relationship with their
television ancestry, namely the family sitcoms that directly preceded this
'Gothic turn'. In order to understand the Gothic family sitcom, we need
to look towards programmes from the previous decade, such as *The
Goldbergs* (CBS/DuMont/NBC, 1949–56), *I Love Lucy* (CBS, 1951–57),
The Adventures of Ozzie and Harriet (ABC [US], 1952–66), *Make Room
For Daddy* (later *The Danny Thomas Show*) (ABC [US]/CBS, 1953–65),
Father Knows Best (CBS/NBC/ABC [US], 1954–63) and *Leave it to Beaver*,
with their cavalcade of bombastic fathers, hapless mothers and brattish
children, getting into 'scrapes' that were resolved by the end of each
episode, thus bringing the family back into harmony. As numerous television critics have noted, these sitcoms provided an image of the all-
American family in 'TV land' which conformed to the safe, suburban
values shared, it was presumed, by television viewers.

It is telling that these family sitcoms are often the programmes used
to define 1950s television *as a whole* (as argued in chapter two), somehow
standing in for all of the programming produced in the United States
during this period, within popular memory (and in popular journalism).
This vernacular canonicity underlines the significance of the genre
within the collective, national psyche, as a group of programmes which
shaped, or at least defined, what it meant to be an American in the post-
war era. John Hartley's definition of the family sitcom emphasises this
cultural work:

> Family sitcoms specialised in the drama of *family comportment*. They
> were distinguished from serials and drama series by their focus on
> internal family roles . . . Family or domestic sitcoms were perhaps the
> bedrock of broadcast television. They were what you grew up on, gently
> and amusingly teaching two important skills: how to watch television
> (media literacy); and how to live in families with tolerant mutual accom-
> modation, talking not fighting (life skills). (Hartley, 2001: 66)

Correspondingly, the Gothic family sitcom concentrated on the latter
skill ('how to live in families with tolerant mutual accommodation'),

building on the themes and issues of earlier family sitcoms while gently poking fun at them. The following analysis will therefore examine the extent to which *The Addams Family* and *The Munsters* subverted the family sitcom as a conservative form, asking whether their playfulness with the family values and gendered stereotypes of the family sitcom challenged or venerated the institutions and identities they satirised.

As well as being judged against the traditional family sitcom, *The Addams Family* and *The Munsters* also need to be understood as part of a cycle of fantastic family sitcoms, or what David Marc calls 'the magicom' (1997: 107). As a precursor to this cycle, *The Beverley Hillbillies* (CBS, 1962–71) was perhaps the first sitcom to send up conventional family values. Following this programme, the mid-1960s saw a slew of fantasy family sitcoms. In the first of these, *My Favorite Martian* (CBS, 1963–66), Martin the Martian (Ray Walston) was adopted by reporter Tim O'Hara (Bill Bixby) as his Uncle Martin; as a ratings hit for CBS, this sitcom prompted a search for other similar programming. The following years produced *Bewitched*, featuring a young witch negotiating her supernatural powers and her duty as a 'good wife'; *My Living Doll* (CBS, 1964–65) in which Dr. Robert MacDonald (Bob Cummings) trained Rhoda the android (Julie Newmar) to be the perfect woman; *My Mother the Car* (NBC, 1965–66), a short-lived sitcom in which the central protagonist's mother is reincarnated as a car; and *I Dream of Jeannie* (NBC, 1965–70), which, in a similar vein to *Bewitched*, featured Barbara Eden as Jeannie, a Genie 'bride' to her new master, Major Nelson (Larry Hagman). Given that, as Spigel notes, 'increasingly over the 1960s these [fantastic family sitcoms] . . . accounted for the mainstay of the genre while the classic nuclear family suburban sitcoms had virtually disappeared by 1966' (1997: 58), it is inaccurate to argue that they somehow subverted mainstream television culture in the United States. In effect, the 'magicom' replaced the traditional family sitcom for a brief period, and, as we shall see in the following analysis, their differentiation was, at times, perhaps quite superficial.

In the Gothic family sitcom, comedy rests upon the closeness between the macabre and the everyday: laughter is constantly inspired by the fact that these are monsters that worry about their weight, the schooling of their children, the love lives of their family and friends, the state of their neighbourhood and how they will pay their bills. We might therefore argue that this is *uncanny* comedy, in which humour is found in the meeting of the ordinary (heimlich) and the extraordinary (unheimlich), though this label reformulates the meaning of the uncanny somewhat. To recap the central tenet of Freud's delineation of the uncanny, '[t]he uncanny is that class of frightening which leads back to what is known of old and long familiar' (1990: 340). Through this proposition, Freud isolates the congruence of that which is both familiar and strange, known and unknown, in uncanny fictions, producing a sense of fear or disgust, and noting the destruction of boundaries between the imagined and the real in the uncanny text. However, Freud goes on to argue that generic context is also important to the uncanny effect, and that narrative devices and images which might be understood as uncanny in, for example, the tales of E.T.A. Hoffman, might not have the same impact in more fantastical literature. Whereas Freud refers to the fairy tale as his primary example of a genre where uncanny images and events are no longer frightening, we might equally argue that the 'magicom' has the same contextualising effect:

> In fairy tales, for instance, the world of reality is left behind from the very start, and the animistic system of beliefs is frankly adopted. Wish-fulfilments, secret powers, omnipotence of thoughts, animation of inanimate objects, all the elements so common in fairy stories, can exert no uncanny influence here; for, as we have learnt, that feeling cannot arise unless there is a conflict of judgement as to whether things which have been 'surmounted' and are regarded as incredible may not, after all, be possible; and this problem is eliminated from the outset by the postulates of the world of fairy tales. (Freud, 1990: 372)

In the Gothic sitcom, the conjunction of the everyday and the supernatural produces laughter rather than fear, as the viewer fully accepts the possibility of their coexistence within this generic context. For example, in both *The Addams Family* and *The Munsters*, the Gothic house becomes comedic through the supernatural transformation of everyday objects. Again, we might read this device as relating to the uncanny. Drawing on Jentsch's delineation of the uncanny (1995), Freud catalogues 'doubts whether an apparently animate being is really alive; or conversely, whether a lifeless object might not be in fact animate . . . the impression made by waxwork figures, ingeniously constructed dolls and automata' (1990: 346) as potentially uncanny, though he remains unconvinced by Jentsch's argument that this uncertainty is the primary cause of uneasy feeling in uncanny literature. However, in the Gothic sitcom, we can see these uncanny devices being employed to non-uncanny effect: in *The Munsters* episode 'A Walk on the Mild Side' (Kayro-Vue Productions, 1964), for example, Grandpa Munster's experiments with an enlarging machine in his underground lab cause the house to become 'possessed'. In a montage sequence which cuts between the lab and other rooms in the house, Herman's electric shaver becomes snake-like and attacks him (see figure 4.1), Lily is showered with toast and coffee in the kitchen from an errant toaster and electric coffee pot, a joint of meat spins out of

4.1 Animating the inanimate: 'A Walk on the Mild Side',
The Munsters (Kayro-Vue Productions, 1966).

control in the rotisserie, and Marilyn's hair drying cap inflates to the size of a beach ball, pulling her head around the room. In the Munster household then, supernatural power is channelled through the household's electric circuit and everyday appliances, making gags out of the incongruence between the supernatural horror and family sitcom genres.

Self-reflexively, television viewing itself is shown to be generically subversive within individual episodes of *The Munsters*. For example, the episode 'Rock-a-bye Munster' (Kayro-Vue Productions, 1964) begins with Herman, Grandpa and Igor the bat watching TV, although it is not at first clear that this is what they are doing. With the camera tracking past their faces, illuminated by the TV screen out of shot, it appears as if they are watching a gruesome experiment in Grandpa's lab, with a plethora of whirring gadgets in the rear of the shot (see figure 4.2). As an off-screen voice asks 'Gentlemen, shall we begin the operation? Scalpel', Herman answers 'Pulse rate falling'. Again, the off-screen voice requests 'Forceps' and Herman replies 'Breathing laboured', to which the voice responds 'Sutures', and Grandpa concedes 'This is a very dangerous operation'. As Herman gulps 'Oh, I know, just let me concentrate', the off-screen voice says 'You've got to save her Dr. Macy, her father owns the hospital', at which point the laugh track comes in and a cut is made to an image of a TV screen 'on the blink'. At once the scene is transformed into a comedy of television viewing, rather than a gruesome, Frankenstein-esque, horror, as Grandpa announces, exasperated, 'there goes that set again, right in the middle of my favourite comedy'. Television in the Munster household is thus depicted as an object of generic inversion or confusion, whereby a hospital drama is firstly mistaken for a horror show

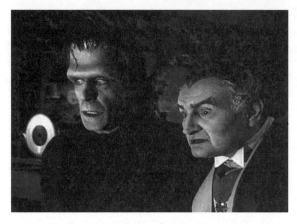

4.2 The Munsters watch Gothic television: 'Rock-a-bye Munster', *The Munsters* (Kayro-Vue Productions, 1964).

(by the viewer), and is then mistaken for a situation comedy (by Grandpa Munster). As Herman directs Grandpa to 'try another channel', cuts are made from the diegetic viewers to a TV Western, a slapstick train crash and a line of chorus girls from an early variety show, all showing on the Munster's TV set. Herman explains the dated nature of this programming by telling Grandpa that he 'shouldn't have repaired [the TV] with those war surplus radar parts', suggesting that the TV set has also become haunted, having taken on supernatural qualities enabling it to receive broadcasts from the beginning of the television service. This representation is in line with Jeffrey Sconce's account of popular cultural representations of American television in the 1950s and early 1960s as a 'haunted medium':

> Television brought with it a new form of 'visual' program flow, making it more than an extraordinary medium linking the invisible voices of the living and the dead, the earthling and the alien. With its illusion of fully formed realities of sound *and* vision adrift in the ether, narrative worlds to be accessed and realized through the antenna, television came to be conceived, not only as an electrical extension of human sight, but as an uncanny electrical space in and of itself. (Sconce, 2000: 16–17)

As this scene progresses, the radar parts are referred to as an explanation when the television starts transmitting scenes from the Munsters' own home: Eddie is shown in a comic scene trying to catch the raven in the cuckoo clock as 'dinner for the cat', and Marilyn and Lily are shown during a 'soap-like' scene in the kitchen, discussing the possibility of a playmate for Eddie. These 'shows within the show' underscore the centrality of the home as the key location of television drama and situation comedy, a spatial organisation which is thus represented in *The Munsters* as both integral to Gothic television text and extending beyond it to the broader television landscape.

While the programmes examined previously in this analysis have been 'straight' drama (perhaps an oxymoron in the realm of Gothic fiction), in the Gothic family sitcom we see a more playful approach to the genre. Fred Botting has highlighted the closeness of the Gothic to its parodic forms:

> It is in the spilling over of boundaries, in its uncertain effects on audiences, that Gothic horrors are most disturbing. That these effects are ambivalent, from the eighteenth century onwards, has been signalled by the capacity of Gothic formulae to produce laughter as abundantly as emotions of terror or horror. Stock formulas and themes, when too familiar, are eminently susceptible to parody and self-parody. (1996: 168)

While the previous chapters of this book have concentrated on Gothic television's ability to produce sensations of anxiety, fear and the uncanny in its viewers, they have not readily dealt with the fact that the genre might also inspire hysterical laughter. In his exploration of the genre, Botting argues that over-familiarity with generic conventions might produce laughter in itself (we see this, for example, in the ironic, cultist spectatorship of re-runs of the Gothic daytime soap opera, *Dark Shadows*), but he also argues that *The Addams Family* and *The Munsters*, as 'comic inversion[s] of everyday American family life' (1996: 168), constitute a separate category of the 'parodic Gothic'. In these instances, the laughter of the Gothic parody is turned squarely towards the representation of ideal homes and families as featured in earlier family sitcoms, thus suggesting that the parodic Gothic is as capable of disarming or exposing domestic ideology as more 'serious' forms of the genre. The attitude towards domestic perfection in these series is, however, ambivalent; as with other fantasy sitcoms from the 1960s, such as *Bewitched* and *I Dream of Jeannie*, which transpose figures from the Gothic genre (witches, spirits, etc.) into the domestic sitcom, *The Addams Family* and *The Munsters* also ironically present rather conservative images of the family as a hallowed, sacred institution, with very traditional parental gender roles established from the outset.

More so than the Gothic dramas previously discussed in this book, the Gothic sitcom was directed towards a *family* viewership, addressing parents and children simultaneously, and underlining the importance of the all-American family unit through its depiction of the families on screen. As Susan Briggs has argued,

From inside their own homes viewers saw as a regular item in programmes portrayals of the family itself, fictional or real. They could identify themselves with what they saw, or they could be shocked or
envious . . . The family was always at the centre of television thinking
and planning: it provided protagonists, situations, and background for
sitcoms, soap operas, and contemporary drama. (1998: 116)

In relation to this argument, it is striking that both Gothic family
sitcoms begin with sequences which underscore the typicality of their
familial representations. *The Addams Family* begins with a title
sequence which replicates the aesthetic of the family portrait: here, the
title sequence shifts between a near static composition of the family
portrait (see figure 4.3), complete with extra-diegetic 'frame' decorated
with barren trees, and shots and short scenes from the sitcom, serving
to underline the fact that this is a family-centric sitcom. *The Munsters*
on the other hand begins with a kind of family pantomime, in which
each of the central characters greets matriarch Lily Munster at the
bottom of the staircase and kisses her goodbye (as they set off to work
or school, it is presumed). Here, again, the title sequence serves to
emphasise the fact that the family on screen is typical and recognisable
to the family viewer. Both series therefore rely on representational
clichés surrounding the family to make the point that they are 'just
regular folks', asking the viewer to read them in relation to their own
families. In short, the title sequences call attention to the 'family-ness'
of these families.

This representation of the family, and the notion of the family as a
viewing body for the Gothic sitcom, has a number of consequences for
these series. In the first instance, there is a very obvious address to the

4.3 The Addams family portrait: *The Addams
Family* (Filmways, 1966–68).

4.4 Merchandising *The Munsters*: 'Rock-a-bye Munster',
The Munsters (Kayro-Vue Productions, 1964).

family as agent of consumption. For example, particularly integral to
The Munsters' success was a direct address to a young audience through
the seductive language of merchandising. In the episode 'Rock-a-bye
Munster', a 'Munster Koach' was introduced (as a birthday present
from Lily to Herman), with the express purpose of producing a look-
alike toy. As John Peel notes, 'the sales of the merchandising rights
proved so phenomenal that the producers were asked to add a second
car later in the series. As a result the Dragula was born' (1994: 18).
Beyond inserting their own tie-in toys into individual episodes, the producers of the show also placed other Universal horror merchandising
firmly on display: for example, in the episode 'Rock-a-bye Munster',
Eddie Munster and his friend Elmer are shown playing with a remote
control Boris Karloff/Frankenstein's monster toy (which Herman mistakes for his own baby), establishing them as diegetic consumers of
Universal merchandise (see figure 4.4). Indeed, later in the same
episode Eddie and Elmer are brought to the front of the house to
admire the Munster Koach, thus emphasising the importance of children for consumers of Universal's horror toys. Again, in the episode
'Herman the Great', Eddie is shown playing with a toy Wolf Man (a
replica of the monster in Universal's film, *The Wolf Man* (US, 1941))
while he watches his father in a wrestling match on television, therefore offering a brand of product placement which speaks directly to the
programme's younger audience as the unlikely consumers of the
Gothic horror genre.

However, coupled with this notion of the family viewer as consumer
lurked a broader concern with the family as threatened institution in an

unstable society, which made the 'Gothicisation' of the family sitcom all the more intriguing. John Hartley has proposed that these sitcoms offer a darker image of the 'other side' of the suburban family, and that somehow their reworking of the traditional family sitcom is tied to the exposure of the less pleasant realities of life which their predecessors glossed over: '[These programmes] tended to suggest that, like modernity, progress, science and reason themselves, the modern suburban family was shadowed by darker and mostly unspoken "others" from pre-modern and irrational traditions' (Hartley, 2001: 66). In a sense then, Hartley argues that the fantasy family sitcom, including its Gothic incarnations, acts as uncanny text, representing the repressed doppelgangers of the families in *Leave it to Beaver* and *Father Knows Best*, and allowing some of the cultural anxieties surrounding the American family to come to the fore.

In her groundbreaking work on the situation comedy genre and US cultural history, Lyn Spigel has argued that the 1960s were characterised by a disappointment in American institutions and lifestyles among liberals and intellectuals, and more widely in popular culture. This sense of being 'let down' by the 'American Dream' was prefigured by the fact that, 'by the end of [the 1950s], Americans were looking backward at the great white hopes that had somehow led them down a blind alley. The utopian dreams for technological supremacy, consumer prosperity, and domestic bliss were revealing their limits in ways that could no longer be brushed aside' (Spigel, 2001: 109). As Spigel's work has more broadly shown us, the gaps between what the post-war discourse of the 'American Dream' promised and the actualities of the urban and suburban experience for the vast majority of Americans, became apparent, and often satirised, in US television during the late 1950s and 1960s, particularly in the sitcom genre. Similarly, John Hartley has proposed that 'sitcoms' attention to the "not-quiteness" of family life, and to some of the grittier issues lurking under suburban consumerism even as audiences lived in it and endorsed it at elections, made them capable of politics' (Hartley, 2001: 66). This notion of the family sitcom as a genre 'capable of politics' speaks to what Jane Feuer has called the 'ideological flexibility' of the genre: 'The sitcom has been the perfect format for illustrating current ideological conflicts while entertaining an audience' (Feuer, 2001: 70).

So what critiques do these programmes provide and to what extent are they 'capable of politics'? The following analysis concentrates on two areas of social critique, beyond the comedic inversion of the 'all-American family' already discussed above: firstly, the fiction of neighbourliness and the representation of suburbia as inclusive, accepting community, and secondly, the gendered division of labour in the North American family, looking at the ways in which both Gothic family sitcoms represent 'motherliness' and feminine conformity. Exploring the fantastic family sitcom, Lyn Spigel draws on Todorov's notion of the fantastic as a genre of hesitation, and his idea that moments of hesitation are integral to the fantastic narrative, in which the reader questions the existence of the supernatural. However, Spigel shifts Todorov's definition somewhat:

> In the fantastic family sitcom, the elements called into question are not the supernatural elements of the story . . . Rather, the moment of hesitation takes place in the realm of the natural. We are, in other words, made to question the 'naturalness' of middle class suburban ideals, especially as those ideals had previously been communicated through the genre conventions of classic suburban sitcoms. (1997: 59)

The Addams Family, for example, calls the 'naturalness of middle class suburban ideals' into question through continual comic inversions of the all-American family, particularly in relation to the parenting of Wednesday and Pugsley. In 'The Addams Family Goes to School' (Filmways, 1964), Gomez and Morticia petition the school board after learning that their children have been reading Grimm's fairy stories in which monsters and ogres are 'slaughtered'; in 'Morticia and the Psychiatrist' (Filmways, 1964) they bring in a child psychologist after learning that Pugsley wants to join the Boy Scouts; and in 'Pugsley's Allowance' (Filmways, 1964), his parents are horrified when Pugsley decides to work rather than living off his trust fund. In relation to these storylines and others, we see this series challenging the traditional sitcom depiction of the family as the primary proponent of the American Dream and a protestant work ethic, engaging viewers in 'a popular dialogue through which they might reconsider [these] social ideals' (Spigel, 2001: 117).

Also central to the social critique on offer here is a comic exploration of the 'neighbours from hell' motif, and the relationship between the monstrous families and their communities. As David Marc proposes, '[*The Addams Family* and *The Munsters*] are about entire families of innocent monsters trying to live their deviant lives among hostile, intolerant "normal" people' (Marc, 1997: 109). In both sitcoms, neighbourly closeness is a constant source of conflict, in line with Spigel's retheorisation of social space in the post-war suburbs:

> [The suburbs] were glorified in popular culture as a new land of plenty – the answer to Depression-era and wartime shortages. Home magazines presented wondrous designs, spacious ranch houses with rolling green

yards, shiny pink appliances . . . [However], cramped quarters took the place of the magazines' spacious ranch homes, and rather than gazing out at rolling green yards, residents found themselves sandwiched between the identical houses of their next-door neighbors. (Spigel, 2001: 110)

Arguably, the comedy of *The Addams Family* and *The Munsters* comes out of this discovery, satirising, or rather rendering literal, the 'neighbours from hell' motif. For example, the first episode of *The Munsters*, 'Munster Masquerade' (Kayro-Vue Productions, 1964), deals directly with the horror of a close community; as with a number of other episodes in the series' two season run, this episode focuses on Marilyn Munster's attempt to get and keep a boyfriend. Unlike the rest of her family, Marilyn is depicted as being 'perfectly normal', the epitome of the blonde-haired, blue-eyed WASP (the character was named after Marilyn Monroe, the ultimate all-American girl). When her boyfriend's parents decide to throw a fancy-dress party, her aunt and uncle grudgingly agree to attend, though Herman grumbles, 'If there's anything that disturbs me Lily, it's the idea of grown people like us dressing up in costume and looking ridiculous'. Tom's staunchly upper-middle-class parents, on the other hand, worry about the coverage their party will receive in the society columns of the local press. Therefore, from the outset, it is the horror of the neighbourhood, the desire to be seen to be doing the right thing by the right people, which provides the comic drive to this episode. Of course, when Lily and Herman arrive at the party, they mistakenly assume that Tom's father isn't in costume, as he is dressed in a Boris Karloff/Frankenstein's monster outfit and therefore closely resembles Herman. Here, then, gags are constructed around Jean Paul Sartre's notion that 'hell is other people', with both families recoiling from the other's way of life, thus producing comedy out of suburban intolerance. Again, in the following episode, 'My Fair Munster' (Kayro-Vue Productions, 1964), the Munsters' next door neighbour proffers protectionist views about the 'state of the neighbourhood' to the postman: 'Since they moved in we have to be prepared for anything . . . this was such a nice neighbourhood until THEY moved in . . . We don't want them wandering over here if you know what I mean', to which the postman replies, 'Keep them in their place, that's the ticket'. The Gothic family sitcom thus offers a comic exploration of xenophobic, protectionist attitudes in the modern suburbs in the mid-1960s. Given this fact, it is perhaps significant that the Munsters are depicted as immigrants to the US, with Grandpa frequently referring to life in the 'old country'. This therefore speaks directly to the notion of the American Gothic as a colonial/postcolonial narrative. In relation to this point, Marilyn Munster is a significant character who embodies social acceptance and tolerance, and is thus positioned as the 'straight' figure at the centre of the narrative, with whom the audience is clearly invited to identify. Although the family consistently jokes about her disappointing 'normality', Marilyn lives among the Munsters as 'social outcasts' and implicitly accepts them as part of her family and her community, thus promoting social tolerance as an ideal.

The two series at the heart of this analysis handle the 'neighbours from hell' motif quite differently; while the Munsters are constantly baffled by their neighbours' unfriendliness and intolerance, *The Addams Family* continually offers comic inversions of the intolerance of their neighbours in suburbia. For example, in the episode 'The Addams Family Tree' (Filmways, 1964), the children are invited to a birthday party at their neighbours' house which prompts the following exchange of dialogue:

Uncle Fester: Where are they going?

Morticia: To the Pomeroy boy's birthday party.

Uncle Fester: You mean those people with the white picket fence and that pink geranium. How could you?

Gomez: There's something to what he says, Morticia. They are a bit peculiar.

Uncle Fester: I'll bet they've got daisies in their back yard.

Gomez: Please don't make me ill.

Morticia: Now, now, we must be tolerant of our neighbours.

Here the joke rests on the recognition of aesthetic intolerance within the suburbs: by openly abhorring the white picket fence, pink geraniums and back-yard daisies of their neighbours, the Addams family invert the 'neighbours from hell' motif, comically criticising their neighbours for their conformity, their 'average-ness'. The protagonists of this programme thus shift between struggling to fit into a suburban community and rejecting those who conform to its standards and values, a position which reflects the *programme's* simultaneous conservatism and social critique.

From the outset of *The Addams Family*, episodes alternate between figures of authority (truant officers, psychiatrists, police officers, local politicians, etc.) trying to police or control the family, and suspicious neighbours resisting change in their neighbourhood, but these comedic conflicts always rest on a representation of the American home as permeable, open to 'invasion' from the outside world, and without any clear sense of domestic or private boundaries. As the following chapter will argue, in the new American Gothic serial, this permeability creates a certain sense of unease or threat; however, in the Gothic family sitcom the permeable home provides an endless stream of situations whereby the 'oddness' of the Addams and Munster families is brought into conflict with agents of normalcy from within their community, to comic effect. As we shall see in the analysis of *The Addams Family* episode 'The New Neighbors Meet the Addams Family' (Filmways, 1964), which ends this discussion of the Gothic domestic sitcom, these programmes produced comedy out of the cramped, claustrophobic suburban situation described by Spigel (2001: 110).

Another important point to consider here, in relation to the social critique on offer in the Gothic family sitcom, is the question of how we read the representation of gender in these programmes. Discussing *Bewitched* and *I Dream of Jeannie*, Spigel argues that these other fantasy family sitcoms offer a conflicting representation of traditional gender roles:

> [These programmes] often seemed to celebrate the sexism of suburbia by respectively featuring a witch and a genie who traded in their powers to live the life of dutiful wives and lovers. On the other hand, however, the collision of two unlikely forms also presented viewers with the possibility of thinking about the social constraints of suburban life. (Spigel, 1997: 58)

Similarly, Rachel Moseley's discussion of the figure of the witch in popular television as 'a discursive site in which the relationship between feminism (as female power), and femininity has been negotiated in historically specific ways' (2002: 403), has argued that these magicoms of the 1960s represent magic and female power in relation to the domestic, privileging maternity and traditional family values. As Moseley examines the relationship between 'feminine allure and magic, witchcraft and *power*' (2002: 404) through the notion of 'glamour', she concludes that present day programmes (such as *Charmed* (Spelling Television, 1998–) and *Sabrina the Teenage Witch* (ABC [US], 1996–2003)),

> have effected the banishment of the powerful and painfully present unruly witch of the second-wave feminist reclamation . . . thereby privileging the conventionally feminine, benign witch . . . The power of contemporary young film and television witches is glamorous, not excessive and bodily; it is respectable . . . , and it is domesticated. In this move, the contemporary teen witch is returned to the realm of the glamorous housewife of texts from *Cinderella* to *Bewitched*, in which magic is harnessed to the production of a clean and orderly (ladylike) self. (2002: 421–2)

The figures of Morticia Addams and Lily Munster, both firmly depicted as vampiric witches alongside a range of stock Gothic characters in their respective Gothic sitcoms, provide an interesting footnote to the representation of magic in the programmes discussed by Spigel and Moseley.

Almost more so than Samantha (Elizabeth Montgomery), the witch-housewife in *Bewitched*, these Gothic witches are contradictory figures who simultaneously embrace and reject traditional, feminine, domestic norms and values. If, as Eric Scharrer has argued, 'joke telling by sitcom characters is a means of expressing power between the sexes' (2001: 23), then the gags that surround these two characters tell us a good deal about the ideological frameworks surrounding these programmes.

Perhaps what is initially striking about both of these witch-like vamps is the sexual *jouissance* that they represent, a factor which is particularly striking in comparison to the asexual partnerships of Samantha and Darin (Dick York/Dick Sargent) in *Bewitched*, and Jeannie and Major Tony Nelson in *I Dream of Jeannie*. Both Morticia Addams and Lily Munster are eminently sexual beings who stir together 'sexuality, house-wifery and death' (Skal, 1993: 282). As Robert T. Garcia has argued, 'a big part of the charm [of *The Addams Family*] was the obvious sexual appreciation [Gomez] had for his wife, Morticia, breaking new ground for television, where sitcom couples regularly slept in separate beds' (1991b: 45). This association of motherhood with sexuality is particularly remarkable given the fact that these shows were made in the mid-1960s pre-sexual revolution, before the publication of Masters' and Johnson's study *Human Sexuality* in 1966, and prior to the impact of second wave feminism which Moseley relates to later incarnations of the glamorous witch in film and television. To a certain extent then, the house is not a space of drudgery for these Gothic heroines, but a play-ground, a space of sexual pleasure, liberation and desire. In reading it as such, we might relate the Gothic family sitcom to the genre of the 'unruly woman' comedy, defined by Kathleen Rowe in her analysis of 'the power of female grotesques and female laughter to challenge the social and symbolic systems that would keep women in their place' (1995: 3). Outlining the significance of this genre, Rowe argues that 'it is the genres of laughter that . . . are built on transgression and inversion, disguise and masquerade, sexual reversals, the deflation of ideals, and the levelling of hierarchies' (1995: 9), and that the unruly woman can therefore be read as an agent of chaos and change. In line with this definition, in the opening episode of *The Addams Family*, 'The Addams Family Goes to School', Morticia is depicted as a powerful figure who dominates the Addams family home, takes great pleasure in her husband and her surroundings, and is afforded a kind of magical control over the entertainment in the home. As she stands in the conservatory, being covered in kisses by an amorous Gomez, she revels in the dirge the butler, Lurch, is playing on the harpsichord. However, as they cross back into the living room, discussing Morticia's latest knitting project, she approaches Lurch and knocks him on the head, causing him to play an up-tempo rock and roll number and offering her a momentary break in her domestic duties as she dances alone around the room with great pleasure. When Gomez returns Lurch to his original tune, Morticia continues to dance a sexy tango with her husband: her power within the domestic space thus allows her to express a sense of *jouissance* and delight in her home.

Further evidence of Morticia's joyful liberation within the domestic space is found in the episode 'Morticia Joins the Ladies League' (Filmways, 1964), which ironically deals with Morticia's desire to conform to traditional, suburban-domestic gender roles and join a group of do-gooder housewives. From the outset of this episode, Morticia articulates a desire to attend to her family and to perfect the role of the good wife and mother: however, we see her constantly shirking her 'domestic responsibilities', getting Lurch the butler to do her laundry, commanding him to play a tune while she decides what to cook, and then getting distracted from her cooking altogether by dancing a tango with Gomez. In the end, a trained gorilla who has escaped from a nearby circus to be with Pugsley takes over the ironing in a moment that symbolises the ridiculousness of domestic convention: while she desires acceptance as the 'perfect wife and mother' within her community, a gorilla doing the housework is less preposterous than Morticia doing it herself! When the women from the Ladies' League come to visit, their tea party is disrupted by the gorilla serving afternoon tea, forcing Morticia to abandon her aspiration to join them (the gorilla is later taken back to the fairground, and is re-branded 'the world's most domesticated gorilla'). In this episode then, the role of suburban housewife is simultaneously venerated and derided: the fantasy of a domesticated gorilla invites the viewer to laugh at the social niceties of the woman's role in suburbia, while Morticia's desire to conform speaks of an essentialised notion of maternity and femininity. As the above episode might suggest then, traditional gender roles are rigidly maintained within the families of the Gothic family sitcom, even while a sense of liberation or *jouissance* is explored. In both programmes discussed here, Morticia and Lily cook, garden, knit and engage in other forms of gender-defined work, even though they have supernatural powers, thus suggesting that housework for women is an essentialised *and pleasurable* skill which is impossible for them to resist. Unlike the women in *Bewitched* and *I Dream of Jeannie*, these housewives rarely use supernatural powers to perform household tasks, though they are as frequently depicted engaged in housework, perhaps explaining why they are discussed less often by feminist media historians.

To close this discussion of the Gothic family sitcom, an analysis of the *Addams Family* episode, 'The New Neighbors Meet the Addams Family' is offered, which draws together the key issues discussed in this chapter. In this episode, broadcast on 13 November 1964, written by Hannibal Coons and Harry Winkler and directed by Jean Yarbrough, a couple of newly-weds move in next door to the Addams family. Throughout the course of this episode we are offered a comedic inversion of the all-American family sitcom, which nevertheless underscores the dominance of the notion of 'neighbourliness' that the family sitcom promoted during this period of broadcasting, and highlights the persistence of domesticated femininity in the US sitcom, whether 'straight' or fantastical. From the outset of the episode, Morticia is depicted as a good housewife and mother, albeit in a bizarre context: in the opening shot of the episode, for example, Morticia lovingly strokes her carnivorous plant while feeding it hamburgers. As she admonishes it ('Now, now Cleopatra, chew your burgers, don't gulp them'), we see a comedic performance of maternity: she 'burps' the plant, saying 'Oh darling, you see what happens when you gulp', thus pantomiming a 'doting mother' in a rather macabre situation. Following this, the scene cuts to Gomez spying on the removal men delivering their neighbours' new furniture, with Gomez commenting on a colonial-style blanket box as 'an item you could do things with'. As well as establishing the 'neighbours from hell' motif then, this scene serves to draw attention to the closeness of the macabre and the everyday yet again, as Gomez reads their blanket box as a 'luxury' coffin.

The new neighbours, Amanda (Cynthia Pepper) and Hubert Peterson (Peter Brooks), are the all-American boy and girl, refugees from the 'straight' family sitcom. If they are wary of meeting their strange new neighbours, the Addams family are also nervous of meeting them, stressing the horror of suburban closeness once again. When they do eventually meet, it is in the Addams' backyard as they wash Pugsley's pet octopus, inverting the image of the all-American family outside washing the family dog at the weekend. Although Hubert is initially friendly towards Gomez and Morticia, his new wife, Amanda, is less forthcoming and more openly suspicious of their strange practices, causing Morticia to sigh 'I had *so* hoped she would be someone I could exchange recipes with', expressing once more her desire for traditional feminine community within the suburban space. Both of the Petersons become more hostile towards their neighbours, however (who, it turns out, are also their landlords), when Uncle Fester arrives in the middle of their living room via a trapdoor in the floor, in a scene which fully visualises the permeability of the suburban home. Here, as elsewhere in this sitcom, gags are built around the invasion of domestic space and the disruption of the domestic idyll (the newly-weds 'nest-making' in their new abode). Conspicuously, trick edits such as the wipe which ends the scene in which Uncle Fester 'breaks in', and a 'twist' edit later in the episode, serve to collapse the space between the two homes on screen (the 'honeymoon cottage' and the Addams family home), emphasising the sense of claustrophobic closeness between the neighbours on which this episode's comedy is based, when these two houses appear in the same frame.

Following Fester's invasion, Gomez and Morticia attempt to repair the neighbourly relationship, again satirising the suburban notion that 'hell is other people'. Discussing the problem with her husband, Morticia opines: 'I think I know what their trouble is. They're lonely . . . Oh Gomez, we've been very selfish. After all, they're newly-weds. I should have been over there a long time ago with a pot of hen-bane soup, some of my dwarf's hair cobbler and marital advice.' Deciding to invite the newly-weds over for a game of bridge, the episode shifts towards domestic, suburban hyperbole: as Amanda looks around the Addams' home, she is cursed by being offered each gruesome *objet d'art* she sees as a house-warming gift, thus underscoring the aesthetic intolerance of close-living in suburbia. The track around their home after they have installed these items emphasises both the closeness and the incongruity of domesticity and horror, and when they eventually escape from their suburban hell, the newly-weds hurt the Addams' feelings by abandoning these unwanted wedding gifts. In this episode then, we see a comic dramatisation of traditional forms of femininity and neighbourliness which essentialises these norms and values. We are constantly reminded that even though this is a monstrous Gothic family who keep a pet octopus and eat 'dwarf's hair cobbler', they share an almost naive desire to be good citizens and to perform their marital and parental roles 'properly'. Therefore, although the Gothic family sitcom has fun with traditional gender roles and the function of the family in American society, they ultimately offer a rather conservative vision of suburbia, much like the family sitcoms that preceded them. As stated above, *The Addams Family* and *The Munsters* were cancelled within weeks of one another (April and May 1966 respectively), though they have remained 'cult classics' ever since, constantly rebroadcast in syndication in the US and abroad. Both series were also revived in one-off specials,[1] later TV series,[2] animated series,[3] feature films[4] and straight-to-video movies.[5] However, it can be argued that within the context of a spate of fantastic family sitcoms in the 1960s, both series had a significant impact in the moment of original broadcast, when they simultaneously satirised and venerated the all-American family.

Dark Shadows: **Gothic soap opera and the fantasy of identification**

> My name is Victoria Winters. There are two great houses at Collinwood. One alive with the present and the other slowly decaying, filled with the dead memories of the past.

To close this chapter on hybrid American Gothic television in the 1960s, we turn now to an examination of the Gothic soap opera, *Dark Shadows*. The piece of dialogue above, taken from the opening of episode 214 of the series (broadcast on 21 April 1967), speaks of the two houses that structure the Gothic soap opera. The first, the home of the Collins family at the centre of *Dark Shadows*' soap narrative, is an ancestral home which is nevertheless filled with the everyday activities of a large, extended family (including the narrator, the family's nanny, played by Alexandra Moltke); the second, a dilapidated mansion in the grounds of the family home, is the centre of the serial's Gothic narrative, and houses Barnabas Collins (Jonathan Frid) (distant relative and vampire) and his henchman, drifter Willy Loomis (John Karlen). These two houses therefore metaphorically represent the generic hybridity of *Dark Shadows*, the unique mixture of the soap opera and the Gothic drama, and the fact that once again the commonplace and the supernatural are inextricably intertwined in this instance of Gothic television.

Dark Shadows was first broadcast a month after the cancellation of *The Addams Family* and *The Munsters*. A daily serial which ran from June 1966 to April 1971, it mingled tales of vampires, werewolves, time travel and parallel universes with the more traditional family saga of the daytime soap opera. The soap was filmed 'as live' on videotape in the studio by creator Dan Curtis' own production company, and broadcast on ABC, Monday to Friday, in the mid-afternoon. There were 1225 episodes in total, alongside two offshoot films, *House of Dark Shadows* (US, 1970) and *Night of Dark Shadows* (US, 1971), 32 paperback novels by Marion Ross, 'games, comic books, (hit) records, wristwatches, posters, postcards, magazines, masks, models, music boxes, puzzles, Viewmasters, chewing gum, and even a *Dark Shadows* cookbook' (Benshoff, 1993: 52). Following its initial broadcast, *Dark Shadows* became the first daytime soap to go into syndication (on local TV stations and PBS) in 1975; there was a revival of the original soap opera in 1991, also titled *Dark Shadows* (Dan Curtis Productions, 1991) but running in a primetime evening slot, which lasted for just 12 episodes, and MPI Video began releasing a series of video (and later DVD) boxsets of the serial in 1989. *Dark Shadows* was also a key programme in the launch of the Sci-Fi satellite channel in 1992, which bought the exclusive rights to air it: between 1992 and 1997, the entire series was re-broadcast twice in a weekday slot, thus recreating the series' initial context of broadcast (albeit on a specialist, narrowcast channel, rather than on ABC, one of the 'big three' US networks).[6]

The soap began as Victoria Winters arrived at the Collinwood mansion to assume her duties as governess to David Collins (David Henesy); it was therefore established as a classic female Gothic narrative from the outset (young woman, relocated from her home, arrives in a threatening house), but became more 'supernatural' as the series progressed, in response to falling ratings. As Dan Curtis remembers:

> When [*Dark Shadows*] was going down the tubes, my kids said to make it scary. I said, 'Why not? I've got nothing to lose.' So I put a ghost on, and when the ghost appeared the ratings jumped, and that's when I started experimenting . . . Who knew?. . . I brought the vampire in and it suddenly became this gigantic hit. Then I thought, 'Now what am I going to do?' I couldn't kill him off, so that's when I turned him into the reluctant vampire. It really caught the imagination of the audience. (Dawidziak, 1990: 24–7)

It is important to remember, in relation to Curtis' claims that the supernatural soap 'caught the imagination' of the viewers, that *Dark Shadows'* narrative initially took place in the present day (of the late 1960s). While the appearance of ghostly and vampiric characters tied the Gothic narrative to the eighteenth and nineteenth centuries, and there were lengthy sojourns into the past of the Collins families in 1967 (which took the narrative back to 1795 for five months), in March 1969 (going back to 1897 for nine months) and a further flashback to 1840 in 1970, the soap was pointedly given a contemporary setting at the outset, which perhaps drew closer parallels between the diegesis and the world of the viewer, only to transport them to earlier times and parallel universes later in *Dark Shadows'* five year run. In fact, we might locate the beginning of *Dark Shadows* within a broader generic cycle of horror in this period identified by Vivian Sobchak:

> From the 1960s onward, family life and social life have continued to converge, partly in response to a number of institutional shifts; within this chronology, horror (as well as science fiction and fantasy) has been transformed into a generic form that includes elements of the family melodrama – a genre whose own representations are driven by an opposing realism. (1996: 146)

One might wonder how this 'dark' programme worked within the daytime schedule, and ask what accounts for the success (and enduring appeal) of a Gothic daytime soap opera. Sam Hall, one of *Dark Shadows'* key writers, noted, 'I never thought the network particularly liked the show. It broke too many daytime rules. They felt it was a cult show; a fad, with no staying power' (Hall, 1990: 41). Just as *The Addams Family* and *The Munsters* fused the family sitcom with Gothic horror, so *Dark Shadows* combined the narrative preoccupations and structure of the soap's 'family saga' with stock characters and situations from a heritage of supernatural Gothic horror. The programme did break 'daytime rules', both in terms of its subject matter and given the fact that it was often literally too dark (with its shadowy graveyards and gloomy rooms) to view in the haze of mid-afternoon light. However, it was conceived of as a daytime soap opera by its producers from the outset:

> Despite the supernatural trappings, the show always remained a soap opera, first and foremost. The storylines always revolved around various love affairs and domestic disputes. In fact, probably the greatest dramatic tension was fuelled by Angélique's unrequited love for Barnabas, which formed a major part of the story arc for several seasons. (Dawidziak and Stevenson, 1996: 32–3)

Certainly, the open-ended soap-style narrative lends itself very well to the Gothic, as a genre of uncertainty. In *Dark Shadows*, the constant hesitation of the soap's cliff-hanger endings produces the suspense essential to the Gothic genre. For example, the appearance of a hand slipping out of a coffin and grabbing at Willy Loomis' throat at the end of a Monday afternoon episode (episode 210, 17 April 1967), which turns out to be the first glimpse of the vampire Barnabas Collins, produces an atmosphere of threat which carries over until the start of the following day's episode. Rather than producing an impression of 'unrecorded existence', identified by Christine Geraghty in relation to the British soap opera's insistence that 'day to day life has continued in our absence even though the problem we left at the end of the previous episode has yet to be resolved' (Geraghty, 1981: 10), *Dark Shadows* provides a threatening sense of suspense between episodes. Rejoining the action a few minutes before the cliff-hanger at the start of the following day's episode, the Gothic soap opera doesn't produce any sense of unrecorded existence here, but, in the context of the soap opera form, with its sense of simultaneity between the diegetic and extra-textual worlds, the hesitation on the vampire's hand at the cliff-hanger suggests an unresolved threat which extends beyond the realm of the text.

Dark Shadows fits easily into the categorisation of soap opera as produced by Gothic scholars. Richard Davenport-Hines, for example, argues that the genre is related to the Gothic in a number of ways:

> Confused paternities, improbable coincidences, melodrama, sudden death, cheap ideas, trivially stereotyped characters. . . . television soap

opera provides the twentieth century equivalent of gothic novels . . .
Both genres provided their consumers with devices by which they could
pretend to be passionate. Their success rests on the understanding that
human beings learn to become adults by acting imitative or emulative
parts; in consequence much human emotion is theatrical, and the private
emotions of most human beings are sustained by inner dialogues of
martyrdom, self-pity, fake heroics and gaudy, mawkish histrionics.
(1998: 144)

In *Dark Shadows*, the stock situations and characters of the daytime soap
are fused with the stock situations and characters of the Gothic genre,
without any internal sense of irony: 'the unique style of *Dark Shadows*
lay in the absurdity of a ludicrous situation performed with complete
conviction by the cast' (Parker, 1990: 17). After an initial sense of hesitation experienced by both viewers of the soap opera and characters
within it, there develops an absolute acceptance of the presence of the
supernatural (vampires, ghosts, lycanthropy, and so on). For example,
when Barnabas Collins (one of the soap's central characters) was introduced during the second year of broadcast, the other characters (and the
viewers) were led to initially believe that he was a distant cousin from
England; here, this hesitation over his true (supernatural) identity is produced through his insistence on his familiarity with Collinwood
through inherited memory, and by the fact that his vampiric activities
are initially implied but not shown on screen. As his true identity as an
ancient vampire is gradually revealed, however, it quickly becomes
accepted and absorbed into the everyday goings-on of the soap narrative.
In relation to Todorov's delineation of the subcategories of fantasy, we
might therefore understand this soap opera as belonging to the 'fantastic marvellous': 'the class of narratives that are [initially] presented as
fantastic and end with an acceptance of the supernatural' (Todorov, 1975:
52). In fact, as the serial developed, it moved even further towards a
purely marvellous narrative, whereby vampirism and haunting became
everyday and commonplace.

As well as insisting on its position as legitimate soap opera, the producers of *Dark Shadows* were very careful to situate their programme
within a heritage of Gothic literature. According to Lara Parker (who
played Angélique in the serial),

> People were willing to be moved, to be stirred by the classics – and I don't
> know if they are any more. Dan Curtis never stopped using the classics
> that were so beloved in *Dark Shadows*. He borrowed from *Jane Eyre*, *The
> Turn of the Screw*, *Frankenstein*, *Dr Jekyll and Mr Hyde*, and *Dracula*. These
> plots were constantly being reinvented. No other show has ever done
> that. The whole idea of using the intensity, the complexity, the emotional

depth and passion of Gothic literature was unique. (Henessey-Derose and McCarty, 2003: 40)

Indeed, Curtis went on to become somewhat of a Gothic auteur for television, creating a series of made-for-TV movies of both original teleplays and classic Gothic adaptations.[7] There is a particularly strong link between *Dark Shadows* and the genre of female Gothic literature discussed at length in the previous chapter. For example, the opening episode of the soap introduces Victoria Winters, who acts as an ongoing narrator at the beginning of each subsequent episode, arriving in Collinwood as the governess to the Collins family. As an orphan looking for a sense of personal history, Winters provides an emotional centre for the early part of the soap opera, which strongly reflects the female Gothic narrative tradition. Like Marian in *The Woman in White* (see the previous chapter), Victoria opens the ongoing soap narrative with an interior monologue (delivered in voice-over) which underscores the importance of feminine subjectivity:

> My name is Victoria Winters. My journey is beginning; a journey that I hope will open the doors of life to me and link my past with my future. A journey that will bring me to a strange and dark place, to the edge of the sea high atop Widows Hill. A house called Collinwood. A world I've never known with people I've never met. People who tonight are still only shadows in my mind who will soon fill the days and nights of my tomorrows.

Here the emotional intensity and implied conspiratorial closeness between young female protagonist and viewer are writ large across this melodramatic opening scene. During this monologue, cuts are made between stock exterior shots of Victoria's journey (a train, the moon, the stately home at Collinwood) and a close-up of her face as she sits on the train, with the camera slowly zooming into her view of the window. As her speech finishes, the scene cuts to a shot of breaking waves, accompanied by a soaring, string-laden vibrato soundtrack, marking this opening as a moment of melodrama, and establishing Victoria's intense anticipation of her life to come, as well as a pervading sense of threat. The image of deep water is seen at the beginning of a number of the female Gothic adaptations discussed previously,[8] and can be seen as a metaphor for the young woman's narrative journey and emotional state: here, the coupling of romantic images (the moonlit train, a full moon, a mansion house and the crashing sea) with shots of the young woman at the centre of the Gothic narrative reinforces the close connection between the genre, femininity, and excessive desire and anxiety. Narratively and structurally then, *Dark Shadows* is connected in a number of ways to the female Gothic genre.

Like the programmes previously discussed in this chapter, one can argue that, to a certain extent, *Dark Shadows* explores prevalent cultural anxieties, or 'taps into' a potential sense of identification between viewer and text. Harry M. Benshoff's work on this serial 'views popular culture as an arena wherein different ideals and ideologies may circulate, coexist and even conflict' (1993: 51), and he takes on the 'fan scholar' position to explore the possibilities for subversive/transformative readings of the text. Conversely, or perhaps in tandem with Benshoff's analysis, it will be argued in the conclusion of this chapter that textual analysis of *Dark Shadows* also provides us with an image of Gothic television 'worrying at' domestic space, domestic invasion and the threatened and/or threatening home. Benshoff's work on this series has primarily engaged with the viewing positions taken up by fans of the programme, drawing on empirical research into the fan cultures surrounding the show.[9] He argues that his research into *Dark Shadows* opposes the 'idea of a single, static, original "text"' (1993: 52) by looking at fan fiction and productions deriving from *Dark Shadows*. Furthermore, Benshoff seeks to capture the heterogeneity of the soap opera's audience: 'Besides the expected soap opera audience of housewives (and to a lesser extent college students), *Dark Shadows* was also watched by children of all ages' (1993: 53). Post-broadcast, Benshoff also identifies an active gay and lesbian subculture organised around the programme, arguing that this viewing body confirms Henry Jenkins' notion that 'fandom is a vehicle for marginalised subcultural groups (women, the young, gays, and so on) to pry open space for their cultural concerns within dominant representations' (Jenkins, 1991: 174). Although Benshoff's approach differs radically from the analysis offered in this exploration of Gothic television and, indeed, he believes that his audience research 'problematise[s] theories of popular culture which posit a universal subject constructed by the text' (1993: 52), his findings are nevertheless illuminating in relation to the following investigation, which seeks to define the pleasures in identification offered to the viewer by the Gothic soap opera. While Benshoff argues that this can only be done through an analysis of the fan activity that surrounded this programme after its initial broadcast, it will be argued that certain viewing positions are *recorded into Dark Shadows*, suggesting a variety of available pleasures and fears for the home viewer. If, as Benshoff has argued, '*Dark Shadows* afforded [viewers] a place of comfort and/or a fantasy of power' (1993: 53), then the analyses that follow uncover the textual strategies that promote these sensations or approaches from within the text itself.

The discussion of *Dark Shadows*' place in the daytime schedule above might suggest that the rest of daytime fiction lies firmly within the realm of the real, and that daytime would therefore be an unusual location for genres of fantasy, such as the supernatural Gothic. On one level this is true but, on another, the soap opera has always been a space of fantasy and melodrama. Here, Ien Ang's work on the US soap opera, *Dallas* (CBS, 1978–91), is particularly illuminating, in which she reads the US primetime soap opera as a genre of fantasy:

> Fiction is not a mere set of images to be read referentially, but an ensemble of textual devices for engaging the viewer at the level of fantasy . . . Fantasy is an imagined scene in which the fantasising subject is the protagonist, and in which alternative scenarios for the subject's real life are evoked . . . Fictions are collective and public fantasies; they are textual elaborations, in narrative form, of fantastic scenarios which, being mass-produced, are offered ready-made to audiences. (1997: 162–3)

While Ang speaks directly of a primetime, not daytime, soap, she categorises television fiction *in general* here as 'collective and public fantasies' which invite viewers into a system of fantastical identification, drawing 'alternative scenarios for the subject's real life', in which they may imagine other realms and worlds beyond their own experience. In essence then, the theoretical framework that Ang provides for thinking about the viewing of soap opera goes some way to explaining the enduring popularity of *Dark Shadows*, as a work of melodramatic fantasy in which a world radically different from our own can be imagined, and therefore inhabited.

Ang's delineation of the soap narrative as melodrama is useful here, given that, as identified above, melodrama can be seen as the generic link between *Dark Shadows*' two hybrid genres, the soap opera and the Gothic drama. Firstly, Ang argues, personal life becomes *the* central narrative focus of the melodrama (Ang, 1997: 158). As in soap opera, the Gothic narrative rests on familial drama (confused paternities, abandoned children, dark inheritances and family curses), and intensely subjective narration serves to emphasise emotion and personal crises: a Gothic soap opera might therefore be seen as the logical conclusion of both genres. Ang also argues that convoluted plotting is another key melodramatic element of soap:

> A second major melodramatic feature of soap opera is its excessive plot structure . . . To the critical outsider this may appear as a purely sensationalist tendency to cliché and exaggeration – a common objection levelled at melodrama since the late nineteenth century. It is important to

note, however, that within the fictional world of the soap opera all those extreme storylines . . . are not treated in a sensational manner, but are taken entirely seriously . . . Their role is metaphorical, and their appeal stems from the enlarged emotional impact they evoke . . . An excess of events and intensity of emotions are inextricably intertwined in the melo-dramatic imagination. (1997: 159)

Here Ang could just as easily be describing Gothic plotting as that of the soap opera, or what Eve Sedgwick describes as 'the difficulty the story has in getting itself told' (1986: 13). As discussed in chapter two, in relation to spectacular horror drama, the Gothic drama (in literature, theatre, film and television) has always been seen as a sensationalist, excessive genre, both narratively and aesthetically. In light of this, *Dark Shadows*' supernatural storylines are the ultimate in melodramatic cliché, combining Gothic exaggeration with that of the traditional tele-vision soap. Emotional excess is also located in performance in *Dark Shadows*, in which the actors produce a kind of hybrid performance style which combines daytime drama convention with a more theatri-cal heritage of Gothic performance. As Lara Parker remembers, '*Dark Shadows* was wonderfully theatrical and romantic. Many of the perfor-mances . . . were larger than life. Most of us were stage actors, not soap opera actors. We were trained to make emotions broad and powerful, rather than internalised and underplayed' (Parker, 1990: 16). This expansive, at times gestural and expressionistic performance style, was one of *Dark Shadows*' key points of stylistic differentiation within the daytime schedule, and emphasised a sense of melodrama in the show's aesthetic.

Finally, Ang argues that the unending soap opera form is inherently melodramatic: 'here a basic melodramatic idea is conveyed: the sense that life is marked by eternal contradiction, by unsolvable emotional and moral conflicts, by the ultimate impossibility, as it were, of recon-ciling desire and reality' (Ang, 1997: 160). In *Dark Shadows* this eter-nal lack of conclusion is particularly emphasised by the flexibility of time and heavy use of flashback throughout the series' five year run: the fact that many of the actors played several different characters, caught up in similar romantic and familial intrigues, in the different time frames of the soap opera (1795, 1840 and 1897, as well as the present day), suggests an eternal lack of conclusion and 'unsolvable emotional and moral conflict' which extends into a much greater 'unrecorded existence' of the past, as well as beyond the end of the soap's narrative. Given that '[melodramatic characters are] victims of forces that lie beyond their control' (Ang, 1997: 160), this eternal repe-tition and coincidence provides an *uncanny* narrative structure, in which, it is suggested, characters are bound to repeat past mistakes and deeply unhappy relationships. The yearning and unrequited love that permeate *Dark Shadows'* narrative structure are a testament to such a sentiment.

This soap opera can also be defined as melodramatic in a more literal sense, in relation to the use of music, which is closely tied to emotion and feeling throughout. The melodramatic mode is utilised in the depiction of the threatened victim-heroine, for example: during an illness brought on by a vampiric attack in episode 229 (11 May, 1967), waitress Maggie Evans (Kathryn Leigh Scott) stumbles about her room silently, wracked with a mixture of desire and terror, and accompanied by the sound of music and wolves. In a scene we have come to understand as an identifying moment of the Gothic television narrative, Maggie is depicted exploring her own domestic space in dread and horror, with a tremulous 'horror' theme offering an impression of her inner turmoil. This depiction of Maggie's suffering thus raises important questions about the viewing pleasures of *Dark Shadows*, specifically 'what does the Gothic soap opera offer its viewers in terms of serial pleasure?' and 'why is it so engaging?'

Harry M. Benshoff's work has suggested that there is 'a whole constellation of factors to which the fans [of *Dark Shadows*] respond' (1993: 52); ranging from an enjoyment of the hybrid Gothic-soap form to valuing *Dark Shadows* 'for its depiction of a "pure and complete fantasy world"' (1993: 52). Benshoff's subjects thus position themselves in, and in relation to, the text in a number of ways. As with the female Gothic dramas discussed in the previous chapter, this leads us back to the question of identification; as actor Lara Parker suggests, 'the fascination for *Dark Shadows* lay in the ability of those in the audience to identify with the characters. You may ask how one can possibly identify with a witch, or a ghost, or a vampire? We have nothing in common with these appalling creatures . . . or do we?' (Parker, 1990: 17). Parker's formulation, a rather dramatic rhetorical question, raises an interesting point here. *Dark Shadows'* particular brand of the 'fantastic-marvellous', the blending of stock characters and narrative events from the soap opera and the Gothic genre, therefore bringing into congruence the ordinary and the supernatural, might be seen to render viewer identification somewhat mystifying. However, it also might tell us that there is no straight connection between representation and reality when it comes to the construction and reception of television fiction and fantasy.

Again, Ang's work on the soap opera is useful here. Her discussion of viewer identification with Sue-Ellen (Linda Gray), a character

from the US soap, *Dallas*, explores the questions and problems raised by female viewers identifying with such a tragic, 'melodramatic
heroine':

> the position from which Sue Ellen fans seem to give meaning to, and
> derive pleasure from, their favourite *Dallas* character seems to be a rather
> melancholic and sentimental structure of feeling which stresses the
> down-side of life rather than its happy highlights; frustration, desper-
> ation, and anger rather than euphoria and cheerfulness. (1997: 157)

Deconstructing earlier feminist accounts of the 'role/image approach' to
identification, which propose that women should look to strong, independent, untroubled role models, presupposing a rather straight connection
between representation and reality, Ang argues that melodramatic
identification offers more complex positions and pleasures. There are, she
proposes, two possible readings of melodramatic identification:

> On the one hand, sentimental and melodramatic feelings of masochism
> and powerlessness, which are the core of the melodramatic imagina-
> tion . . . Identification with these feelings is connected with a basic, if not
> articulated, awareness of the weighty pressure of reality on one's subjec-
> tivity, one's wishes, one's desire. On the other hand, identification with
> a melodramatic character also validates these feelings by offering women
> some room to indulge in them, to let go as it were, in a moment of
> intense, self-centred abandon. (1997: 164–5)

It is the indulgence of melodramatic identification which, I would
argue, lies at the heart of *Dark Shadows*. A series of tragic characters at
the centre of the narrative provide multiple points of connection (and
therefore identification) for the viewer: the orphaned young woman
on the verge of self-discovery (Victoria Winters), the struggling matriarch (Elizabeth Collins Stoddard), the confused teenager (Carolyn
Collins), even the reluctant vampire (Barnabas). Each of these characters can be read as a melodramatic figure with whom we are encouraged
to identify, given that they are each positioned as the narrational centre
of the soap opera at key moments throughout its run, and their stories
are constructed to elicit viewer sympathy and engagement.

As with other programmes discussed in this exploration of Gothic
television, fear is constructed in *Dark Shadows* around a series of familiar images, most notably the image of the Gothic house, and yet, according to Ien Ang's reading of the vicarious nature of the melodramatic
imagination, this is fear which might also be experienced as a kind
of pleasure: identification with the threatened home and family therefore becomes a wilful abandonment to domestic trauma. Given the

restrictions of its studio production, *Dark Shadows* appears rather like a chamber drama, with its action confined to a limited number of mainly interior (and mainly domestic) settings. Although this setting might, on the one hand, be seen as a marker of the paucity of the programme's production values and the economic intransigence of daytime television drama production, it also produces a certain 'domestic' aesthetic in keeping with the narrative's main themes and concerns. For example, if we look at the episodes surrounding a key moment in the soap's history, when vampire Barnabas Collins returns to his ancestral home, we see the house as both the key location of family history and traumatic memory within the Gothic narrative, and also as a site of domestic horror, built around the image of the home under threat of invasion.

Following Collins' exploration of his old house, young David Collins reports to the rest of the family that 'it seems as though he was haunting the rooms instead of just walking through them': indeed, several episodes are dominated by the vampire wandering through rooms in the house, discussing its significance within family history. When governess Victoria Winters tells him 'to me this house has always been a reminder of the enterprise of the people who settled here' (see episode 214), Barnabas delivers a long monologue which speaks of the American Gothic's identity as postcolonial narrative:

> Yes, in a way you're right. The design and construction of this house represented a marriage of the elegance of Europe and the vigour and enterprise of a new world. The foundations were made from rocks left behind by glaciers thousands of years ago. The beams and supports were cut from ancient local forests. The plaster walls were made from crushed clam shells and horsehair. Bricks were imported from Holland. That dusty chandelier was brought over from France . . . That faded wallpaper was especially designed by a Belgian artist. The parquet floors were installed by an Italian craftsman, the mouldings were the effort of a Spanish craftsman.

While this dialogue is primarily designed to demonstrate the vampire's uncanny familiarity with the house's construction (the other characters still believe that he is a distant cousin from London with an expert knowledge of family history, rather than an ancient vampire), it also underscores the relationship between the 'old' and 'new' worlds that is so central to the American Gothic narrative. Here, the colonial moment is said to have produced a haunted artefact (the house), imbued with a sense of a national, as well as familial, past, and an inheritance which is not eradicated through the passing of time. When Barnabas goes on to speak of the house's significance in their particular family history, however, we also see domestic space as a representation of the American Gothic's more quotidian, familial concerns in *Dark Shadows*:

> The beautiful exterior belies the hatred and distrust that lived beneath this roof. Nothing was ever real here. The love and happiness that one would expect was never lived in the lives of those that lived here . . . This room saw much hatred. Saw families divide and devour each other. On these stairs, a father and son hurled words at each other, words that would lead to the death of the son.

The house is thus depicted as an emotionally 'loaded' location within the Gothic soap opera

As suggested above, houses are also depicted as threatened spaces in *Dark Shadows*, most obviously through that iconic image of the vampire narrative: the open window. The vampire narrative is particularly well suited to Gothic television in this respect, given that it is a cycle within the Gothic genre which is defined more generally by the permeability of the house (the vampire's ability to enter bedrooms, to slip in and out of people's everyday lives leaving infection and death behind). In *Dark Shadows*, for example, the connection between Barnabas Collins and his second victim, waitress Maggie Evans, is represented through the trope of the permeable home. Not only is it suggested that he continually enters her bedroom at night (through the recurring image of the open patio doors next to her bed as each morning breaks), but also, after their initial meeting, Barnabas is able to watch Maggie from afar, his view rendered 'televisual' in its literal sense by the token that he possesses 'distant sight'. Here, we revisit the horror of the American neighbourhood in the 1960s, discussed above in relation to the Gothic family sitcom: Barnabas' 'night visits' and his ability to see over great distance mean that we are again shown a community in which there are no hard and fast boundaries between public and private space.

Episode 227 (9 May 1967), for example, begins with an exterior shot of Maggie's home, warmly lit from the inside, establishing the 'normality' of this domestic space. A cut is then made to close-ups dissolved together of Maggie's hands wringing her bed covers and her face wracked with turmoil, anticipating the moment of domestic horror to come. As she clutches at her throat, the camera tracks up and around to the patio doors in her bedroom, accompanied by the sound of heartbeat-like timpani drums and a low wind instrument which plays a musical warning that Maggie is under threat, as the shadow of the vampire crosses over the net curtains covering her doors, again building the anticipation of an imminent attack. A slow track up the door as it opens reveals Barnabas' face, as the moment of horror is realised and he enters

her room to stand over her bed, grinning in the gloom of the evening and
baring his fangs. As elsewhere in Gothic television then, the climax of
horror is found in domestic invasion: we need not see his first bite (the
scene cuts to the title sequence before this occurs), as the vampire's entry
into the home is horror enough for a domestic (daytime) audience.
Following the credit sequence, the exterior shot of the house is repeated,
this time in daylight rather than dusk, and a cut is then made to the open
door of the young woman's bedroom: therefore, while the attack takes
place during an ellipsis created by the credit sequence, the viewer is
immediately reminded that this is the site of domestic invasion.
Furthermore, on two occasions during this episode, and elsewhere in the
series, Barnabas' 'televisual' sight is also marked as an act of domestic
invasion. In a moment which strongly resembles Nosferatu's (Max
Schreck's) stalking of Ellen (Greta Schröeder) in Murnau's *Nosferatu*
(Germany, 1922), cuts are made between a close-up of Barnabas' leering
face at the window of his own house, suggesting that he can *see* his victim
(see figure 4.5), and Maggie's bedroom, where she in turn reacts, suggesting the uncanny sensation of being watched. Later, this closeness
without proximity is intensified by the use of a slow dissolve which places
the voyeur (Barnabas) and the object of his intense gaze (Maggie) in the
same frame (see figure 4.6).

In both these instances, editing is utilised to create a sense of extreme
anxiety around domestic invasion, and, arguably, to record into the text
a potentially intense moment of identification in which the viewer fears
for Maggie's safety from the comfort of their own home. Like the Collins
household discussed above then, other homes in this Gothic soap opera
are configured as permeable households, in which boundaries between
public and domestic, inside and outside, remain worryingly blurred.

4.5 The televisual sight of the vampire: episode
227, *Dark Shadows* (Dan Curtis Productions Inc.,
1967).

4.6 Bringing vampire and victim together: episode 227, *Dark Shadows* (Dan Curtis Productions Inc., 1967).

This representation of domestic space in earlier American Gothic television thus also prefigures the narrative preoccupations of the programmes discussed in the following chapter.

While all three of the programmes discussed at length in this chapter were very much 'of their time', unique explorations of the domestic Gothic from a number of different positions, it is possible to locate the legacy of these unusual instances of hybrid Gothic television from the 1960s in current programme making in the US. For example, *Buffy the Vampire Slayer* (20th Century Fox Television, 1997–2003) and its spin-off series, *Angel* (20th Century Fox Television, 1999–2004), perhaps the most famous and successful examples of parodic, hybrid Gothic television in recent years, have not been discussed at any great length in this book. This decision is taken partly because there already exists a wealth of critical literature on *Buffy the Vampire Slayer* and its spin-off, with several articles discussing *Buffy*'s relationship to the Gothic genre specifically (see Callander, 2000; Davis, 2000). As Robert A. Davis argues,

> In one sense, the literary and cinematic ancestry of *Buffy the Vampire Slayer* seems self-consciously clear. Episode by episode the program makers mischievously invoke the full catalogue of gothic horrors, knowingly parading an endless series of monstrous exhibits whose thoroughbred credentials from the archives of gothic fiction and film make them instantly recognisable to the viewing audience. (2000)

Davis and Callander both argue that *Buffy the Vampire Slayer* is indeed Gothic at its core, citing a range of visual and narrative references to the genre within the series to construct their arguments. *Buffy*'s narrative clearly relates to some of the central issues dealt with in this delineation of Gothic television, particularly those questions about gender and the Gothic genre raised in this book. Indeed, in a second season episode entitled 'Halloween', Buffy puts on a haunted costume (an eighteenth century ball gown) which transforms her into a vulnerable Gothic heroine! As a post-feminist text (Moseley, 2002), *Buffy the Vampire Slayer* worries at many of the anxieties surrounding femininity and independence which are generic to the Gothic heroine, and, like the long-running Gothic series drama discussed in the following chapter, *Buffy* also explores the burgeoning fear of home invasion. In this series, the threatened domestic space is one of the focal centres of the serial narrative in which the young heroine struggles to look after her home and younger sister while defending it from a wealth of supernatural enemies. Other teen TV dramas, such as those discussed by Rachel Moseley (2002) (e.g. *Charmed*, *Sabrina the Teenage Witch*) can also be understood as hybrid Gothic texts, fusing the narrative preoccupations of the teen drama with the stock characters and imagery of the Gothic. However, it is to the televisual Gothic serial drama that we now turn in the following chapter.

Notes

1 *Hallowe'en With the New Addams Family* (CBS, 1977), *The Munsters' Scary Little Christmas* (20th Century Fox Television, 1996), *The Munsters' Revenge* (NBC, 1981).
2 *The Munsters Today* (The Arthur Company, 1988–91), *The New Addams Family* (Fox Family Channel, 1998–99).
3 *The Mini-Munsters* (ABC [US], 1973), *The Addams Family* (Hanna-Barbera Productions, 1973–75), *The Addams Family* (ABC [US], 1992–93).
4 *The Addams Family* (US, 1991), *Addams Family Values* (US, 1993).
5 *The Addams Family Reunion* (US, 1998).
6 A very thorough production history of *Dark Shadows* is offered in Kathryn Leigh Scott's *The Dark Shadows Companion: 25th Anniversary Collection* (1990).
7 For example: *The Night Stalker* (ABC [US], 1972), *The Night Strangler* (ABC [US], 1973), *Frankenstein* (ABC [US], 1973), *The Turn of the Screw* (ABC [US], 1974).
8 E.g. *Rebecca* (Carlton, 1997), *The Turn of the Screw* (United/Martin Pope/WGBH Boston, 1999), *The Haunting of Helen Walker* (Norman Rosemont Productions, 1997).
9 Benshoff contacted fans through fanzines, initiating correspondence and sending out questionnaires, as well as analysing fan fiction (both literary and videographic).

Televisuality and the new American Gothic

5

In addition to its reappearance on European television, the Gothic flourished in many and diverse areas of North American culture during the 1990s. Christoph Grunenberg, curator of a major exhibition entitled *Gothic* at the Institute of Contemporary Art, Boston, Massachusetts, noted that:

> A predilection for the Gothic has deeply affected all areas of contemporary life – from 'high' literature to 'schlock' science fiction, mystery, and romance novels; penetrating art, architecture, design, fashion and graphic design; to be found in advertisements and on record covers; present in popular music of today as in the revival of Gregorian chants and medieval hymns; and, most pronounced, making its daily appearance in film and television, where an obsession with sex, crime and the proclivities of twisted yet clever serial killers has developed into one of the most popular categories in mainstream entertainment. (1997: 210)

Grunenberg, who explains this predilection as 'a true fin de siècle spirit of cultural pessimism and spiritual malaise' (1997: 208), is joined by other cultural commentators in unpacking the Gothic's renaissance in the US during the final decade of the twentieth century. For instance, Mark Edmundson finds the discourses of the Gothic present in 'media renderings of the O.J. Simpson case, in [America's] political discourse, in our modes of therapy, on TV news, on talk shows like *Oprah*, in our discussions of AIDS and of the environment', concluding that, 'American culture at large has become suffused with Gothic assumptions, with Gothic characters and plots' (1997: xii). I wish to examine the Gothic trend in North American television drama during the 1990s and into the twenty-first century, a trend identified as originating in the groundbreaking serial drama, *Twin Peaks* (Lynch-Frost Productions, 1990–91). This long-form serial is described by Lenora Ledwon as '[tapping] the full potential of the "Television Gothic" . . . [utilising]

familiar Gothic themes and devices such as incest, the grotesque, repetition, interpolated narration, haunted settings, mirrors, doubles and
supernatural occurrences' (1993: 260). Created by David Lynch and
Mark Frost, the drama centres on Special Agent Dale Cooper's (Kyle
MacLachlan's) investigation of the murder of prom queen, Laura
Palmer (Sheryl Lee), interweaving a plethora of quirky sub-plots and
allusions to other texts and genres. Like the programming discussed in
the previous chapter, *Twin Peaks* deconstructs the concept of the
'American Dream' through the Gothic narrative, highlighting the gap
between the 'dream' of the all-American family as a sacred institution
and the 'reality' of lives lived in fear.

We will then see how the Gothic mode subsequently flourished at the
turn of the century in a number of long-running Gothic series and
serials. These programmes included *The X-Files* (10:13, 1993–2002),
Poltergeist: The Legacy (PMP Legacy Productions, 1996–99), *Profiler*
(NBC, 1996–2000), *Brimstone* (Warner Bros. Television, 1998–99), *The
Others* (NBC, 2000), *Carnivale* (HBO, 2003–5) and *Kingdom Hospital*
(ABC [US], 2004), to name a few of the more high profile examples. For
the sake of brevity, this examination of US Gothic television will focus
on two further serials as case studies. The first of these, *American Gothic*
(CBS, 1995–96), is a serial drama set in the fictitious South-Carolinian
town of Trinity, focusing on the struggle between the evil Sheriff Buck
(Gary Cole) and the saintly ghost of Merlyn Temple (Sarah Paulson), the
girl murdered by Buck in order to gain access to her brother Caleb
(Lucas Black), born after Buck raped their mother. The other case study
in this chapter is *Millennium* (10:13, 1996–99), a Gothic cop serial
following the fortunes of an ex-FBI profiler, Frank Black (Lance
Henrickson) as he investigates numerous serial murders and the shady
'Millennium Group'. Both these latter serials, made for different networks in the heyday of this trend, are representative of new American
Gothic television. These serials will also be discussed in relation to the
'problem' of horror on television, and the moralising which surrounds
the role that television entertainment plays in public (and private) life in
the US and beyond.

Twin Peaks: the new American Gothic

Lenora Ledwon was perhaps the first person to use the descriptor
'Television Gothic' in her insightful analysis of *Twin Peaks* (1993). In this
article, which views television as the 'ultimate medium of Gothic
enquiry', Ledwon engages with Eve Sedgwick's inventory of Gothic

narrative convention and image repertoire (Sedgwick, 1986), providing a list of the serial's Gothic characteristics according to Sedgwick's
schema:

> The woods around *Twin Peaks* are a wild and mysterious landscape . . .
> The Bookhouse Boys are a secret, quasi-mystical institution. Sub-
> terranean spaces exist (Owl Cave), as do resonant silences, guilt and
> shame, nocturnal landscapes and dreams. Strange fires occur . . . The
> flickering torches of the charnel house are replaced with the cold glare
> and strobe effect of fluorescent lights in the morgue. Discovered manu-
> scripts (Laura Palmer's diary) and mediated narratives (Cooper's tapes)
> abound. Cooper's quest for knowledge and his decision to sell his soul
> qualify him as a Faust-like figure. And, of course, the unspeakable
> occurs: rape, incest, and murder. The most antisocial of crimes intrude
> into the sanctuary of domesticity. (1993: 262)

While this listing of Gothic characteristics is useful in thinking about
how the serial conforms to the conventions of the genre in its traditional,
literary forms,[1] we can think beyond this when looking at *Twin Peaks'*
identity as Gothic television. 'Gothic television', in this context, becomes
a critical category to define programming in which fear is the sustaining
emotion, translated to the viewer through the creation of a certain 'mood'
(melancholy, dread, the uncanny), and through an emphasis on impressionistic renditions of (troubled) subjectivities which can be seen across
all recent Gothic television. Admittedly, 'mood' is difficult to define and
discuss in a precise and scholarly way; the following analysis does,
however, attempt to do this through a detailed analysis of the mise-en-
scène of *Twin Peaks*.

From the outset of *Twin Peaks*, a mood of melancholy and desolation
is established which permeates the serial as a whole. The title sequence,
a montage of Twin Peaks' pastoral and industrial scenery, depicts a
world without people which resounds with a harrowing emptiness. As
both Jason Jacobs (2001) and Jostein Gripsrud (1995) have argued, a
television programme's title sequence is both essential in acting as an
audio-visual signal to the viewer that the show is about to start, and also
establishes the aesthetic identity or 'style' of the programme in shorthand from the outset: 'The title sequence of a show is its self-
presentation and self-promotion . . . Since they are designed to identify
a particular show, they will try to capture and express a particular
affective mode which the producers wish to associate with it' (Gripsrud,
1995: 183–4). In *Twin Peaks*, this 'affective mode' or mood is one of deep
sadness, expressed through the slowness of a montage sequence which
presents an image of small-town America where people (and the home)
are absent. In the serial, 'home' is the source of trouble, and thus in the

title sequence, this familiar locale of small-town America is 'unspeakable' and pointedly missing from the montage of familiar spaces in the town. Accompanied by Angelo Badalamenti's haunting theme tune, the title sequence eloquently encapsulates the mood of the show. Badalamenti recalls: 'David [Lynch] said, "I've got a TV show to do, and the music should be slow, dark, brooding, haunting. It should start with an anticipatory melody, then build slowly up to a climax – a climax that's slow and tears your heart out" ' (Hartman, 2005). The programme's title track, a slow, romantic melody, is tinged with this brooding darkness described by Badalamenti. This opening sequence is also tied to the punctuating shots of the town's waterfall and of Douglas firs blowing in the wind which recur throughout the serial. The pastoral is therefore understood as an absence of the human and the social in the serial, and refers to the deep sense of loneliness and isolation experienced by *Twin Peaks'* central characters.

The title sequence of *Twin Peaks* also establishes the serial's colour palette, with its muted brown and sepia tones, further assisting in the creation of a recognisable mood or tone for the show. Here, the brownness of the title sequence reflects the brownness of many of the central locales of the drama (such as the Palmers' house). Brownness has many potential connotations in this serial: it suggests a sense of depression and degradation (America is dull brown, not red, white and blue, in *Twin Peaks*); it links the narrative to a problematic/troubling sense of the past (the sepia tone inspires echoes of early photography); and the brown tones also suggest a fecundity which links the everyday spaces of *Twin Peaks* to the site of horror at the heart of the serial (the rural site of Laura Palmer's murder). Conversely, red and coral tones are also used within the serial to create an unsettling sense of warmth and homeliness at odds with the events which unfurl in *Twin Peaks*. As Duwayne Dunham, director of several episodes, notes: '[I made] this a very ordinary place . . . One of the things [shooting through coral filters] gives you [is] a very, kind of warm, comfortable feeling, a warm look. The exteriors are rather misty, rainy, snowy, cold, you know, more distant. This [colour] makes it a little more homey.'[2] On *Twin Peaks*, shooting styles and colour schemes were set by David Lynch from the outset of the serial (Lynch actually only directed the first and last episodes, and a further four in between), and a serial style was carefully replicated throughout the serial by subsequent directors. The use of colour was particularly significant on the show, and, unusually, Lynch oversaw the network transfer of the finished programme from 35mm film, to ensure that these striking red and brown tones weren't adjusted out of the transfer from the film print. Director of photography, Frank Byers, recalls that

[Lynch told us] that he wanted a warm, comfortable look on the 'outside' so the inside could be turbulent – things happening on the inside meaning the story happened within this veneer of warmth and comfort. He would say 'Well I'm trying to create a mood here', and that look had to do with what David said was *the* mood, and the mood was very important to him.[3]

Here, then, we see colour being used in a deliberate and expressive way to establish mood and tone within the American Gothic serial.

In *Twin Peaks*, certain shooting techniques also serve to enhance and underscore this mood of unease. For example, characters and spaces within the Palmers' house are frequently shot from a low angle to convey a sense of burden and anxiety. Perhaps the most emblematic shot in relation to this (and one that recurs in Sarah Palmer's visions) is a low angle shot of the staircase and ceiling fan. This offers an aesthetically unsettling representation of the domestic space, as do extreme close-ups of everyday objects within the home, such as the ceiling fan or the needle on a record, rendering the familiar strange and evoking the uncanny within the domestic space. This shooting style frames and emphasises the performances offered within *Twin Peaks*, which also have a large impact on the mood/tone of the drama. This is a serial full of characters over-emoting – Deputy Andy's constant crying, Nadine's aggressive psychosis, Sarah Palmer's hysteria – which translates into a hyperbolic, melodramatic performance style. For example Leland Palmer, the father of Laura Palmer (and, as we will later discover, her killer), appears in a scene at his house in the third episode, 'Zen, or the Skill to Catch a Killer' (Lynch-Frost Productions, 1990), in which this combination of colour, shot composition and excessive performance style creates a mood of domestic horror. Shot from a fairly low angle, Leland appears to fill the room, which we will later understand as a visualisation of his threatening presence within the domestic space. As he dances manically with his daughter's photograph, his expression is fixed into a mask of excessive emotion (see figure 5.1). Here, then, a mood of domestic terror is created through a combination of the brown colour palette, an unusual, unsettling shooting style, and exaggerated, melodramatic performance.

As suggested in the introduction to this section, *Twin Peaks* is also a drama about the exploration of extreme subjective states and, as such, the serial's visual style is markedly impressionistic at times; dreams, visions and hallucinations are all rendered in the first person, in psychical point-of-view moments which disrupt the more prosaic shooting and editing style of the rest of this drama. A striking example of this is Agent Cooper's dream sequence of the 'Red Room',[4] in which he encounters a dancing dwarf speaking backwards forwards, the doppelganger of Laura

5.1 Domestic terror: 'Zen, or the Skill to Catch a Killer',
Twin Peaks (Lynch-Frost Productions, 1990).

Palmer talking in riddles, and a one armed man delivering a poetic monologue direct to camera. The sequence, composed of flash edits in which several objects/people are revealed too quickly for the viewer (and Cooper) to make any sense of them, is an incoherent, impressionistic rendition of Cooper's eccentric subjectivity. Glen Creeber has argued that these moments reflect a broader move away from social realism within television drama:

> Television drama has seen a shift away from the depiction of external social/political realities to a more self-reflexive, multidimensional and subjective form. Dramas like . . . *Twin Peaks* . . . certainly appear to dispense with more traditional notions of 'naturalism'; their heightened levels of fantasy constructing a narrative universe in which social reality itself is continually set against subjective, individual and multiple perspectives. (2004: 14)

In the context of Gothic television, programme makers have consistently explored new ways of translating the unconscious to the screen, in order to represent the extreme states of feeling/emotion associated with the Gothic genre.

Arguably, *Twin Peaks* had a huge impact on the aesthetic of American television drama as a whole in the early 1990s, beyond the initiation of a cycle of Gothic serial dramas. Robin Nelson suggests that '*Twin Peaks*, so its advocates allege, has almost single-handedly effected a paradigm shift in TV drama, changing its (sur) face for ever' (Nelson, 1997: 236); this shift has been viewed as a move towards stylish, intelligent, 'knowing' drama, discussed below in relation to John Thornton Caldwell's concept of 'televisuality' (1995). As with the other serials discussed in this chapter, *Twin Peaks* marked a move away from 'network, catch-all, "lowest common denominator" programming to niche marketing of specific products to attract different segments of the audience at different times of the day' (Nelson, 1997: 236). In the case of *Twin Peaks*, this niche audience was assumed to have a good deal of cultural capital and a high level of media literacy, in order to make sense of the programme's dizzying network of allusions and complex plotting, a select, but lucrative, viewer group in the eyes of advertisers.

It is this allusionism which has particularly marked *Twin Peaks* out as 'postmodern' in the eyes of many commentators. The allusion to other texts and genres is both understood as a fundamental appeal to a knowledgeable viewer, able to identify a plethora of references and parodies, and also anchors the drama within the postmodern moment. Within the lexicon of postmodernist criticism, the generic hybridity of the Gothic drama is understood as intertextual 'bricolage', one of the identifying traits of the 'postmodern'. Genres as diverse as the detective genre, the forensic/police procedural drama, the soap opera, the sitcom, the horror film, the 'juvenile delinquent' film of the 1950s, the teen melodrama, the TV commercial, the Western and film noir are present within *Twin Peaks*, interwoven to produce a text which, at first glance, defies easy generic categorisation. Jim Collins has argued that there is something medium specific about the nature of *Twin Peaks*' generic hybridity, that television *per se* is intertextual in its constant flow of programming: 'the ongoing oscillation in discursive register and generic conventions describes . . . the very act of moving up and down the televisual scale of the cable box' (Collins, 1992: 347–8). Here then, the 'flow' of television itself is understood as an example of postmodern intertextuality, whereby diverse medium-specific genres are juxtaposed with one another. Collins subsequently argues that *Twin Peaks* somehow distils the very essence of television's supertext, incorporating these references and juxtapositions into the fabric of the serial itself.

However, perhaps there is more to say about this intertextuality or generic hybridity than that it is simply 'postmodern'. As Glen Creeber proposes, 'as "postmodern" as this "polysemic" world might seem, its constant generic "bricolage" finally reveals more than simply a *depthless* postmodern commodification'[5] (2004: 53). In short, this generic hybridity creates *meaning* in the context of the Gothic text, particularly by highlighting the tension between the surface and the reality of American life: as Lenora Ledwon has argued, '[Lynch] brings the horrid and the normal into juxtaposition until the viewer is unsure what is normal anymore'

(1993: 263). In terms of the serial's complex generic identity, the 'horrid' is represented by references to the detective genre, horror movies, film noir and the Gothic on the one hand, and, on the other hand, the 'normal' is found within allusions to the soap opera, the sitcom and the teen romance genre, for example. Taking a scene from the '*Twin Peaks* Pilot' (Lynch-Frost Productions, 1990) to illustrate this point, we see a clear blending of the generic traits of the teen 'high school' drama and the crime-procedural drama to Gothic effect. The scene in which the police enter the local school to investigate Laura's death begins with a sense of generic normalcy within the teen drama: we see Audrey Horne (Sherilyn Fenn) changing her sensible shoes for some kitten heels at her locker, Bobby Briggs (Dana Ashbrook) arrives, 'goofing off' in the corridor, and class begins with the standard 'registration' scene. In effect, this opening announces the ordinariness of the school and the events taking place within it. However, even before the school's principal announces Laura's murder over the tannoy, the very 'normal' space and narrative of the teen drama begin to transform. On seeing the police at the door, and following a glance at Laura's empty seat, her best friend Donna (Lara Flynn-Boyle) begins to sob uncontrollably, marking a dramatic shift in performance style beyond the emotional histrionics of the teen drama. Then, during the principal's announcement, cuts are made between shots of the principal, shots of the classroom and a slow track down the broad corridor of the school, one of the key generic spaces of the teen drama, poignantly empty of teenagers and echoing with the sorrow and devastation of the moment (see figure 5.2).

Like the montage of the show's title sequence, it is the emptiness of this shot which speaks so eloquently of the drama's central themes of loneliness and despair. The scene then closes with a zoom into the trophy cabinet where Laura's prom photo is placed in the centre, followed by a cut to a closer zoom into the photograph. The slowness of this zoom in the context of the scene serves to underscore the horror of this moment in which the ordinary and the everyday of the American high school are turned upside down through murder (and, as we will later learn, incest and domestic violence). Here we see the generic transformation of the identifying spaces of a 'benign' generic text – the teen drama – through the expression of the extreme emotions of fear and sorrow particularly associated with the Gothic horror film.[6]

Clearly one of the most 'affective' generic relationships in *Twin Peaks* is that of the soap opera and Gothic horror. In particular, the place of the diegetic soap opera, 'Invitation to Love', is significant in drawing parallels and connections between television's 'everyday' fare (the daytime soap opera) and the primetime Gothic serial. The device of the 'programme

5.2 The space of the teen drama transformed: '*Twin Peaks*
Pilot', *Twin Peaks* (Lynch-Frost Productions, 1990).

within the programme' is used particularly heavily in the first season of
the show, where characters are frequently depicted watching the soap at
key moments in the narrative of *Twin Peaks*; indeed, the diegetic soap
opera very obviously echoes the narrative of *Twin Peaks*. On occasion,
these moments can be viewed as *Twin Peaks* poking fun at itself (as in the
moment when Laura's cousin Madeleine arrives (played by Sheryl Lee,
who also plays Laura), and the title sequence of 'Invitation to Love'
announces 'Starring Selena Swift as Emerald and Jade' just before
Madeleine's entrance). However, as well as producing comedy, this
moment also points towards the inherent Gothicism of the soap opera, as
a genre which frequently revisits the trope of the doppelganger.

Within *Twin Peaks*, the viewing of 'Invitation to Love' also points
towards the uncanny quality of television viewing, in the soap opera's
ability to echo and reflect the 'real lives' of the *Twin Peaks* characters.
Another instance of this is seen when Sarah Palmer describes her vision
of her daughter's missing necklace being removed from its hiding place,
when a cut is made directly to a shot of a necklace in 'Invitation to Love'
(in episode five, 'The One-Armed Man' (Lynch-Frost Productions, 1990)).
Here the presence of the text within the text emphasises an uncanny connection between the real and televisual worlds (once removed). From this
shot of the TV screen, we cut to Lucy's (Kimmy Robertson's) face,
enthralled, as the Sheriff's secretary watches the soap at work. The
sequence then satirises the image of the over-involved soap opera viewer:
as the Sheriff (Michael Ontkean) arrives and asks what's been going on,

Lucy gives him a full synopsis of the soap's convoluted plot, comedically dramatising the over-involved viewer's presumed inability to separate fact from fiction, to which Sheriff Truman responds, 'No what's been going on *here*'. This reference to other medium-specific genres such as the teen drama and the soap opera thus produces an uncanny effect in *Twin Peaks*, which speaks of a split between 'the homely and clean-cut life of the town's *conscious* veneer . . . and the dark and possibly *"unconscious"* influences of the town's dangerous underbelly' (Creeber, 2004: 54).

One of the products of this intertextuality is the historical indeterminacy of *Twin Peaks*: the serial refers heavily to the 1950s within its mise-en-scène but also obviously takes place in the present. In the context of the Gothic drama, this historical indeterminacy can be understood as an uncanny device. Reflecting the overriding concerns of the narrative, the past constantly 'haunts' the present aesthetically within the drama's mise-en-scène. As argued in the previous chapter of this book, the 1950s have been understood as the Gothic drama's historical 'other' from the 1960s onwards, and, like the genres discussed above (the teen drama, the soap opera), the decade has become 'shorthand' for sentiments of normality, ordinariness and all-American family values within American Gothic television. It is therefore highly appropriate that the 1950s aesthetically 'haunt' the 1990s in *Twin Peaks*. As with other examples of the American Gothic discussed in this book, *Twin Peaks* repeatedly evokes 'old-fashioned' notions of the 'American Dream' in order to undercut them. We see this, for example, in Agent Cooper's speech to the gathered townspeople towards the end of the '*Twin Peaks* Pilot', where a US flag and a wall frieze of the mountains stand behind him as he emphatically tells the gathered audience that the killer may 'come from this town'. In this sequence, metonymic images of the American Dream (the flag, pastoral imagery) underscore the sentiment that this is a flawed ideology, underlining the fact that the threat to the townspeople comes from within: this is both part of Lynch's worldview and endemic of American Gothic television's major preoccupations as outlined in this analysis of the genre.

The representation of the American family has been particularly singled out for discussion in critical approaches to *Twin Peaks*, with the spectre of child abuse and domestic violence 'standing for' the collapse of the 'American Dream'. As Randi Davenport has argued,

> *Twin Peaks* horrified us because it held a mirror up to the American family and what we saw when we gazed upon it was a brutality that made many of us sick. *Twin Peaks* is thus unsettling because it disruptively implicates its audience in the family violence that it simultaneously suggests is a customary, even banal, feature of the average, middle-class American family. (Davenport, 1993: 255–6)

Davenport goes on to state that 'If *Twin Peaks* is "about" the horrors of incest, it is equally about the horror of the secret life of the American family'(1993: 258), and Lenora Ledwon concurs: 'What is so frightening about the Television Gothic? The fact that it returns to the domestic sphere something repressed yet familiar – the spectres of incest and family violence' (1993: 264). Ultimately, there may be something television specific about the representation of family violence and domestic abuse in *Twin Peaks*. As Diane Stevenson points out, these are themes which have permeated Lynch's film work but 'it is only in *Twin Peaks* that Lynch allows himself explicitly to bring out the incestuous violence right in the midst of the middle-class home' (Stevenson, 1995: 74). As has been argued throughout this book then, television offers the ideal medium on which to deconstruct the prevalent myths about the sanctity of American family life through the Gothic narrative. The concluding part of this chapter will subsequently investigate the legacy of this representation in the televisual Gothic drama serial.

Televisuality and the American Gothic

The examination of *American Gothic* and *Millennium* offered in the close of this final chapter has a dual focus, reflecting the broader concerns of this study. Firstly, echoing the examination of British Gothic anthology television offered in chapters one and two of this book, this analysis will ask how American Gothic television drama of the 1990s continued to push the technological possibilities and limitations of television production, seeking to further outline a correlation between medium innovation and the representation of the supernatural within Gothic television drama. Secondly, this analysis of *American Gothic* and *Millennium* will close by scrutinising the familial Gothic narrative and associated preoccupations with the home and family evident in both these serials. In conclusion it will be argued that in the context of the television industry in the US, the mirroring of families on screen and families at home ultimately evoked fears about television, the Gothic narrative and the morality of entertainment.

As a theoretical framework for the first part of this analysis, John Thornton Caldwell's delineation of the *televisual* aesthetic of US television in the 1980s and 1990s will be cited as an important starting point (Caldwell, 1995). Gothic serials such as *American Gothic* and *Millennium* 'tapped into' and flaunted the potential of certain nascent production technologies in order to realise a more 'realistic' representation of the supernatural. Although neither of these serials was seen as a total commercial success in terms of Nielsen ratings points,[7] both serials were seen as artistically/creatively successful, drawing in a small discerning audience with an appreciation for the eccentricities and innovations of both programmes. While I am wary of making claims for the quality or 'excellence' of either of these programmes, it is clear that they represent creative responses to the challenges of representing the supernatural on television.

There has been a long tradition of using the supernatural Gothic to demonstrate or 'show off' innovations in audio-visual media. For example, in his long-ranging study of the pre-history of cinema, Laurent Mannoni argues that 'Diabolical subjects were one of the commonest themes of lantern imagery over a long period [roughly, the thirteenth to the eighteenth century]' (2000: 110). Both Mannoni and Terry Castle (1995) go on to discuss the Gothic spectaculars of the late eighteenth century, such as the phantasmagorias of Paul Philidor and Étienne-Gaspard Robert (aka Robertson), which offered graphic and dramatic demonstrations of new technologies that afforded still images the appearance of animation and movement.[8] As Marina Warner concurs,

> When showmen staged the first moving pictures . . . the relationship of this new invention to fantasy (as opposed to reality) seemed its most marvellous property . . . The new, moving flux of images held out the enthralling possibility of passing beyond the visible to the (normally) invisible, from the real to the supernatural. (1993: 14)

Just as in the Gothic dramas of the London patent theatres of the eighteenth and nineteenth centuries, where skill in stage design was often demonstrated by the tricks and traps which allowed for a visualisation of the supernatural,[9] so the inventors of early projection technologies demonstrated the full possibilities of their products through Gothic representation. Furthermore, while it would be inaccurate to suggest that the Gothic mode was the only way in which early cinema technology was showcased, it is true that certain film pioneers demonstrated their new art through cinematographic tricks of supernatural representation (see Gunning, 2001). Examples of this range from Georges Méliès' work, in films such as *Le Manoir du diable* (1896) where supernatural characters 'magically' appeared and disappeared within the frame through trick edits, to G.A. Smith in the UK, and his 1898 films *The Corsican Brothers*, *Photographing a Ghost* and *Faust and Mephistopheles*. Here we begin to see a relationship developing between technological innovation and the Gothic genre: the spectres of Robertson's phantasmagorias, the ghosts of the eighteenth century London patent theatres, and the disembodied

floating heads of George Méliès' 'trick' cinematography are all a testament to this fact.

The argument that Gothic serial drama in the US made during the
1990s showcased innovations and changes within the television industry evokes a characterisation of the industry prior to and during this
decade which has been carefully outlined in John Thornton Caldwell's
Televisuality (1995). This book offers a convincing account of the way in
which North American television 'had retheorized its aesthetic and pres-
entational task' (1995: 4–5) in the 1980s and early 1990s. In this study,
Caldwell outlines the complete overhaul of what he terms the era of 'televisuality', relating these seismic changes to transformations of production technologies and programming strategies, as well as
reconfigurations of both the organisation of the industry and the role of
the audience:

> Television has come to flaunt and display style. Programs battle for
> identifiable style markers and distinct looks in order to gain audience
> share within the competitive broadcast flow . . . The stylistic emphasis
> that emerged during this period resulted from a number of interrelated
> tendencies and changes: in the industry's mode of production, in pro-
> gramming practice, in the audience and its expectations and in an eco-
> nomic crisis in network television. (1995: 5)

Caldwell thus argues that the proliferation of 'televisual' shows during
the 1980s occurred as a response to the threat posed towards the 'big
three' (ABC, CBS and NBC) by the nascent Fox network and the
encroaching presence of cable channels, manifesting the need for distinction in much the same way as the major film studios of 1950s
Hollywood had done thirty years earlier: in production extravagance and
excess.

Caldwell's *Televisuality* asserts that 'special' or event television was
produced during this period as a response to competition, and locates
a great degree of the programming's stylishness in its signature producers, who functioned as a 'promotional marquee; a spotlit entrée
for programming seasons on their respective networks' (1995: 11). He
isolates three kinds of televisual auteurs: the 'showcase producers'
offering 'marquee signatures [as] network banner carriers', 'mainstream conversion producers' who 'acquired mannerisms [and] embell-
ished genres' and 'auteur-imports' from the cinema who produced
'cinematic spectacle' and were seen as 'visionary émigrés' (1995: 16). In
the serials at the centre of this analysis, David Lynch and Aaron
Spelling's roles as co-producers of *Twin Peaks* represent a blend of the
imported, visionary auteur and the 'mainstream conversion producer',

and, to a certain extent, their professional identities embody the oppos-ing poles of the Gothic narrative's hybrid generic identity: at the time of broadcast, Spelling was famous for executive producing teen melo-drama and soap opera in the States (e.g. *Beverley Hills 90210* (Spell-ing Television, 1990–2000), *Dynasty* (Aaron Spelling Productions, 1981–89)), whereas Lynch was more readily associated with the Gothic horror of films like *Eraserhead* (US, 1977) and *Blue Velvet* (US, 1986). On the other hand, *Millennium* clearly played upon executive producer/ writer/director Chris Carter's status as a 'showcase producer' from the outset, with print ads published in the national press leading up to the beginning of the serial in October 1996 highlighting Carter's pre-vious success on the Fox network, announcing a new serial 'from the creator of *The X-Files*'. *American Gothic* also offered a production team which might be seen as a mix of 'mainstream conversion' and 'auteur import'. The name most readily associated with the serial was that of Shaun Cassidy, who was credited as producer and writer but might be more accurately viewed as *American Gothic*'s 'creator', as the initial concept of the show had also been developed by Cassidy. As a rather unusual 'mainstream conversion', Cassidy had not moved from pro-ducing mainstream television, but starring in it, as Joe Hardy in the hit TV series *The Hardy Boys Mysteries* (ABC [US], 1977–79); Cassidy's fame was also associated with his position as a teen heartthrob in the 1970s, with a successful pop career. On the other hand, the role of exec-utive producer on *American Gothic* was credited to Sam Raimi, who had already had a good degree of success with the production of gore-filled horror films such as the *Evil Dead* films (US, 1982 and 1987) and *Darkman* (US, 1990). At the time, Raimi might well have been seen as a 'visionary émigré' within the Gothic/ horror genre, although he has become associated with historical fantasy on television more latterly, acting as executive producer on shows such as *Xena: Warrior Princess* (MCA Television Entertainment Inc./ Renaissance Pictures/Studios USA Television/Universal Television, 1995–2001) and the *Hercules* mini-series franchise (MCA Television Entertainment Inc./Renaissance Pictures/Studios USA Television/ Universal TV, 1994–99). Caldwell's notion of the producer as a 'promotional marquee' therefore accurately characterises the role of the producer/executive producer in the selling of the serials discussed in this chapter.

Two versions or 'strains' of televisual television are described in Caldwell's analysis: the videographic and the cinematic. Whereas video-graphic televisuality[10] is more usually associated with non-fictional tele-vision genres and 'trash' television competitions and quizzes, Caldwell's notion of the 'cinematic ecstasies' (1995: xi) of television in the 1980s and 1990s is most pertinent to this analysis of Gothic television:

> The cinematic refers, obviously, to a film look in television. Exhibitionist television in the 1980s meant more than shooting on film, however, since many nondescript shows have been shot on film since the 1950s. Rather, cinematic values brought to television spectacle, high production values, and feature style cinematography. (1995: 12)

Twin Peaks, *Millennium* and *American Gothic* can all be described as cine-matically televisual television: they were made for North American tele-vision during an era of intensifying competition, relied on the creative status of those producing to sell the serials, they each demonstrate a highly complex visual style, and the latter two programmes in particu-lar fully utilised, and indeed challenged, the technology available for television drama production in the US during the 1990s, enabled in part by the relatively large budgets for serial drama.[11] Subsequently, the cine-matically stylish televisual Gothic clearly demonstrates a relationship between distinction/showcasing within the television schedule and the Gothic genre. For example, Edward J. Fink's discussion of *American Gothic* as an extremely televisual production loaded with special effects, details the complexities of the creative process behind producing *American Gothic* during an era of what he describes as a 'digital revolu-tion' (1996: 9), arguing that the introduction of digital technology into the programme-making process '[allowed] the creative team time to explore more options with special effects' (1996: 11). To this end, the Gothic serial's high production values and inflated expenditure were flaunted through the representation of the supernatural happenings of the narrative.

Similarly, the producers of *Millennium* also proclaimed that their modes of production and their visual style were both innovative and inherently cinematic. While arguing that the production team was pushing the boundaries of television, Chris Carter, David Nutter (direc-tor of the '*Millennium* Pilot' episode (10:13, 1996) and several subse-quent instalments) and Peter Wunstorf (director of photography on the '*Millennium* Pilot') all argued that *Millennium* represented US television drama's move towards the cinematic. Christopher Probst reported the following in *American Cinematographer*:

> Fresh from his resounding success with the paranormal-shock series *The X-Files*, writer/executive producer Chris Carter is determined to push the boundaries of prime-time television's sensibilities even further into uncharted territory with his new show, *Millennium* . . . Inspired by such psychological thrillers as *Angel Heart*, *Silence of the Lambs*, and *Se7en*,

Carter and Nutter set out to find a cinematographer with a fresh eye and
the ability to render a look never before seen on television. (1996: 46–7)

Millennium's cinematic-ness was highlighted as a clear point of its distinction from other television drama, offering a style of Gothic horror
'never before seen on television'; indeed, the slick, cinematic Gothic is
knowingly referred to within the mise-en-scène of the '*Millennium*
Pilot', which opens on a sequence set in a strip club. This milieu, set
apart from the cosy homes and work spaces of American television
drama, is reminiscent of a similar setting in the film *Se7en* (US, 1995),
and is accompanied by the track 'Piggies' by the band Nine Inch Nails,
whose track 'Closer' was referenced in the title music to *Se7en*. Here the
low key lighting, the dark, saturated colours, and the filth and degradation of the mise-en-scène are strikingly similar to the 'look' of *Se7en*'s
crime scenes (see figure 5.3).

This rather knowing referencing of a highly visible and popular
example of Gothic cinema of the 1990s might be read as an acknowledgement of the serial's status as 'cinematic TV' (as is the risqué subject
matter and near-nudity on display here). Caldwell's study highlights a
number of production innovations which enabled this cinematic stylishness: new film stocks, electronic/non-linear editing, developments
in motion/camera control, and so on. To draw this discussion of televisuality to a close, the impact of these particular technological innovations on the representation of the supernatural will be considered,
responding to Caldwell's suggestion that 'programs could tie acute stylistic looks to alternative narrative worlds' (1995: 55).

5.3 Cinematic horror on television: '*Millennium* Pilot',
Millennium (10:13, 1996).

Perhaps the most obvious point to make in relation to the question of how US television became seen as 'cinematically stylish' during the 1980s and 1990s is that this 'film look' was reliant, in the first instance, on the use of film stock. During this period, there was a marked increase in filming on film for television, particularly in the genres of primetime fantasy drama and commercial advertising. Caldwell notes that the ability to shoot a new kind of darkness on television was seen by production personnel as a particular sign of prestige:

> When primetime DPs [Directors of Photography] boasted that 'of course, not everything on television is shot at ten footcandles [i.e. at an extremely low light]', they were both showing off that they could shoot primetime at that unheard of level of darkness and also making stark contrasts to earlier, prestige production stocks. (1995: 84)

Clearly, this darkness is demanded in the production of Gothic television: the milieu of *Millennium*'s rain-soaked Seattle is a distinct testament to this. As Catherine Johnson (2000; 2005) has argued in her analysis of Chris Carter's earlier series, *The X-Files*, it is precisely this burgeoning darkness which both provides the serial with its signature 'look' and also indicates the serial's sense of quality or prestige. Carter reinforced this association of darkness with quality (and also cinematic-ness) in an interview coinciding with the transmission of the '*Millennium* Pilot': 'In this genre, there's a tendency to go with surreal lighting techniques: macabre, high-key, glowing stuff. But I wanted the new show to be as real as possible, to create natural lighting situations – no fake sources – while keeping it good and dark and cinematic' (Probst, 1996: 46).

Advances in editing techniques also enabled a greater level of experimentation in the post-production processes of programme making during this era, allowing for the creation of hyperactive and visually dense television images. In the televisual era, non-linear and random access electronic editing systems 'encouraged, or fed, the televisual appetite for stylistic volatility and infinite formal permutations' (Caldwell, 1995: 82–3), enabling the kind of densely layered images and montage-style flashbacks and flashforwards which became the key stylistic markers of Gothic television in the 1990s. This 'visually dense' layering of images is particularly evident, in both *American Gothic* and *Millennium*, in the impressionistic rendering of supernatural subjectivity or other 'psychical' points of view (dream sequences, flashbacks, premonitions, hallucinations, 'second sight', etc.), where fast edited montage and image layering techniques make the image noticeably 'strange'. As Fink describes, 'On *American Gothic*, a single image might have consisted of four or more layers of composited video' (1996: 14). In fact, these sequences can be viewed as more technically complex versions of the flashback montages endemic in Gothic television as a whole (as discussed in chapter three). However, in the era of televisual television, new production technologies, particularly non-linear editing, enabled greater depth and more complexity in the construction of character subjectivity and psychical point of view, thus marrying televisual style to the narrative concerns of the genre (the return of the repressed, mental breakdown and trauma).

Throughout *American Gothic*, many of the central characters are linked to at least one of these sequences of supernatural point of view. In the '*American Gothic* Pilot' episode (CBS, 1995) for example, one of the first of these hyper-dense sequences takes place as Caleb Temple's cousin Gail (Paige Turco) arrives in town to look after her newly orphaned relative. During the course of the episode the viewer learns that Gail is herself an orphan, having lost both her parents in a fire at the Trinity Guardian (their workplace); it is also implied that this event somehow involved the sinister town Sheriff. As Gail kneels at her parents' graveside, two fast edited sequences of overlaid images are interspersed with facial close-ups of Gail to underline the fact that the montages come from her subjective position. The following shot list outlines the fifty-four second sequence:

Shot one: (A mournful piece of orchestral music, played on violins and wind instruments, continues throughout each shot) Facial close-up of Gail talking to her parents' graves: 'I always wanted to come back. Guess I was just too afraid' (7 seconds)

Shot two: (Sounds of wind and echoing screams continue to shot six) Long shot of the Temples' house at night as lightning flashes (0.8 seconds)

Shot three: Eye-level exterior tracking shot towards the window of Merlyn's bedroom (0.8 seconds)

Shot four: Repeat shot two (0.8 seconds)

Shot five: Jump cut to medium long shot of the same as lightning strikes (0.8 seconds)

Shot six: Dissolve to medium close-up of Caleb which slowly dissolves (0.8 seconds)

Shot seven: Repeat shot one: 'There's a little boy here who's in the same situation I was and he's going to have a lot of questions. Questions I don't think I can answer. Maybe if I understood what happened to you' (24 seconds)

Shot eight: (Sounds of breaking glass and fire continue to shot eleven) Extreme close-up of a gravestone, with a partial US flag visible behind (0.4 seconds)

Shot nine: Long distance travelling shot of a sunset through trees (0.6 seconds)
Shot ten: Extreme close-up of a photo in a frame of a family in front of the Trinity Guardian store front dissolves to shot eleven (0.6 seconds)
Shot eleven: Extreme close-up of fire (0.6 seconds)
Shot twelve: Repeat shot one: 'I need to know the truth. Please help me' (8 seconds)
Shot thirteen: Symmetrical medium shot from behind Gail of her kneeling in front of the graves – a small US flag sits behind her father's grave (3 seconds)
Shot fourteen: Repeat shot one: ''Cause this time I'm not leaving "'til I find it" (6 seconds).'

This short sequence introduces techniques which are commonly used throughout the serial. The psychical point-of-view sections (shots two to six and eight to eleven) utilise patterns of quick cutting and dissolves (shots six to seven and ten to eleven) to suggest Gail's confusion and to represent a 'sixth sense'. Later in the serial other formally disruptive techniques such as the use of slow-motion photography, stop-motion photography, colour distortion, blue-screen shooting and negative images are all combined during sequences of supernatural subjectivity, particularly when assigned to the evil Sheriff. In these moments, it is suggested that his supernatural 'power' can be conveyed in the 'strangeness' of his sight, when the rules of continuity editing and film processing in the television drama are temporarily broken. In the graveyard, Gail experiences images which either she did not witness but the audience did (shots two to six), or images which she 'remembers' from the serial's back story, which the audience have not yet witnessed (the family portrait (shot ten) and the fire (shot eleven)). Therefore, these unusual point-of-view sequences have multiple purposes within the structure of the serial narrative: they suggest supernatural or psychical sight (premonitions, the 'evil eye', hallucinations, etc.); they allow for the incorporation of images which are not directly linked to narrative events but which speak to the narrative on a thematic level (such as the recurrence of the raven motif in Sheriff Buck's point-of-view sequences, suggesting a sense of evil); and they act as a kind of storytelling 'shorthand' whereby unseen parts of the back story may be sketchily 'filled in' or earlier parts of the narrative may be economically recapped. This latter use of the psychical montage sequence, a visual representation of the 'return of the repressed' becomes particularly useful towards the later episodes of a long-running, twenty-two week serial, in that a 'previously on *American Gothic*' sequence can be integrated into the diegetic space and time of the narrative. This notably occurs in episode sixteen, 'Dr. Death Takes a Holiday' (CBS, 1996), whereby a lengthy montage of images from the serial is interspersed with pictorial representations of the devil in a visualisation of Dr. Matt Crower's (Jake Weber's) mental disintegration. Here, it can be argued, the generic conventions of Gothic television and the conventions of the long-running serial drama format come together.

If, as proposed in the introduction to this book, Gothic television produces a sense of the uncanny through its returns and repetitions, it can be argued that the formal organisation of the television serial strengthens this sense of 'uncanny return'. The serial drama, in which the narrative returns to the same characters, locations and situations each week, relies precisely on a repetitive structure to re-identify the series (such as repetition of certain graphics or a particular credit sequence) and to re-familiarise the viewer with the 'story so far' (through expositionary dialogue and the 'last week on *American Gothic*' recap). Richard Dyer has argued that this 'mix of repetition and anticipation, and indeed the anticipation of repetition . . . underpins serial pleasure' (1997: 14). However, in the context of serials like those discussed in this chapter, this serial pleasure is also underpinned by a kind of serial uncanniness, whereby the repetitions of the serial reinforce an uncanny feeling of *dreadful* recognition.[12] This is not to argue that all serial television is uncanny in its structural repetitions or returns: rather, that the serial form lends itself particularly well to a drama of the uncanny in which the processes of viewer recognition strengthen a feeling of uncanniness. As Freud suggests, '[repetition] does undoubtedly, subject to certain conditions and combined with certain circumstances, arouse an uncanny feeling' (1990: 358–9). In the context of Gothic television, these 'conditions and circumstances' are the narrative preoccupations with the supernatural and the uncanny.

In *Millennium*, the use of this supernatural point-of-view sequence is even more prevalent, and provides what Chris Carter has described as 'the visual conceit of the show'.[13] Here Carter implies that these psychical points of view provide *Millennium* with the distinctiveness or 'branding' essential to a programme's success within the era of televisuality. These sequences are used frequently in the show to connote three different subjective positions: the telepathy of the central protagonist, Frank Black (a kind of super-empathy with the killer's own point of view as he 'detects' snatches of crime-scene detail); the terrified point of view of the victims, whom, it is suggested by the broken-ness of these sequences, have been frightened out of 'coherent' sight; and the psychical point of view of the criminal mind, which, it is implied, is either too sick or too evil to see as 'normal' humans do. As with *American Gothic*, the sequences in *Millennium* are also marked by a kind of formal experimentation not seen elsewhere in the serial, using innovative production techniques to render the psychical point of view as 'othered' within the programme's broader aesthetic. In the '*Millennium* Pilot', for example, these sequences were shot on 16mm Video News film[14] (although other film, video and photographic stocks were experimented with later in the serial), a film usually used for news or documentary filming which gave the sequences a rough, grainy quality as opposed to the slick, cinematic-looking 35mm footage used for the main narrative.[15] Peter Wunstorf, director of photography on the '*Millennium* Pilot' episode, describes a system of 'in camera' edits that made these sequences appear jumpy and distorted:

> The killer doesn't see the world the way the rest of us do, so I had to figure out how to make his point of view different . . . During filming we would start and stop the camera, creating a lot of flash frames and providing edit points . . . We felt this would be an effective way to give a distorted point of view without going over the top. (Probst, 1997: 74)

Here the experimentation with film stocks and shooting processes, as detailed above, both creates a 'visual conceit' for the serial (as suggested by Carter) and marks out a moment of narrative interpolation, a standard device of the Gothic narrative wherein the central narrational perspective is interrupted by another. For instance, in the '*Millennium* Pilot', the first interpolation of supernatural subjectivity comes as Frank Black stands over the body of the dead stripper (Kimm Wakefield). As Black prevents the mortician from opening the body bag, a cut is made from a low angle medium shot of him barely looking at the body to a series of images, edited 'in camera' and accompanied by screams and the sound of breaking glass. Here we see shots of the young woman struggling against the camera (representing the position of the killer), lasting only a second, followed by a return shot of Black's face in close-up, and then a second sequence, this time accompanied by heavy breathing and showing the blood spattered carpet and the top of the stripper's face, again lasting only a second (see figure 5.4). Following the second sequence, a cut is made back to Black, in close-up, as he mutters, 'She was decapitated'. It will be argued in the conclusion of this chapter that this sequence, and the other moments of supernatural subjectivity in *Millennium*, serve to suggest, rather than graphically depict, extreme violence. However, in the context of this analysis of the formal experimentation and 'stylishness' of the televisual Gothic, we can view sequences such as the one described above as providing the 'visual signature' of the show, evidencing the conjunction of expressivity and innovation within the Gothic television drama.

5.4 Supernatural sight: '*Millennium* Pilot',
Millennium (10:13, 1996).

Other important technological developments in relation to the representation of the supernatural are those which can be described under
the umbrella term 'motion control'. These devices, such as computer
programmed cameras, Steadicam, Camrail, robotic controlled studio
cameras, jib arms and motorised cranes are, according to Caldwell, 'all
alike in one important way: they physically take the camera away from
the camera operator's eyes and move it through space in very fluid ways'
(1995: 80). The impact of this kind of movement is that it lends itself to
the representation of a subjectivity which is, in Caldwell's words, 'eerily
non-human' (1995: 80). Through computer/robotic/motorised operation, subjectivity is dislocated from actual human subjectivity and thus,
within the realm of Gothic television particularly, can be more easily
aligned to super-human or supernatural sight. One might therefore
argue that this technology is taken to its natural conclusion on Gothic
television, whether through the representation of ghosts, demons or
other supernatural beings, or through the depiction of a psychical rather
than physical terrain. Indeed, if, as Caldwell argues, 'the televisual
image no longer seems to be anchored by the comforting, human eye-
level view of the pedestal-mounted camera, but floats like the eye of a
cyborg' (1995: 18), one might quite easily replace his cyborg analogy
with that of the spirit, and read these as developments in the possibility
of representing supernatural subjectivity. This technique is most pronounced in *American Gothic*, both in the evocation of Merlyn Temple's
angelic spirit and in the suggestion of Sheriff Buck's supernatural omniscience over the town of Trinity.

Another important innovation in television production which radically enabled the production of cinematically televisual television in the

latter half of the decade is the rise of computer generated imagery. The introduction of digital technology whereby computer generated images are relatively easily sutured into the 'real world' of a programme, has revolutionised the possibilities of representation on television, allowing for the 'believable' depiction of the fantastic/supernatural, while also being employed within more traditionally realist or non-fictional genres.[16] As well as leading to further specialisation (and subsequent fragmentation) within the television production industry (studios are often employed by producers to produce their particular 'speciality' effects),[17] the use of CGI may be seen as evidence of television's increasing budgets and the lure of visually spectacular television with a certain cinematic stylishness for the television viewer. CGI effects in *American Gothic* include the 'materialisation' as if from nowhere of Merlyn's angel-spirit, or the morphing of her face on to various other characters and objects (see, for example, the sequence in the episode 'Inhumanitas' (CBS, 1996), in which she 'possesses' a statue of the Virgin Mary (see figure 5.5)). These are uncanny techniques whereby the dead appear from out of the ether, and inanimate objects are brought 'to life', and can be seen as a visualisation of the automata or 'living dolls' which Jentsch (1995) locates as a key source of the uncanny in his essay on the subject. Here, the computer generated image is both central to the thematic concerns of the drama and also acts as a sophisticated stylistic flourish, differentiating *American Gothic* from other television dramas. This delineation of the 'technological ecstasies' of recent American Gothic television thus

5.5 CGI representation of the uncanny: 'Inhumanitas', *American Gothic* (CBS, 1996).

suggests that these serials offered a high level of visual stylishness, but that this was at the service of the key concerns of Gothic television, as outlined in this study and revisited below.

American Gothic and the family narrative

As discussed in the previous chapter, the American Gothic is inextricably linked to notions of the home and family as formulated within national ideology (the 'American Dream'), and has frequently been understood as a genre which exposes the 'other side' of more benign representations of domesticity. In North American culture, this 'other side' of the American Dream is often represented regionally, in relation to the southern states of America. Teresa A. Goddu, for example, writes that 'identified with Gothic doom and gloom, the American South serves as the nation's "other", becoming the repository for everything from which the nation wants to disassociate itself' (1997: 3–4). A. Robert Lee concurs: taking 'The Fall of the House of Usher' as the Southern Gothic's 'founding text' (1998: 217), Lee argues that Poe's story offers 'a long supposed perfect Gothic image of "The South", the Deep South that is, shot through with brooding family darkness and a deeply inward sense of the past as burden . . . Here, indeed, was another kind of American "house" replete with its ghosts [and] inverted desire,' (1998: 217–18). The television serial *American Gothic* clearly draws on this association of the 'Deep South' with the Gothic representation of the family and the family home.

Returning to the notion that the American Gothic is somehow a manifestation of the 'underside' of the American Dream, we might look towards the ways in which *American Gothic* demonstrates an awareness of the duality of American family life in the Deep South. In the opening sequence of the '*American Gothic* Pilot', in which Sheriff Buck's voice-over is played over a sunny, soft focus montage of quotidian activity in Trinity, this conflict between the surface and the 'underside' of the American Dream is dramatised. As the camera pans past picket fences and wooden swings, an image of small-town bliss and neighbourly (racial) harmony is created, established in order to make the following sequence all the more shocking (in which Buck enters the Temple house and murders the young Merlyn). During this montage, Sheriff Buck ironically offers the following: 'Now I've heard it said that the American Dream is a thing of the past. That the basic tenets of home, job, and family are slipping away. Well, not in my town. Where I come from that dream is still a reality. 'Course, you have to know who's boss.' This opening of the serial therefore draws precisely on the aforementioned duality of images of domestic perfection and familial harmony; here the picket fences and housewives sweeping their front porches represent the façade of American idealism, when viewed in conjunction with the Gothic's representations of domestic and family life. In the context of *American Gothic*, this duality is immediately presented to the viewer as the episode cuts from the opening montage to the establishing shot of the Temples' house. At this point a sunny long shot of the family home is quickly transformed, through stop-motion photography, into a dark, night-time shot of the same, in a matter of a couple of seconds. If the house is read as a metonym for 'family' and its associated values, then this short sequence visualises both sides of the American Dream as presented in the American Gothic: the sunny façade and its dark underside.

The basic premise of the serial, established from the outset, is very much in keeping with the delineation of the American Gothic offered above and in the previous chapter. As a serial immersed in the guilty secrets of family pasts and the conflict between family life as it appears and as it actually *is*, *American Gothic* presents the classic American Gothic narrative. During the serial's twenty-two week run, the viewer learns that Caleb is Sheriff Buck's illegitimate son, conceived as Caleb's mother was raped and his sister traumatised by witnessing the event. In the '*American Gothic* Pilot' episode, Caleb's father (the man who raised him) attacks his daughter, Merlyn (whose mental state means she cannot stop reliving the traumatic rape), and then is arrested by Sheriff Buck, who secretly finishes off the father's attack by killing Merlyn himself. In prison, Caleb's father is goaded into suicide by Buck who, it appears, has a supernatural ability to control others, and Caleb runs from the Sheriff under the guidance of his sister's spirit, pursued by Buck, and also his cousin Gail and Dr. Matt Crower, all of whom want to look after him. Throughout the serial then, the impact of the events of the '*American Gothic* Pilot' episode continues to shape the narrative, thus keeping the familial past at the centre of the serial. Even within the opening episode, the backstory of family trauma is reconstructed when Caleb runs away from Sheriff Buck and back to his family home.

During Caleb's return home, the computer generated angelic spirit of Caleb's dead sister appears, and proceeds to reveal to Caleb what family life was like before his mother's rape. At this point in the narrative, the living room is transformed, using the computer generated 'molecular' effect which also brings about Merlyn's materialisation, into the happy family home it once was, in order to show Caleb how he was conceived (and to fill in some more of the backstory for the viewer) (see figure 5.6).

5.6 CGI return of the repressed: '*American Gothic* Pilot', *American Gothic* (CBS, 1996).

With Caleb superimposed in the left hand foreground of the shot, the degraded living room behind him is transformed into a warmly lit, soft-focus shot of Caleb's mother reading to his sister as a young girl, creating an image of 'family' more suited to a TV 'movie of the week'. However, as the Sheriff arrives and proceeds to attack his mother, camera movements become more frenzied, with whip pans and fast zooms undercutting the apparently idyllic image of home until Caleb screams 'No!' and closes his eyes, thus dissolving the image. This audio-visual reconstruction of the moment of family trauma therefore acts as a dramatisation of the central conceit of the American Gothic: that homely perfection is only found on the surface, and that families are continually threatened by the exposure of grisly ancestral secrets.

Throughout the serial, Merlyn continues to return after her death as Caleb's guardian angel, to protect him from the evil which lies dormant in Caleb's soul due to his genetic parentage, and which may be awoken by the influence of Sheriff Buck on his life. As such, this serial is very much focused upon the generic struggle between good and evil, in the form of the struggle to overcome genetically inherited behaviour. Whereas Sheriff Buck as a father figure presents Caleb with a set of innate supernatural abilities and a proclivity towards evil, Dr. Crower and other 'good' characters (Merlyn, his foster-carer Miss Holt, etc.) present a highly moral version of family and child rearing, in which care triumphs over genetics. In essence, the story of *American Gothic* is the story of the conflict between inherited and learned behaviour. Beginning with the opening episode, this struggle is represented in a rather simplistic duality between two characters. Here then, the American Gothic is presented as a morality tale, in which the issues of family, paternity and inheritance are played out, and in which concerns over genetics replace the more usual European Gothic preoccupation with issues of monetary inheritance (see *The Woman in White* (BBC1, 1997) or *The Wyvern Mystery* (BBC1, 2000), for example).

Subsequently, a highly conservative and morally idealistic notion of 'family' and 'care' is implied, even within a genre which highlights the 'other side' of family life. The episodic structure of the serial not only allows for the presentation of an extended narrative of guilt and fear surrounding the Temple family, but also introduces weekly storylines which focus on the trauma of the other families in Trinity being manipulated by the satanic forces of Sheriff Buck, with each episode providing a self-contained American Gothic parable. For example, in the fourth episode, 'Damned If You Don't' (CBS, 1995), the Brown family are taunted by Buck through the reappearance of Wash Sutpen (Muse Watson), let out of prison after killing a man who he believed had had sex with his daughter. When Sheriff Buck tells Sutpen that Carter Brown (Steve Rankin) was in fact the man having an affair with his daughter, the released man threatens to do the same to Brown's own daughter and eventually goads Brown into killing his own wife. Again, in later episodes, families are torn apart by guilty secrets, broken family oaths, infidelity and domestic violence, all stock narratives of American Gothic television. In these episodes and others, as in the meta-narrative of *American Gothic*, the family is constantly depicted as the site of past transgressions and a traumatic revisitation of history.

Millennium: strangers in the house

While *Twin Peaks* and *American Gothic* offer family-centred episodic narratives which are recognisable as American Gothic narratives, drawing on plots, characterisations and imagery which are easily identifiable within nationally specific Gothic convention, *Millennium* may initially seem more elusive in terms of generic categorisation. Essentially a police procedural serial killer drama, *Millennium* developed from season to season, latterly becoming associated with Carter's own brand of paranoid, government-conspiracy drama, and his earlier show, *The X-Files*. However, in the first season of *Millennium* (in which the boundaries of the serial's initial generic identity were set), the focus was once again placed on the threatened American family, plagued by monstrous villains and guilty secrets, a focus which, it has been argued, is characteristic of new American Gothic television. While *Twin Peaks* and *American Gothic* take the threat to the American family as coming from within its own confines, *Millennium* is primarily concerned with narratives of domestic invasion, in which the home and the family unit are seen as prey for external forces of evil. These 'forces of evil' are frequently found in the form of the most common Gothic villain of the twentieth century: the serial killer. While all three seasons of the show focused on Frank Black's investigation of serial killing and serial killers, the formative season of *Millennium* concentrated most fully on these figures and the threat which they posed to the sanctity of 'normal' family life (and particularly the detective's own family), alongside other, more supernatural, threats.

As well as centring on the grisly detail of serial killing, *Millennium* focuses on the home life of detective Frank Black, and in doing so it 'sets up the stakes' of domestic invasion within the American Gothic narrative. From the outset of the serial, the viewer is presented with an image of Black's home and family life which is almost allegoric in its idealistic representation. As Richard Dyer has argued:

> Just as in the Westerns and gangster films of yore, home is the realm of normal reproductive sexuality at stake in the hero's engagement with the killer's abnormal destructive world. He is protecting home from what the killer represents, doing his bit to make the world safe for women and children. The potential invasion of the home is the deepest anxiety in . . . *Millennium* (where it provides a running weekly cliff-hanger). (1997: 17)

Dyer's comparison with Westerns and gangster films is insightful. Here the duality of the American Gothic, the simultaneous appearance of an ideal home and family and the acknowledgement that this ideal is not stable or safe, is writ large throughout each episode of *Millennium*. In the opening episode, Frank Black explains the motive for his work with serial killers: 'I'm here because I have a wife and a kid and I want them to live in a place where they can feel safe'. As discussed in the previous chapter, this representation of a rather saccharine version of North American domesticity within the American Gothic narrative is not a new phenomenon, as Karen Halttunen's work on eighteenth century murder narratives has shown (1998). In the 1990s however, sentimentalised depictions of domesticity were most frequently represented with deep conviction on television (in situation comedies and soap operas, for example), and therefore perhaps it is fitting that a proliferation of narratives of domestic murder should also appear on this medium.

Each time the Black family is introduced in *Millennium*, brightly lit, relatively soft-focus images are used which seek to create a sentimental image of the family. The programme's makers have adamantly stated that different kinds of cinematography were essential in marking the duality between 'home' and the criminal spaces of the serial. According to Peter Wunstorf, director of photography on the '*Millennium* Pilot', 'Gary Wissner and David [Nutter] had been already talking about a motif for the show, which was a sort of heaven and hell concept, with heaven being Frank's home life . . . That idea was then reflected in the art direction and lighting' (Probst, 1996: 48). This concept is also confirmed by Chris Carter: 'When we go to the [Black's] house, we want the photography to help create the feeling of a safe place. So you don't want the camera circling or whip-panning. You want all of the moves to be as normal and as comforting as possible' (Probst, 1996: 52). This notion of visually 'marking out' the family spaces of *Millennium*, by using different film stocks, brighter lighting and static, familiarising camerawork, is also reflected aurally within the serial. Mark Snow, the musical director of the serial, created an incidental score for the serial whereby the sanctity of the Blacks' yellow house is reinforced by a change in tone of the extra-diegetic music: when the narrative returns to the house, the score frequently becomes 'lighter' or more upbeat than the suspenseful, mournful violin theme used in the serial to denote moments of fear or sadness.

Each episode of *Millennium* is based on a similar structure, shifting back and forth between the crime scene and Black's family home. By using this alternating structure, the polarity between the two spaces of the narrative is repeatedly emphasised. However, as well as emphasising the distance between the family home and the spaces of criminality, the dual format of the narrative also seeks to emphasise a certain closeness between these spaces. Editing techniques are often used to accentuate this closeness by moving from one space to the other using matches on image or action, thus drawing a visual comparison between the scenes. In the second episode of *Millennium*, 'Gehenna' (10:13, 1996), when Black first visits a crime scene in San Francisco where a large amount of burnt human remains have been found, an extreme close-up of a human ear is shown lying in a pile of ashes. Subsequently, when the action returns to the 'Yellow House' in the following scene, the first interior shot is again a close-up of an ear, this time that of Black's daughter, Jordan (Brittany Tiplady), being licked by her dog. While this is not a direct match on image (a direct cut from the first 'ear shot' to the second), visual echoes of the crime scene in San Francisco can be seen to enter into the domestic setting here. Moments such as this thus allow for a dissolution of boundaries between the family home and the site of crime, with the binary plot structure drawing comparison, rather than contrast, between these two spaces.

The central horror in this first season of *Millennium* is found, unsurprisingly, in the moments in which the sanctity of the Black home is penetrated by the criminal 'other' of the Gothic narrative, and the distance drawn between Black's family and the outside world no longer exists. Even in the serial's title sequence, this fear is invoked by a montage of images suggestive of domestic invasion, coupled with sinister, ambiguous shots of unidentifiable shadowy figures. *Millennium* is punctuated throughout by moments in which Frank believes his family to be in danger from those he is stalking, and this fear is brought to a climax towards the end of the first season in the episode 'Lamentation' (10:13, 1997), where a serial killer's wife, Lucy Butler (Sarah Jane Redman), and two other figures which 'supernaturally' appear at the same time as her (a sinister-looking man-woman and devil-like creature), break into the Blacks' house, terrifying Catherine and Jordan, and killing Frank's friend, Detective Bob Bletcher (Bill Smitrovich). At this point in the narrative, the futility of the detective's attempts to keep the evil of a society under threat from serial murder from infiltrating the safety of his family home is clear.

It is not only the detective's family who are threatened by an externalised evil in *Millennium*, however: episode after episode, victims are attacked within the confines of their home, thus building up a kind of 'domestic victimology' whereby an image of the North American home as a safe space is no longer valid. Whether in affluent, middle-class neighbourhoods, or more typical suburban dwellings, the family home is depicted as a permeable space which is easily infiltrated by serial murderers and, in some cases, the supernatural forces of evil. In 'Paper Dove' (10:13, 1997), for example, it is the very ordinariness of the victim's home, and the ease with which the killer enters it, which highlights the horrific moment within this particular version of the televisual Gothic. At the beginning of this episode, the viewer is introduced to both the killer (Henry Dion (Mike Starr)) and the victim (Amy Lee Walker (Angela Donahue)) to the sounds of rock singer Wayne Kramer's 'Stranger in the House', as he follows her home from the supermarket. A series of shots inside the victim's house confirm the 'everyday-ness' of her activities: a close-up of her finger automatically keying the code on the security system key pad, followed by shots of her putting her groceries away. The act of putting the shopping away, as an ultimately quotidian moment, frames the ensuing horror as a disruption of everyday activity. Indeed, unknowingly, believing that it is her husband who has just entered the house, she chats to the killer about what kind of cheese and crackers she bought at the supermarket. Cutting from these shots of banal domesticity as Amy realises that her husband is not talking back, a slow pan from her point of view takes in the sight of the deranged killer standing in her kitchen wearing nothing but a pair of rubber wading trousers. This moment thus stresses the very commonplace nature of the domestic activity which is so easily and startlingly infringed upon by horror here: in *Millennium*, the serial killer is most certainly at home within the domestic space.

Gothic television's focus on domestic space has been examined elsewhere in this book: in chapter three, for example, it was argued that certain formal techniques, such as the use of character-specific subjective camerawork and sound recording, and a repeated emphasis on the house as a Gothic location, drew a parallel between those domestic spaces on screen and those in which the drama was to be watched. In *Millennium*, a similar correlation is also drawn by the programme makers, who expressly wished to make a connection between the image on screen and the 'model viewer' at home. As with the female Gothic adaptations discussed in chapter three, *Millennium*'s makers also acknowledged the importance of point of view in creating viewer-protagonist identification within Gothic television, as a way of suturing the model viewing into the narrative. As David Nutter explains, 'one of the things that Chris Carter has instilled in me is that point of view is so very important. You always have to ask, "Who are you with in this scene?" . . . Rather than just sitting back observing the event, I think the camera should be part of the characters' (Probst, 1996: 50). Furthermore, Nutter states that the serial's visual design was aimed at blurring the line between the homes on screen and the domestic viewing spaces:

> The new film stocks can see so much and pick up so much image, and the effect I wanted to achieve was that when people were in their house at night and the lights were off and they were watching the show, that the black on the side of the screen would bleed off and make the audience feel like they're part of the show, that they're part of the story. (Vitaris, 1997: 25)

Here, the potential of the dark spaces of the programme to 'bleed off' into the homes of the serial's viewers highlights the aims of the Gothic drama made for television: to suggest a congruence between the domestic spaces on screen and the domestic reception context.

Millennium, and other televisual Gothic serials which place the family home at the centre of their narratives, refute Ellis Cashmore's argument that the domestic viewing context provides a 'safe space' from which to view endangered characters on screen:

> There is a nice tension in watching a crime show: in identifying with figures who are perpetually at risk. Perhaps it is the kind of risk we crave as a contrast to our own society . . . We, as viewers, are able vicariously to

share the risk in the safety of our own homes and with a reasonable certainty that the morally right characters will come to no harm. (1994: 171)

In the context of *Millennium* at least, this reasonable certainty, that
morally right characters in the safety of their own homes will come to no
harm, is undercut by the serial's relentless insistence on the randomness
and ordinariness of the victims selected, many of whom are taken
directly out of their family homes by a seemingly endless stream of serial
killers. With a clear emphasis on shared point of view between detective,
victim and viewer, and the intentional suturing of the domestic spaces
(on screen and off), the serial potentially sets up a thrilling 'it could be
me' response in the model viewer which defies Cashmore's cosy image
of television watching. Therefore Gothic television drama takes on new
meaning (and arguably a greater propensity for viewer 'affect') when
watched at home. Throughout the publicity campaign for *Millennium*,
the serial's creator, Chris Carter, insisted that this point of connection
between victims' and viewers' homes was entirely justified, seeing the
representation of the family home under threat as a kind of public
service. In conversation with Alan Yentob, then outgoing controller
of BBC1,[18] Chris Carter announced the following at the Edinburgh
Television Festival:

> What I am concerned about is content because I think that the climate
> of American television right now is very anti-reality . . . I'm flying in the
> face of that. I think that what I am doing is very responsible to the world
> we live in. By telling these stories I am addressing the world and educat-
> ing people. I hope this is a show that seeks to do more than entertain.
> (Yentob and Carter, 1996: 2)

Carter's statement here implicitly builds upon the 'it could be me'
impulse: by arguing that *Millennium* reflects the realities of domestic life
in the United States, the programme's creator sees the depiction of serial
killers who target families in their own homes as a kind of public service,
warning his viewers of the dangers of everyday life. While these kinds of
attacks in the 1990s were, in actuality, extremely unlikely, it is clear that
Millennium's programme makers wished to highlight the closeness of the
diegetic world to the 'real world' to give their programme an 'edge', albeit
in the somewhat spurious guise of providing a public service.

Family viewing

Chris Carter's defence of his serial brings this analysis of Gothic serial drama towards its conclusion, by raising the issue of the concerns

surrounding television, the Gothic narrative and the morality of consuming tales of family trauma and serial murder as entertainment. On a thematic level, what *Twin Peaks, American Gothic* and *Millennium* share, both with each other and with other contemporaneous Gothic television dramas in the US, is a certain tangible anxiety built around the domestic spaces of the diegesis. This anxiety of domestic invasion, coupled with these serials' dramatisation of what could be termed 'supernatural sight' or uncanny vision, might, in fact, be read as textual enactments of ongoing concerns surrounding domestic space and television's position within the home.

To place these concerns into their proper context, one need only look to the thriving debates surrounding 'family viewing' which proliferated during the late 1990s, mainly fuelled by the religious right-wing in the US, to see why serials such as *American Gothic* and *Millennium* might wish to align themselves with a public service ethos and discourses of moral propriety. Anxieties around television viewing led to the establishment of the 1996 Telecommunications Law in the US, outlining, among other proposals, plans for a ratings system for television programmes and concerns about family viewing and the responsibilities of programme makers and television manufacturers. The findings of this Congressional bill also prompted the production of various television 'nannying' technologies such as the V-Chip (a chip placed in a television, VCR or satellite box which receives ratings codes broadcast by the networks and which blocks the reception of 'inappropriate' broadcasts), TVGuardian (a set-top 'profanity filter' which plugs into the television set), and the Weemote (a programmable remote control which only gives access to 'suitable' channels),[19] as well as widespread publicity campaigns regarding responsible parenting and television access. One of the most vociferous committees behind the campaign for 'family television' was the 'Parents' Television Council', who widely reported damning accounts of television programming in the United States during the 1990s on all the major news channels and aired concerns about what Mark Seltzer has described as the rise of a 'pathological public sphere' (2000: 101).

In relation to Gothic television, much of the criticism levelled at programmes such as *American Gothic* and *Millennium* cited the serials' disruption of family programming as the main point of contention against the shows. Once again, we might look towards *American Gothic*'s serial creator, Shaun Cassidy, given that so much was made in the press of the contrast between Cassidy's earlier television persona (as a teen heart throb from popular seventies family show, *The Hardy Boys Mysteries*) and the 'dark' content of *American Gothic*. For example, Colson Whitehead, discussing the censorship of the '*American Gothic* Pilot' in *The Village*

Voice, commented that 'maybe it was the fact that the show was created by former teen heartthrob Shaun Cassidy, and the censors weren't ready to see him da doo ron ronning into the macabre' (1995: 35). The conflict between the Gothic show and traditional family-led programming in the United States was also personified in the casting of Gary Cole as Sheriff Buck; Cole's most recent role before *American Gothic* had been Mike Brady, father of the family in *The Brady Bunch Movie* (US, 1995), a nostalgic film spin-off of the anodyne family-values sitcom *The Brady Bunch* (ABC, 1969–1972). This incongruity, between 'family television' and the Gothic, was also knowingly referred to within the serial itself: as Sheriff Buck visits Caleb's father in jail in the '*American Gothic* Pilot', he enters whistling the theme tune to another classic family show, *The Andy Williams Show* (NBC, 1962–71), thus ironically highlighting the distance between a Gothic serial, created by a 'Hardy Boy' and starring a 'Brady', and the saccharine, family-focused sitcom so perennially popular on primetime North American television.

As well as authorial incongruity, *American Gothic* was also seen as a bold commissioning decision on the part of CBS, one of the 'big three' networks in the US and a company more traditionally associated with 'lighter' family programming at the time. Although *American Gothic* was broadcast on Fridays at 10.00 p.m., after the watershed and outside 'family viewing' hours, it was still scheduled in a high profile Friday night slot, on a major network. As Colson Whitehead notes, 'Perhaps what was so beguiling about *Gothic* initially was that the gruesomeness usually banished to television's margins – cable, syndication, Fox – had been sucked into primetime, with a real primetime budget' (1995: 35). CBS issued a warning before the first episode of *American Gothic*, stating that the show was possibly unsuitable for a 'family audience': 'CBS . . . was so spooked about what middle America might think – and the opportunities it might provide for politicians to fulminate about V-chips – that the opening episode was preceded by an "advisory", a warning that viewers might not like what was to follow' (Jivani, 1996: 157). While one could read this pre-show warning as a disingenuous move to attract viewers through prohibition, perhaps it also provided the first evidence of CBS' squeamishness about its new show. *American Gothic*'s producers have suggested that the programme's eventual 'failure' on its initial broadcast[20] can be explained by the show's incongruity on CBS, and that CBS' foray into the televisual Gothic was an ill-advised desire to imitate Fox's success with their hit paranormal serial, *The X-Files*:

> *American Gothic* appeared ready to handle the throng of viewers which CBS was certain would be tuning in after *The X-Files*. The network was

looking to change its image and was hoping that the offbeat series would help them make such a transition . . . [Shaun Cassidy] 'If you look at CBS now you'll see that they want to be a very traditional, homespun place . . . When we went to CBS the network was in a state of transition and for five minutes they thought they wanted to be Fox'. (Eramo, 1997: 13–14)

This brief summary of *American Gothic*'s commissioning, scheduling and reception thus suggests that those concerns about family viewing outlined above had a great impact on American Gothic television.

Arguably, the producers of Gothic television show themselves to be acutely aware of these concerns surrounding family viewing, and, to a certain extent, all of the programmes discussed in this chapter pre-empted or responded to criticism by dramatising concerns surrounding viewing within their ongoing narratives. One need only look towards the anxiety that surrounds the act of looking in *Millennium* to find a textual enactment of the potential of the Gothic image to corrupt. In this serial, Frank Black's hallucinations are often described as both a gift and a curse, and can be read as a form of 'watching' which directly refers to the act of television viewing: the facts that Black need not be present at a murder to witness it, that he experiences death/murder vicariously rather than 'first hand' and that certain objects within the crime scene 'transmit' these images to him, all suggest that his visions are both supernatural and 'like television'. Similarly, in *Twin Peaks*, Sarah Palmer's 'visions' of her daughter's killer suggest a supernatural, television-like sight, an ability to see beyond 'the real'. Throughout the narrative, she is depicted as a 'viewer', her over-involvement in what she sees causing hysterical reactions, and thus she performs the role of viewer 'at risk'. If we read these visions as a kind of self-referential comment on the propriety of watching murder narratives, then this ambivalence clearly offers comment on the concerns surrounding family viewing within Gothic television's diegesis.

American Gothic also performs a kind of textual enactment of the anxiety of looking. For instance, the serial frequently returns in flashback to the scene in the opening episode when the Sheriff's deputy, Ben Healy (Nick Searcy), accidentally oversees Buck murdering Merlyn Temple through her bedroom window, to the point at which these visions nearly drive him mad. Also, in the sequence discussed above where Caleb's sister's spirit returns home and recreates her own moment of horror, both children watching from the edge of the 'vision' are shown in extreme close-up in a traumatised state, witnessing this act of profound violence. When Caleb simply asks his sister 'why?', she replies 'because you have to know the truth'. Echoing this sentiment, Shaun Cassidy suggested that he too was showing 'life as it really is', in a CBS press conference at Universal Studios following a showing of the opening episode for television critics:

> Right, there are seventy children a week, according to the National Council of Domestic Violence, that are killed in their homes by parents or guardians . . . This is a real issue, and we're not a political show, certainly . . . But when you're talking about an issue like that, I would hope that it is shocking. And I would hope that it causes discomfort. And I would hope within the context of our show, we can address those issues and actually use it as a forum, because the world is scary right now. There's a lot of this going on. (Gothic Phantom)

Here, as with Carter and *Millennium*, Cassidy expresses a kind of 'public service' approach to family viewing and the appropriateness of the Gothic narrative for television, just as he dramatised these anxieties within the serial's narrative.

So the question of how to deal with these problems of morality and broadcasting standards remains an issue. Just as television personnel struggled with these problems in the UK in the 1950s (see the opening of chapter one), so Gothic television in the United States in the 1990s continued to seek to find a way around representing horror within a domestic context. Perhaps this issue is reflected in both *Millennium* and *American Gothic*'s ironic, self-referential antagonism towards their own medium, both in the depiction of television as negative force within North American culture, and in the representation of television as a point of access through which the horrifying/terrifying may enter the domestic space. In *Millennium*, for example, television is to blame for kidnap,[21] is constantly disparaged by Frank Black, and is repeatedly shown within the diegesis as sensationalising or trivialising violence. For example, as Black lies in bed with his wife in the episode 'Dead Letters' (10:13, 1996), a cut is made from the police station to a TV image from a 'real crime' show, the edge of the screen barely visible within the frame. Following this cut, the channel is switched to a chat show. Here, then, the diegetic channel hopping emphasises the use of crime as entertainment, while simultaneously depicting the television set as a point of entry for the criminal narrative into the home. At this point, and others like it, *Millennium* is both highly self-referential and simultaneously morally outraged by its own medium (and perhaps even its own genre).

Ultimately, *American Gothic* dealt with the problem of its suitability within a 'family medium' through its rather ostentatious sense of 'morality', whereby each episode was clearly assigned 'good' characters who 'win through' by behaving according to traditional 'family values'. It is through this treatment of the 'episode as parable' format, and through the serial's depiction of the other, 'good' side of the American

Gothic narrative, that the serial attempted to escape from the relentless bleakness of the genre. The presence of angels in the serial can be understood as redemptive, for example, tapping into an aspect of Gothic culture in the 1990s described by Mark Edmundson as 'the culture of facile transcendence . . . inspired by the belief that self-transformation is as simple as a fairy-tale wish' (1997: xv). *Millennium*, on the other hand, ultimately reverts to the suggestive, restrained visual style of earlier Gothic television to answer the problem of broadcasting standards and family viewing. The serial's central visual conceit (the supernatural points of view discussed above) allowed for a representation of extreme violence and serial murder which, like the ghost stories on British Gothic television in the 1960s and 1970s, 'showed less and suggested more'. These montage sequences rather judiciously represented violence and gruesomeness on screen in a suggestive, non-graphic, way, thus avoiding the censorship of television's regulatory bodies and fears for the family viewer. For example, looking back at the first of Frank Black's 'visions' in the '*Millennium* Pilot' episode, the series of shots, jumpily edited 'in camera' and accompanied by screams, the sound of breaking glass and heavy breathing, only show a limited number of images (the young woman struggling against the camera and the blood spattered carpet and the top of the stripper's face), and do so in a matter of seconds, thus avoiding the graphic depiction of the murder which is subsequently described as a decapitation. Several formal techniques render this montage (and others) as suggestively indistinct (fast editing, blurry, handheld camerawork, non-synchronous sound, etc.), and therefore, while the overall effect of the montage sequences is horrific, the viewer is not actually privy to the act of horror. The viewer is in fact twice removed from the moment of horror, as it is neither depicted 'first hand' within the narrative, nor is it depicted 'second hand' in an easily readable or viewable way. Chris Carter explicitly cited this use of the impressionistic montage as a 'way round' broadcasting standards: 'We don't show all that much on the show . . . We show things in flashes. They're impressionistic; they're not graphic, and it's what we don't show that is the more interesting part of the show' (Vitaris, 1997: 26). To conclude this examination of Gothic television then, it is clear that in moments such as the 'vision' discussed above, the identifying formal techniques of the televisual Gothic concurrently mark out *Millennium*'s visual stylishness, allow for a representation of the American Gothic which is very much grounded within the quotidian spaces of the family home, and ultimately appease those concerns surrounding family viewing and the morality of viewing the Gothic narrative, by reverting to techniques of suggestion established much earlier in the history of the genre.

Notes

1 Indeed, it is possible to add to Ledwon's list: for example, Laura Palmer's psychiatrist, Dr. Jacobi, can be read as the 'mad doctor' typical of Gothic fiction, with the mysterious Log Lady acting as its supernatural seer; Laura Palmer's tape, produced for her therapist, might be viewed as a further example of interpolated narration, and so on.

2 Extract from director's commentary (episode 01), *Twin Peaks Season One* DVD (Playback/Universal/Republic Pictures, 2002).

3 Extract from director of photography's commentary (episode 03), *Twin Peaks Season One* DVD (Playback/Universal/Republic Pictures, 2002).

4 First seen in the third episode, 'Zen, or the Skill to Catch a Killer' (Lynch-Frost Productions, 1990).

5 Original emphasis.

6 More recently, a cycle of 'Gothic teen dramas' has appeared on US and UK television, perhaps initiated by the success of *Twin Peaks* and later *Buffy the Vampire Slayer* (20th Century Fox Television, 1997–2003). Shows such as *Point Pleasant* (20th Century Fox Television, 2005) in the US and *Hex* (Shine, 2004–) in the UK similarly centre on the teenager as troubled figure, 'haunted' by a sinister familial past.

7 *Millennium* premiered in the States 'with some of the best numbers for the season' (Genge, 1997: xi), but ratings soon fell, even though 'what numbers it was pulling in were all in the right demographics, that lucrative market between 18 and 49 years old' (Genge, 1997: xii). Similarly, *American Gothic* was viewed as a critical success which was not reflected in its viewing figures: 'although *American Gothic* was embraced by critics as well as viewers the series was, unfortunately, not the success that CBS was counting on so far as ratings go' (Eramo, 1997: 13).

8 'The pictures shown were animated and mobile, appearing to rush towards a terrified audience who were certainly not used to such an assault of images. In addition, the macabre show devised around this new type of projection heightened the impression of unease and fear in the spectators' (Mannoni, 2000: 136).

9 Such as the Pepper's Ghost trick (circa. 1860–90), which enabled a live actor's spectral image to appear on stage during a play, via a system of under-floor lights and mirrors (see Ranger, 1991).

10 Videographic televisuality is described as 'an appreciation for multiple electronic feeds, image-text combinations, videographics, and studios with banks of monitors that evoked video installations' (Caldwell, 1995: 13).

11 *American Gothic* was made for an average of $1 million per episode, and *Millennium* was given an 'almost unheard of budget for a television program' (Genge, 1997: 10) at $1.5 million per episode.

12 I make this argument in relation to the Danish Gothic hospital drama, *Riget/The Kingdom*, elsewhere (see Wheatley, 2002).

13 Taken from an interview which precedes the 'Pilot' on its commercial video release in the UK (released by 20th Century Fox Home Entertainment on 26th January, 1998).

14 Eastman Kodak 7240 and 7250 Ektachrome colour reversal film, most commonly used for news and documentary filming.

15 Using Eastman Kodak EXR 5293 for day interior and exterior shots and 5298 for the night-time interiors and exteriors.

16 E.g. the fantasy flourishes of romantic comedy *Ally McBeal* (20th Century Fox Television, 1997–2002) or the recreation of dinosaurs and animals for the BBC's natural history programmes, starting with *Walking with Dinosaurs* (BBC1, 1999).

17 For example, the special effects company Vision Art in Los Angeles was employed by the makers of *American Gothic* solely for the purpose of creating the computer

generated 'molecular' effect of Merlyn's spirit's exits and entrances, whereby her body gradually appears, molecule by molecule, on screen (see figure 5.5 for another example of this technique).

18 A channel which had, under the direction of Michael Jackson, rejected the serial on the grounds of its 'unsuitable' content.

19 See, for example, http://www.familysafemedia.com, where a range of these devices are sold and promoted.

20 *American Gothic* was eventually removed from CBS' schedule, with the latter six episodes unbroadcast until the show was later syndicated.

21 In 'The Wild and the Innocent' (10:13, 1996) a young girl's baby is sold by her step-father in order to pay for an enormous widescreen TV.

Conclusion

In conclusion, Gothic television can be characterised by the meeting of two houses: the textual domestic spaces of Gothic television (haunted houses, decaying mansions, permeable family homes under threat from within and without) and the extra-textual domestic spaces of the medium (the homes in which Gothic television is viewed). This book has examined the dialogue between these two houses, arguing that structures of identification are laid in place which potentially render the Gothic on television as one of the most affective of genres. In the previous chapter of this book, for example, I argued that representations of domestic space in new American Gothic television are inherently tied to the assumed domestic contexts of the programmes' reception, reflecting on anxieties around television's status as a potentially invasive medium, and the 'problem' of family viewing. Therefore, it has been proposed that it is possible to look to the very fabric of the programmes in question to create a picture of the 'model viewer', who is 'recorded into' the texts of Gothic television.

On the other hand, however, the two houses at the centre of this study of Gothic television might be viewed as the two distinct bodies of criticism which provide the theoretical framework for this book, in that a productive dialogue has been created here between Gothic studies and television studies. While it might be (correctly) assumed that these are radically divergent fields of academic study, there are striking points of convergence between the two disciplines which, it is hoped, have been made apparent through this analysis of Gothic television. Indeed, these two disciplines are most clearly joined together by the concept of the uncanny. While the uncanny's relationship to the Gothic genre is well documented, to the point at which the two terms become almost synonymous, or indivisible, in certain areas of criticism, television studies' use of the uncanny as a pivotal concept within the understanding of television as a medium is less visible. However, if we look at the meta-analyses of television which have characterised its academic study, we see that the specific nature of broadcast television is located precisely within the terms of the uncanny, in that many explorations of television as medium rest precisely upon viewing the object of study as the meeting point of the familiar/everyday with the unfamiliar/extraordinary (a meeting which also defines the uncanny). To take a recent example of such an analysis of television to illustrate this point, we can look to John Ellis' notion of 'witness' (2000) to understand how television studies utilises the terms (if not the term) of the uncanny.

In his book *Seeing Things: Television in the Age of Uncertainty*, Ellis argues the following:

> The twentieth century has been the century of witness. As we emerge from that century, we can realise that a profound shift has taken place in the way that we perceive the world that exists beyond our immediate experience . . . [Television] has brought us face to face with the great events, banal happenings, the horrors and the incidental cruelties of our times. Perhaps we have seen too much. Certainly, 'I did not know' and 'I did not realise' are no longer open to us as a defence. (2000: 9)

Ellis qualifies television's ability to 'witness' by defining three eras of television broadcasting (the eras of scarcity, availability and plenty), delineating the purest form of witness in the era of scarcity, when the limited choice of broadcast television guaranteed a large domestic audience for individual programmes:

> Television allowed its viewers to witness remote events as they happened. Television provided its audiences with a powerful sense of co-presence with the events it showed. It provided them with a sense of togetherness in separation from their fellow audience members. It reached its audiences in their homes. Television made the act of witness into an intimate and domestic act. (2000: 32)

While Ellis argues that the act of viewing as witness is less united in the 'era of plenty' (i.e. in the age of stratified, digital, multi-channel television viewing at the beginning of the twenty-first century), he concludes that it remains an important aspect of broadcast television, arguing that '[television] will be distinguished by its continuing, crucial, social role of working through the emotions provoked by the process of witness' (2000: 178).

What the above description of John Ellis' work provides us with is an image of television studies' deployment of the terms of the uncanny. Ellis makes a strong case for the fact that television is characterised by its delivery of extraordinary events into the homes of its viewers, arguing that 'the great events, banal happenings, the horrors and the incidental cruelties of our times' *reach into* the domestic spaces in which a televi- sion set is located. It therefore seems to me that in describing broadcast television, Ellis describes the uncanny, whereby the unfamiliar (death, horror) is brought into the locale of the familiar (the home), almost to the point at which the unfamiliar becomes simultaneously familiar to the domestic viewer (we become used to seeing war, famine and other atrocities on television). To this definition of television studies' inherent use of the terms of uncanniness, we might also add that the medium's repetitive structures and built-in systems of recognition, also isolated within television studies as one of the medium's defining characteris- tics, can be identified as uncanny. If, as Freud proposes in his treatise on the uncanny, 'involuntary repetition . . . surrounds what would otherwise be innocent enough with an uncanny atmosphere' (1990: 359), then the repetitive patterns of television production and schedul- ing (as described in Raymond Williams' seminal study of the medium (1975), to give a prominent example) might also be seen as uncanny. I am not arguing here that television *as a whole* is inherently uncanny. Rather, I am proposing that television studies has, to this point, implic- itly taken up the terms of the uncanny to describe the nature of broad- cast television, and therefore the uncanny provides the initial point of dialogue between Gothic studies and television studies. Furthermore, the anxieties surrounding the broadcast of Gothic television identified in this book (fears about bringing death/horror into the domestic viewing space) might be seen as indicative of broader concerns around the propriety of television viewing as a whole.

At the time of this book's completion, there have been a number of new studies of television drama which engage in an analysis of Gothic or horror television, suggesting an increased interest in the genre within television studies. Eric Freedman's discussion of *Buffy the Vampire Slayer* (20th Century Fox Television, 1997–2003), for example, takes a similar stance to this book, arguing that, 'with the movement from film to television, horror and science fiction genres have literally invaded the domestic sphere and opened up the family room to the horrific world outside of this traditionally private and safe domain' (2005: 159). Like the analysis of *Twin Peaks* (Lynch-Frost Productions, 1990–91) offered in the previous chapter of this book, Freedman's analysis of the generic hybridity of *Buffy* finds the combination of the teen melodrama and horror particularly affective:

> Horror, science fiction and fantasy fit readily into the highly coded land- scape of melodrama for adolescent viewers, for individually and together

the generic elements of each form works towards expressing the anxieties of inbetween-ness – a metamorphosing body caught between child-
hood and adulthood. (2005: 161)[1]

Discussing *Buffy*'s sister show, *Angel* (20th Century Fox Television,
1999–2004), Matt Hills and Rebecca Williams have also argued that
horror television has become a prevalent form, though they identify
Angel as more generically traditional than *Buffy*, using Barbara Creed's
(1993) notion of the abject to understand *Angel*'s specific brand of
horror, looking at the ways in which abjection is visually and narratively
present, but restricted, within television horror.

Several contributors to Kim Akass and Janet McCabe's (2005) collection on the HBO show *Six Feet Under* (HBO, 2001–) have also identified this long-form serial as Gothic television or, more specifically, as an
American Gothic text (see Bundy, 2005; Merck, 2005; Heller, 2005).
Dana Heller, for example, argues that '*Six Feet Under*, although not a
Gothic text in the strict sense, employs distinctly Gothic conventions in
its study of psychic and cultural dislocation, or the "turns and tenden-
cies in the dismantling of the national subject"' (2005: 73), while
Mandy Merck focuses on the show's connection to the uncanny: '[Its]
narratives of "death and dead bodies . . . the return of the dead, and . . .
spirits and ghosts" invoke the thematics of the uncanny in what Freud
described as "the highest degree"' (2005: 63). The identification of *Six
Feet Under* as Gothic television is interesting; it would certainly seem to
me that, along with a number of other programmes recently identified
as 'quality US television', such as *The Sopranos* (HBO, 1999–2006) and
Desperate Housewives (ABC, 2004–), *Six Feet Under* refers to the Gothic
genre in its desire to distinguish itself as 'different', 'quirky' and 'more
intelligent' in some way, its ruminations on death and family trauma
(both staples of Gothic television) understood as its markers of 'quality'.

It is hoped that during the course of this study, it has become clear
that Gothic television provides us with moments of textual richness
within the flow of broadcast television. Many of the programmes discussed in this study have been characterised, to a greater or lesser
extent, by a sense of creativity and experimentation on the part of the
programme makers, as they responded to the challenges of presenting
the Gothic (and the supernatural and uncanny) on the small screen.
While the project of defining 'quality television' will be left to others,
I would however make a strong case here that many, if not all, of the
programmes I have looked at have been complex, nuanced pieces of
television drama and comedy which are open to the kind of close
reading I have employed here. As argued in the introduction to this

book, the analysis offered in this book is not intended to be definitive or objective, but rather it should be viewed as my own subjective reading of the texts, intended to open up a critical dialogue and debate on the subject of Gothic television. It is perhaps paradoxical, given that this book has looked at one of the most formulaic of genres, to conclude that Gothic television is actually less standardised and formulaic than other genres of television fiction, but perhaps this sense of richness and diversity comes from the fact that this book has worked towards the critical construction of the genre, rather than looking at a genre already identified within production and viewing practices. Conceivably, if Gothic television were to become more widely recognised as a category of television drama, the genre could quickly become standardised. Indeed, the recent bevy of supernatural serials on US television discussed in the last chapter of this book have a certain self-regenerative quality, guaranteeing that innovation and formal experimentation soon become repetitive and mundane.

There will be those who disagree with the selection of texts I have identified as 'Gothic' here, or that feel that I have not paid enough attention to what they might see as the ultimate, or definitive, example of Gothic television. That this will certainly occur testifies to the validity of my argument that Gothic television is a useful and recognisable generic category. However, in conclusion, perhaps the project of defining the Gothic as a television *genre* has, paradoxically, limited the full usefulness of the term 'Gothic television'. By paring the definition down to identify a certain genre of television fiction, perhaps I have also closed down the usage of the term in a restrictive way. Alternatively, by discussing 'Gothicness' on television, and locating the appearance of the Gothic as both a genre *and* a mode, a more inclusive, though less precise, definition of Gothic television can be produced which, for example, embraces instances of Gothicism in factual, as well as fictional, television (see Probyn (1993) and Edmundson (1997), for example). Discussing this problem in relation to the study of Gothic literature, Anne Williams proposes to see the Gothic as a 'complex', selecting this descriptor for its multiple meanings, as an adjective ('consisting of interconnected or interwoven parts . . . involved, intricate or complicated'), a noun ('a whole composed of interconnected parts') and as a psychiatric term ('a connected group of repressed ideas that compel characteristic or habitual patterns of thought, feeling, or action') (see Williams, 1995: 23). By categorising Gothic television as a complex rather than a genre, we might begin to see a much broader picture of Gothic programming, opening up the space for a discussion of occurrences and instances of the Gothic across a wider range of texts and genres. It is thus hoped that this book provides a series of starting points, rather than conclusions, in the study of Gothic television.

Note

1 This argument is similar to one proposed by Moseley (2001) in her history of the teen series.

Teleography[1]

Programmes

The Addams Family, US, Filmways/ABC, 1964–66.
Producer: David Levy/Nat Perrin.

The Addams Family, US, Hanna-Barbera Productions/Halas and Batchelor Cartoon Films, 1973–75.
Producer: Joseph Barbera/William Hanna/Iwao Takamoto, Director: Joy Batchelor/John Halas/Charles A. Nichols.

The Addams Family, US, ABC, 1992–93.
Producer: Buzz Potamkin, Writer: Lane Raichert/David Schwartz.

The Adventures of Ozzie and Harriet, US, ABC/Stage Five Productions/ Volcano Productions, 1952–66.
Producer: Ozzie Nelson et al.

The Adventures of Sherlock Holmes, UK, Granada, 1984–85.
Producer: Michael Cox/John Hawkesworth.

Alfred Hitchcock Presents, US, CBS/Revue Studios/Shamley Productions/ Universal TV, 1955–62.
Producer: Joan Harrison/Alfred Hitchcock, Creator: Alfred Hitchcock.

Alice in Wonderland, UK, BBC1, tx. 28.12.1966.
Producer: Jonathan Miller, Writer: Lewis Carroll/Jonathan Miller, Director: Jonathan Miller.

Ally McBeal, US, 20th Century Fox Television/David E. Kelley Productions, 1997–2002.
Producer: David E. Kelley et al., Creator: David E. Kelley.

American Gothic, US, CBS/Renaissance Pictures/Universal TV, 1995–96.
Producer: Sam Raimi/Robert G. Tapert/Shaun Cassidy, Creator: Shaun Cassidy.

The Andy Williams Show, US, Barnaby Productions/NBC, 1962–71.
Producer: Norman Lear/Bud Yorkin.

Angel, US, 20th Century Fox Television/Mutant Enemy Inc./Kuzui Enterprises/Sandollar Television, 1999–2004.
Producer: Joss Whedon et al., Creator: Joss Whedon.

Armchair Mystery Theatre, UK, ABC, 1960–65.
Producer: Leonard White.

Armchair Theatre, UK, ABC/Thames, 1956–74.
Producer: Dennis Vance/Sydney Newman/Leonard White.

Ballykissangel, UK, BBC Northern Ireland/Ballykea/World Productions, 1996–2001.
Producer: Robert Cooper/Tony Garnett, Creator: Kieran Prendiville.

Batman, US, ABC/20th Century Fox Television/Greenway Production, 1966–68.
Producer: William Dozier/Howie Horwitz.

The Beverley Hillbillies, US, Filmways/CBS, 1962–71.
Producer: Martin Ranshoff/Al Simon, Creator: Paul Henning.

Beverley Hills 90210, US, Spelling Television/Torand Productions Inc./Fox Network, 1990–2000.
Producer: Aaron Spelling et al., Creator: Darren Star.

Bewitched, US, ABC/Ashmont Productions/Screen Gems Television/ Sidney Sheldon Productions, 1964–72.
Producer: Harry Ackerman, Creator: Sol Saks.

The Brady Bunch, US, ABC/Paramount/Redwood Productions, 1969–74.
Producer: Sherwood Schwartz.

Brideshead Revisited, UK, Granada, 1981.
Producer: Derek Granger, Writer: Evelyn Waugh/John Mortimer, Director: Charles Sturridge/Michael Lindsay-Hogg.

Brimstone, US, Warner Bros. Television/Fox, 1998–99.
Producer: Chad Hoffman/Ian Sander, Creator: Ethan Reiff/Cyrus Voris.

Broadway Television Theatre, US, WOR-TV, 1952–54.
Producer: various.

Buffy, the Vampire Slayer, US, 20th Century Fox Television/Mutant Enemy Inc./Kuzui Enterprises/Sandollar Television, 1997–2003.
Producer: Joss Whedon et al., Creator: Joss Whedon.

Carnivàle, US, HBO, 2003–5.
Producer: Daniel Knauf et al., Creator: Daniel Knauf.

Charmed, US, Spelling Television/Northshore Productions Inc./ Paramount Pictures/Viacom, 1998–.
Producer: Constance M. Burge et al., Creator: Constance M. Burge.

Children of Green Knowe, UK, BBC1, 1986.
Producer: Paul Stone, Writer: Lucy M. Boston/John Stadelman, Director: Colin Cant.

Chiller, UK, Yorkshire, 1995.
Producer: Lawrence Gordon Clark/Peter Lover.

Christopher Lee's Ghost Story for Christmas, UK, BBC1, 2000.
Producer: Richard Downes, Writer: M.R. James/Ronald Frame, Director: Eleanor Yule.

The Clifton House Mystery, UK, HTV, 1978.
Producer: Leonard White/Patrick Dromgoole, Writer: Daniel Farson/Harry Moore, Director: Hugh David/Jeffrey Milland/Terry Miller.

Coronation Street, UK, Granada Television, 1960–.
Producer: various, Creator: Tony Warren.

Count Dracula, UK, BBC2, tx. 22.2.1977.
Producer: Morris Barry, Writer: Bram Stoker/Gerald Savory, Director: Philip Saville.

Crossroads, UK, ATV, 1964–88.
Producer: various, Creator: Hazel Adair/Peter Ling.

The Culture Show, UK, BBC2, 2004–.
Producer: Julian Birkett/Edward Morgan.

Dallas, US, CBS/Lorimar Television, 1978–91.
Producer: Leonard Katzman et al., Creator: David Jacobs.

Dark Shadows, US, Dan Curtis Productions Inc./ABC, 1966–71.
Producer: Dan Curtis et al., Creator: Dan Curtis.

Dark Shadows, US, Dan Curtis Productions Inc./MGM Television, 1991.
Producer: Dan Curtis, Creator: Dan Curtis.

Dead of Night, UK, BBC2, 1972.
Producer: Innes Lloyd.

Desperate Housewives, US, ABC/Touchstone Television/Cherry Productions, 2004–.
Producer: Mark Cherry et al., Creator: Mark Cherry.

Doctor Who, UK, BBC1, 1963–.
Producer: various, Creator: Sydney Newman.

Dr Terrible's House of Horrible, UK, Baby Cow Productions/BBC2, 2001.
Producer: Graham Duff/Steve Coogan/Henry Normal, Writer: Graham Duff/Steve Coogan/Henry Normal, Director: Matt Lipsey.

Dynasty, US, Aaron Spelling Productions Inc./ABC/Richard and Esther Shapiro Productions/The Oil Company, 1981–89.
Producer: Aaron Spelling et al., Creator: Esther Shapiro/Richard Shapiro.

Eastenders, UK, BBC1, 1985–.
Producer: various, Creator: Tony Holland/Julia Smith.

The Edgar Allen Poe Centenary, UK, BBC, tx. 6.10.1949.
Producer: Douglas Allen, Writer: Edgar Allen Poe/Joan Maude/Michael Warren, Director: Douglas Allen.

Father Knows Best, US, ABC/NBC/CBS/Rodney Young Productions/Screen Gems Television, 1954–60.
Producer: Eugene B. Rodney, Director: William D. Russell/Peter Tewksbury.

Frankenstein, US, ABC/Dan Curtis Productions Inc., tx. 16.1.1973.
Producer: Dan Curtis, Writer: Dan Curtis/Sam Hall/Richard H. Landau/Mary Shelley, Director: Glenn Jordan.

Garth Merenghi's Darkplace, UK, Avalon Television/Channel 4, 2004.
Producer: Richard Grocock, Writer: Matthew Holness/Richard Ayoade, Director: Richard Ayoade.

The Georgian House, UK, HTV, 1976.
Producer: Leonard White/Patrick Dromgoole, Writer: Jill Laurimore/Harry Moore, Director: Derek Clarke/Terry Harding/Sebastian Robinson/Leonard White.

A Ghost Story, UK, BBC, tx. 31.10.1947.
Producer: uncredited.

Ghost Story for Christmas, UK, BBC1, 1971–78.
Producer: Rosemary Hill, Creator: Lawrence Gordon Clark.

Ghosts, UK, BBC2, 1995.
Producer: Ruth Baumgarten.

The Goldbergs, US, CBS/DuMont Television Network/Guild Films/NBC, 1949–56.
Producer: Gertrude Berg, Writer: Gertrude Berg, Director: Marc Daniels.

Hallowe'en With the New Addams Family, US, CBS/Charles Fries Productions, tx. 30.10.1977.
Producer: Charles Fries/David Levy, Writer: George Tibbles, Director: David Steinmetz.

Hammer House of Horror, UK, Cinema Arts International/Chips Productions/Hammer Film Productions Ltd./ITC, 1980.
Producer: Brian Lawrence/David Reid/Roy Skeggs.

Hammer House of Mystery and Suspense, UK, Hammer Film Productions Ltd./20th Century Fox Television, 1984.
Producer: Brian Lawrence/Roy Skeggs.

The Hardy Boys Mysteries, US, ABC/Glen A. Larson Productions/Universal TV, 1977–79.
Producer: Glen A. Larson.

Haunted, UK, ABC, 1967–68.
Producer: Michael Chapman.

Haunting of Helen Walker, UK, Rosemont Productions Ltd., tx. 11.4.1997.
Producer: Nick Gillott/Tom McLoughlin, Writer: Henry James/Hugh Whitemore, Director: Tom McLoughlin.

Hercules: The Legendary Journeys, US, MCA Television Entertainment Inc./Renaissance Pictures/Studios USA Television/Universal TV, 1995–99.
Producer: Sam Raimi/Robert G. Tapert/Christian Williams, Creator: Christian Williams.

Hex, UK, Shine/Sony Pictures Television International, 2004–.
Producer: Dean Hargrove/Sara Johnson/Elisabeth Murdoch, Writer: Julian Jones/Lucy Watkins, Director: Brian Grant/Andy Goddard.

Hour of Mystery, UK, ABC, 1957.
Producer: John Nelson Burton.

I Dream of Jeannie, US, CBS/Screen Gems Television/Sidney Sheldon Productions, 1965–70.
Producer: Sidney Sheldon, Creator: Sidney Sheldon.

I Love Lucy, US, CBS/Desilu Productions Inc., 1951–57.
Producer: Desi Arnaz.

The Jewel in the Crown, UK, Granada, 1984.
Producer: Denis Forman/Christopher Morahan, Writer: Paul Scott/Ken Taylor, Director: Christopher Morahan/Jim O'Brien.

Journey to the Unknown, UK, ATV/Hammer/20th Century Fox Television, 1968–70.
Producer: Anthony Hinds.

Kingdom Hospital, US, ABC/Touchstone Television/Mark Carliner Productions Inc./Sony Pictures Television, 2004.
Producer: Mark Carliner/Stephen King/Lars von Trier, Writer: Richard Dooling/Stephen King, Director: Craig R. Baxley.

Kolchak the Night Stalker, US, Francy Productions/Universal TV/ABC, 1974–75.
Producer: Cy Chermak/Darren McGavin, Creator: Jeffrey Grant Rice.

Late Night Horror, UK, BBC2, 1968.
Producer: Harry Moore.

League of Gentlemen, UK, BBC2, 1999–2002.
Producer: Jon Plowman/Sarah Smith, Writer: Jeremy Dyson/Mark Gatiss/Steve Pemberton/Reece Shearsmith, Director: Steve Bendelack.

Leave it to Beaver, US, ABC/CBS/Kayro Productions/Revue Studios/ Gomalco Productions, 1957–63.
Producer: Joe Connelly/Richard Lewis/Bob Mosher.

Lights Out, US, Admiral Corporation/Erwin, Wasey and Co./NBC, 1949–52.
Producer: Fred Coe/Arch Oboler/Herbert B. Swope Jr./Ernest Walling.

Make Room for Daddy, US, ABC/CBS/Marterto Productions, 1953–65.
Producer: Sheldon Leonard, Writer: Bob Fisher/Garry Marshall/Ray Singer/Bob Weiskopf, Director: William Asher/Sheldon Leonard.

Matinee Theatre, US, NBC, 1955–58.
Producer: George Cahan/Albert McCleery/Frank Price/Darrell Ross.

Melrose Place, US, Darren Star Productions/Fox Television Network/Spelling Television/Torand Productions Inc., 1997–99.
Producer: Darren Star/Aaron Spelling et al., Creator: Darren Star.

Millennium, US, 10:13/20th Century Fox Television, 1996–99.
Producer: Chris Carter et al., Creator: Chris Carter.

The Mini-Munsters, US, ABC/Fred Calvert Productions, 1973.
Animator: Lew Keller.

Moondial, UK, BBC1, 1988.
Producer: Paul Stone, Writer: Helen Cresswell, Director: Colin Cant.

The Munsters, US, Kayro-Vue Productions/CBS, 1964–66.
Producer: Joe Connelly/Bob Mosher.

The Munsters' Revenge, US, NBC/Universal TV, tx. 27.2.1981.
Producer: Edward J. Montagne, Writer: Arthur Alsberg/Don Nelson, Director: Don Weis.

The Munsters' Scary Little Christmas, US, 20th Century Fox Television, tx. 17.12.1996.
Producer: Leslie Belzberg/John Landis, Writer: Ed Ferrera/Kevin Murphy, Director: Ian Emes.

The Munsters Today, US, The Arthur Company, 1988–91.
Producer: Lloyd J. Schwartz/Bryan Joseph/Arthur Annecharico.

My Favorite Martian, US, CBS/Jack Chertok Television, 1963–66.
Producer: Jack Chertok.

My Living Doll, US, CBS/Jack Chertok Television, 1964–65.
Producer: Jack Chertok/Howard Leeds, Creator: Bill Kelsay/Al Martin.

My Mother the Car, US, Cottage Industries Inc./United Artists Television/NBC, 1965–66.
Producer: Rodney Amateau, Creator: Allan Burns/Chris Hayward.

Mystery and Imagination, UK, ABC & Thames, 1966–70.
Producer: Jonathan Alwyn (ABC)/Reginald Collin (Thames).

The New Addams Family, US, Fox Family Channel/Shavick Entertainment Inc., 1998–99.
Producer: Lance H. Robbins/James Shavick/Victoria Woods.

Night Gallery, US, Universal TV/NBC, 1970–73.
Producer: Paul Freeman, Creator: Rod Serling.

The Night Stalker, US, ABC, tx. 11.1.1972.
Producer: Dan Curtis, Writer: Richard Matheson, Director: John Llewellyn Moxey.

The Night Strangler, US, ABC, tx. 16.1.1973.
Producer: Dan Curtis, Writer: Jeffrey Grant Rice/Richard Matheson, Director: Dan Curtis.

Northanger Abbey, UK, BBC2/A&E Network, tx. 15.2.1987.
Producer: Louis Marks, Writer: Jane Austen/Maggie Wadley, Director: Giles Foster.

Omnibus, UK, BBC1, 1967–2003.
Producer: various.

One Step Beyond, US, ABC/Joseph L. Schenck Enterprises, 1959–61.
Producer: Collier Young, Director: John Newland.

The Oprah Winfrey Show, US, Harpo Productions/HD Vision Studios/HBO, 1986–.
Producer: Oprah Winfrey et al., Creator: Oprah Winfrey.

The Others, US, Dreamworks Television/NBC, 2000.
Producer: John D. Brancato/Michael Ferris/Glen Morgan/James Wong, Creator: John D. Brancato/Michael Ferris.

Out of the Unknown, UK, BBC2, 1965–71.
Producer: Irene Shubik/Alan Bromly.

The Outer Limits, US, Daystar Productions/United Artists Television/Villa di Stefano, 1963–65.
Producer: Leslie Stevens.

Point Pleasant, US, 20th Century Fox Television/Adelstein-Parouse Productions, 2005.
Producer: John McLaughlin/Marti Noxon et al., Creator: John McLaughlin/Marti Noxon.

Poltergeist: The Legacy, US, PMP Legacy Productions/Showtime Networks Inc./Trilogy Entertainment Group, 1996–99.
Producer: Richard Barton Lewis/Grant Rosenberg/Mark Stern, Creator: Richard Barton Lewis.

Pride and Prejudice, UK, BBC/A&E Television Networks Inc./Chestermead Ltd., 1995.
Producer: Sue Birtwistle/Michael Wearing, Writer: Jane Austen/Andrew Davies, Director: Simon Langton.

The Professionals, UK, LWT/Mark One Productions Ltd., 1977–83.
Producer: Brian Clemens/Albert Fennell.

Profiler, US, Sander Moses Productions/Three Putt Productions/NBC, 1996–2000.
Producer: Stephen Kronish/Nancy Miller/Kim Moses/Ian Sander, Creator: Cynthia Saunders.

The Quatermass Experiment, UK, BBC, 1953.
Producer: Rudolph Cartier, Writer: Nigel Kneale, Director: Rudolph Cartier.

Rebecca, UK, BBC, tx. 19.1.1947.
Producer: Harold Clayton, Writer: Daphne du Maurier/Harold Clayton, Director: Harold Clayton.

Rebecca, UK, BBC, tx. 10.10.1954.
Producer: Rudolph Cartier, Writer: Daphne du Maurier/adaptation uncredited, Director: Rudolph Cartier.

Rebecca, UK, BBC1, 1979.
Producer: Richard Benyon, Writer: Daphne du Maurier/Hugh Whitemore, Director: Simon Langton.

Rebecca, UK, Carlton/Portman Productions/ITV/Tele-München, 1997.
Producer: Hilary Heath, Writer: Daphne du Maurier/Arthur Hopcraft, Director: Jim O'Brien.

Riget (The Kingdom), Denmark, Danmarks Radio/Zentropa, 1994.
Producer: Sven Abrahamsen/Philippe Bober/Peter Aalbæk Jensen/Ole Reim/Ib Tardini, Writer: Lars von Trier/Niels Vørsel/Tómas Gislason, Director: Morten Arnfred/Lars von Trier.

Sabrina the Teenage Witch, US, ABC/Hartbreak Films/Viacom/Finishing the Hat/Warner Bros. Television, 1996–2003.
Producer: Nell Scovell et al., Creator: Nell Scovell.

Sapphire and Steele, UK, ATV/Colour Productions, 1979–82.
Producer: Shaun O'Riordan, Creator/Writer: Peter Hammond, Director: Shaun O'Riordan/David Foster.

Saturday Night Stories, UK, BBC, 1948–49.
Producer: uncredited.

Screen One, UK, BBC1, 1985–2002.
Producer: various, Creator: Kenith Trodd.

Six Feet Under, US, HBO/The Greenblatt Janollari Studio/Actual Size Films, 2001–.
Producer: Alan Ball et al., Creator: Alan Ball.

The Sopranos, US, HBO/Brad Grey Television/Chase Films, 1999–.
Producer: David Chase et al., Creator: David Chase.

Strange, UK, Big Bear Films/BBC1, 2002–3.
Producer: Marcus Mortimer, Writer: Andrew Marshall, Director: Joe Ahearne/Simon Massey.

Sunset Beach, US, Aaron Spelling Productions Inc./NBC, 1997–99.
Producer: Aaron Spelling et al., Creator: Josh Griffith, Robert Guza Jr.,
Charles Pratt Jr.

Supernatural, UK, BBC1, 1977.
Producer: Pieter Rogers, Writer: Robert Muller/Sue Lake.

Suspense, US, CBS, 1949–54.
Producer: Martin Manulis.

Tales of Mystery, UK, A-R, 1961–63.
Producer: Peter Graham Scott.

Tales of Tomorrow, US, George F. Foley/ABC, 1951–53.
Producer: Mort Abrahams/George F. Foley/Richard Gordon.

Thriller, US, Hubbell Robinson Productions/NBC, 1960–62.
Producer: Hubbell Robinson/William Frye/Fletcher Markle/Maxwell Shane.

Thriller, UK, ATV/ITC/ABC [US], 1973–76.
Producer: Brian Clemens, Creator: Brian Clemens.

Tom's Midnight Garden, UK, BBC1, 1989.
Producer: Paul Stone, Writer: Julia Jones/Philippa Pearce, Director:
Christine Secombe.

The Troubleshooters, UK, BBC1, 1965–72.
Producer: John Elliot/Peter Graham Scott, Creator: John Elliot.

The Turn of the Screw, US, ABC/Dan Curtis Productions Inc., tx. 15.4.1974.
Producer: Dan Curtis/Tim Steele, Writer: Henry James/William F. Nolan,
Director: Dan Curtis.

Turn of the Screw, UK, United Film and Television Productions/Martin Pope
Productions/WGBH Boston, tx. 26.12.1999.
Producer: Michael Buck/Rebecca Eaton/Tim Vaughan, Writer: Henry
James/Nick Dear, Director: Ben Bolt.

The Twilight Zone, US, CBS/Cayuga Productions, 1959–64.
Producer: Rod Serling.

Twin Peaks, US, Lynch-Frost Productions/Spelling Entertainment/Twin
Peaks Productions Inc./ABC, 1990–91.
Producer: Mark Frost/David Lynch/Aaron Spelling et al., Creator: Mark
Frost/David Lynch.

Ultraviolet, UK, World Productions, 1998.
Producer: Sophie Balhetchet/Bill Shapter, Writer: Joe Ahearne, Director: Joe
Ahearne.

Urban Gothic, UK, Blackjack Productions/Columbia TriStar Television/
Golden Square Pictures, 2000–1.
Producer: Steve Matthews/Victor Glynn, Creator: Tom De Ville.

Wagon Train, US, NBC/ABC/Revue Studios/Universal TV, 1957–65.
Producer: Howard Christie/Richard Lewis.

Walking With Dinosaurs, UK, BBC1/Pro 7, 1999.
Producer: Tomi Bednar Landis/John Lynch, Writer: Georgann Kane,
Director: Tim Haines/Jasper James.

The Wednesday Thriller, UK, BBC1, 1965.
Producer: Bernard Hepton.

Woman in White, UK, BBC1, 1966.
Producer: David Conroy, Writer: Wilkie Collins/Michael Vosey, Director:
Brandon Acton Boyd.

Woman in White, UK, BBC2/RCTV Inc., 1982.
Producer: Jonathan Powell, Writer: Wilkie Collins/Ray Jenkins, Director:
John Bruce.

Woman in White, UK, BBC/Carlton/WGBH Boston, 1997.
Producer: Gareth Neame, Writer: Wilkie Collins/David Pirie, Director: Tim
Fywell.

The Wyvern Mystery, UK, BBC1/The Television Production Company, 2000.
Producer: Gareth Neame/Ruth Baumgarten, Writer: J.S. Le Fanu/David
Pirie, Director: Alex Pillai.

Xena: Warrior Princess, US, MCA Television Entertainment Inc./
Renaissance Pictures/Studios USA Television/Universal TV, 1995–2001.
Producer: Sam Raimi/R. J. Stewart/Robert G. Tapert, Creator: John
Schulian/ Robert G. Tapert.

The X-Files, US, 10:13 Productions/20th Century Fox Television, 1993–2002.
Producer: Chris Carter et al., Creator: Chris Carter.

Selected episodes[2]

'The Addams Family Goes to School', *The Addams Family*, US, tx. 18.9.1964.
Producer: David Levy/Nat Perrin, Writer: Ed James/Seaman Jacobs,
Director: Arthur Hiller.

'The Addams Family Tree', *The Addams Family*, US, tx. 16.10.1964.
Producer: David Levy/Nat Perrin, Writer: Hannibal Coons/Harry Winkler/
Lou Houston, Director: Jerry Hopper.

'*American Gothic* Pilot', *American Gothic*, US, CBS/Renaissance Pictures/
Universal TV, tx. 22.9.1995.
Producer: Sam Raimi/Robert G. Tapert/Shaun Cassidy, Writer: Shaun
Cassidy, Director: Peter O'Fallon.

'Children of the Full Moon', *Hammer House of Horror*, UK, Cinema Arts International/Chips Productions/Hammer Film Productions Ltd./ITC, tx. 1.11.1980.
Producer: Roy Skeggs, Writer: Murray Smith, Director: Tom Clegg.

'Dracula', *Mystery and Imagination*, UK, Thames, tx. 18.11.1968.
Producer: Reginald Collin, Writer: Bram Stoker/Charles Graham, Director: Patrick Dromgoole.

'Fall of the House of Usher', *Mystery and Imagination*, UK, ABC, tx. 12.2.1966.
Producer: Jonathan Alwyn, Writer: Edgar Allen Poe/David Campton, Director: Kim Mills.

'Frankenstein', *Mystery and Imagination*, UK, Thames, tx. 11.11.1968.
Producer: Reginald Collin, Writer: Mary Shelley/Robert Muller, Director: Voytek.

'Gehenna', *Millennium*, US, 10:13/20th Century Fox Television, tx. 1.11.1996.
Producer: Chris Carter et al., Writer: Chris Carter, Director: David Nutter.

'Ghostwatch', *Screen One*, UK, BBC1, tx. 31.10.1992.
Producer: Ruth Baumgarten, Writer: Stephen Volk, Director: Lesley Manning.

'The House that Bled to Death', *Hammer House of Horror*, UK, Cinema Arts International/Chips Productions/Hammer Film Productions Ltd./ ITC, tx. 11.10.1980.
Producer: Roy Skeggs, Writer: David Lloyd, Director: Tom Clegg.

'The Kiss of Blood', *Late Night Horror*, UK, BBC2, tx. 24.5.1968.
Producer: Harry Moore, Writer: Sir Arthur Conan Doyle/John Hawkesworth, Director: Richard Martin.

'Lo Cal Munster', *The Munsters*, US, Kayro-Vue Productions/CBS, tx. 29.10.1964.
Producer: Joe Connelly/Bob Mosher, Writer: Joe Connelly/Bob Mosher, Director: Norman Abbott.

'Lost Hearts', *Ghost Story for Christmas*, UK, BBC1, tx. 25.12.1973.
Producer: Rosemary Hill, Writer: M. R. James/Robin Chapman, Director: Lawrence Gordon Clark.

'*Millennium* Pilot', *Millennium*, US, 10:13/20th Century Fox Television, tx. 25.10.1996.
Producer: Chris Carter et al., Writer: Chris Carter, Director: David Nutter.

'Morticia Joins the Ladies' League', *The Addams Family*, US, tx. 23.10.1964.
Producer: David Levy/Nat Perrin, Writer: Phil Leslie/Keith Fowler, Director: Jean Yarbrough.

'Mr. Nightingale', *Supernatural*, UK, BBC1, tx. 2.7.1977.
Producer: Pieter Rogers, Writer: Robert Muller, Director: Alan Cooke.

'Munster Masquerade', *The Munsters*, US, Kayro-Vue Productions/CBS, tx. 24.9.1964.
Producer: Joe Connelly/Bob Mosher, Writer: Joe Connelly/Bob Mosher, Director: Lawrence Dobkin.

'My Fair Munster', *The Munsters*, US, Kayro-Vue Productions/CBS, tx. 1.10.1964.
Producer: Joe Connelly/Bob Mosher, Writer: Norm Liebmann/Ed Haas, Director: David Alexander.

'The New Neighbors Meet the Addams Family', *The Addams Family*, US, tx. 13.11.1964.
Producer: David Levy/Nat Perrin, Writer: Hannibal Coons/Harry Winkler, Director: Jean Yarbrough.

'The One-Armed Man', *Twin Peaks*, US, Lynch-Frost Productions/Spelling Entertainment/Twin Peaks Productions Inc./ABC, tx. 3.5.1990.
Producer: Mark Frost/David Lynch/Aaron Spelling et al., Writer: Robert Engels, Director: Tim Hunter.

'The Open Door', *Mystery and Imagination*, UK, ABC, tx. 19.2.1966.
Producer: Jonathan Alwyn, Writer: Margaret Oliphant/George Kerr, Director: Joan Kemp-Welch.

'Paper Dove', *Millennium*, US, 10:13/20th Century Fox Television, tx. 16.5.1996.
Producer: Chris Carter et al., Writer: Walon Green/Ted Mann, Director: Thomas Wright.

'Rock-a-bye Munster', *The Munsters*, US, Kayro-Vue Productions/CBS, tx. 15.10.1964.
Producer: Joe Connelly/Bob Mosher, Writer: Norm Liebmann/Ed Haas, Director: Norman Abbott.

'The Silent Scream', *Hammer House of Horror*, UK, Cinema Arts International/Chips Productions/Hammer Film Productions Ltd./ITC, tx. 25.10.1980.
Producer: Roy Skeggs, Writer: Francis Essex, Director: Alan Gibson.

'Stigma', *Ghost Story for Christmas*, UK, BBC1, tx. 28.12.1977.
Producer: Rosemary Hill, Writer: Clive Exton, Director: Lawrence Gordon Clark.

'Sweeney Todd', *Mystery and Imagination*, UK, Thames, tx. 9.2.1970.
Producer: Reginald Collin, Writer: George Dibdin Pitt/Vincent Tilsley, Director: Reginald Collin.

'*Twin Peaks* Pilot', *Twin Peaks*, US, Lynch-Frost Productions/Spelling Entertainment/Twin Peaks Productions Inc./ABC, tx. 8.4.1990.

Producer: Mark Frost/David Lynch/Aaron Spelling et al., Writer: Mark Frost/David Lynch, Director: David Lynch.

'Uncle Silas', *Mystery and Imagination*, UK, Thames, tx. 4.11.1968.
Producer: Reginald Collin, Writer: J.S. Le Fanu/Stanley Miller, Director: Alan Cooke.

'A Walk on the Mild Side', *The Munsters*, US, Kayro-Vue Productions/CBS, tx. 8.10.1964.
Producer: Joe Connelly/Bob Mosher, Writer: Norm Liebmann/Ed Haas, Director: Norman Abbott.

'Whistle and I'll Come to You', *Omnibus*, UK, BBC1, tx. 7.5.1968.
Producer: Jonathan Miller, Writer: M.R. James/Jonathan Miller, Director: Jonathan Miller.

'Witching Time', *Hammer House of Horror*, UK, Cinema Arts International/ Chips Productions/Hammer Film Productions Ltd./ITC, tx. 13.9.1980.
Producer: Roy Skeggs, Writer: Anthony Read, Director: Don Leaver.

'Zen, or the Skill to Catch a Killer', *Twin Peaks*, US, Lynch-Frost Productions/ Spelling Entertainment/Twin Peaks Productions Inc./ABC, tx. 19.4.1990.
Producer: Mark Frost/David Lynch/Aaron Spelling et al., Writer: David Lynch/Mark Frost, Director: David Lynch.

Notes

1 In some cases, writer and director are not given when these details change from week to week. In most cases, key executive or head producers are cited. For some long-running serials and soap operas, the creator is given where known. All transmission dates given here relate to the initial transmission of the programme in its country of origin. Single dramas or episodes are given their full transmission date, whereas the year(s) of transmission only are given in the case of series or serials.
2 Only episodes discussed in detail are listed separately here.

Filmography

The Addams Family (Barry Sonnenfeld, US, 1991).
The Addams Family Reunion (Dave Payne, US, 1998).
Addams Family Values (Barry Sonnenfeld, US, 1993).
The Amityville Horror (Stuart Rosenberg, US, 1979).
. . . And Now the Screaming Starts! (Roy Ward Baker, UK, 1973).
Asylum (Roy Ward Baker, UK, 1972).
Blood from the Mummy's Tomb (Seth Holt/Michael Carreras, UK, 1971).
Blue Velvet (David Lynch, US, 1986).
The Brady Bunch Movie (Betty Thomas, US, 1995).
Bram Stoker's Dracula (Francis Ford Coppola, US, 1992).
The Corsican Brothers (George Albert Smith, UK, 1898).
The Curse of Frankenstein (Terence Fisher, UK, 1957).
Darkman (Sam Raimi, US, 1990).
Dracula (Tod Browning, US, 1931).
Dracula (Terence Fisher, UK, 1958).
Dracula, Prince of Darkness (Terence Fisher, UK, 1966).
Dragonwyck (Joseph L. Mankiewicz, US, 1947).
Eraserhead (David Lynch, US, 1977).
Evil Dead (Sam Raimi, US, 1982).
Evil Dead II (Sam Raimi, US, 1987).
The Exorcist (William Friedkin, US, 1973).
Faust and Mephistopheles (George Albert Smith, UK, 1898).
Frankenstein (James Whale, US, 1931).
Gaslight (George Cukor, US, 1944).
Der Golem, wie er in die Welt kam (The Golem: How he came into the World) (Paul Wegener, Germany, 1920).
The Hills Have Eyes (Wes Craven, US, 1977).
House of Dark Shadows (Dan Curtis, US, 1970).
The House that Dripped Blood (Peter Duffell, UK, 1971).
Hush, Hush Sweet Charlotte (Robert Aldrich, US, 1964).
The Innocents (Jack Clayton, UK, 1961).
I Remember Mama (George Stevens, US, 1948).
Inside Daisy Clover (Robert Mulligan, US, 1965).

It's Alive (Larry Cohen, US, 1973).

Das Kabinett des Dr. Caligari (*The Cabinet of Dr. Caligari*) (Robert Wiene, Germany, 1919).

Kiss of the Vampire (Don Sharp, UK, 1964).

The Last House on the Left (Wes Craven, US, 1972).

Lilith (Robert Rossen, US, 1964).

Le manoir du diable (*The Devil's Castle*) (Georges Méliès, France, 1896).

Meet Me in St. Louis (Vincente Minnelli, US, 1944).

Mildred Pierce (Michael Curtiz, US, 1945).

Der müde tod (*Destiny*) (Fritz Lang, Germany, 1921).

Night of Dark Shadows (Dan Curtis, US, 1971).

Night of the Demon (aka Curse of the Demon) (Jacques Tourneur, UK, 1957).

Night of the Living Dead (George A. Romero, US, 1968).

Nosferatu – eine Symphonie des Grauens (*Nosferatu – a Symphony of Horrors*) (F. W. Murnau, Germany, 1922).

The Omen (Richard Donner, US, 1976).

Photographing a Ghost (George Albert Smith, UK, 1898).

Rebecca (Alfred Hitchcock, US, 1940).

Rosemary's Baby (Roman Polanski, US, 1968).

Se7en (David Fincher, US, 1995).

Silence of the Lambs (Jonathan Demme, US, 1991).

The Spiral Staircase (Robert Siodmak, US, 1946).

Texas Chainsaw Massacre (Tobe Hooper, US, 1974).

The Two Mrs. Carrolls (Peter Godfrey, US, 1947).

The Wolf Man (George Waggner, US, 1941).

Bibliography

Abbott, S. (2005) *Reading* Angel: *The TV Spin-off With a Soul*, London: IB Tauris.

ABC Television Ltd. (1967) 'ABC Television and its programmes 1956–67 in support of its application for appointment as programme contractor', British Film Institute Library, London (hereafter BFI Library), ITC collection, unpublished document (April).

Akass, K. and McCabe, J. (eds) (2005) *Reading* Six Feet Under: *TV to Die For*, London: IB Tauris.

Allen, R. C. (ed.) (1992) *Channels of Discourse, Reassembled*, New York: Routledge.

Altman, R. (1999) *Film/Genre*, London: BFI.

Ang, I. (1997) 'Melodramatic identifications: television fiction and women's fantasy', in C. Brunsdon, J. D'Acci and L. Spigel (eds) *Feminist Television Criticism: A Reader*, pp. 155–66.

Anon. (1968a) 'Have a drink on Dracula', *TV Times* (16 November), p. 9.

—— (1968b) 'Review: *Late Night Horror*', *Sunday Telegraph* (26 May), p. 35.

—— (1977) 'Review', *Glasgow Herald* (27 June), p. 25.

—— (1987) 'Television', *Daily Telegraph* (16 February), p. 13.

Bailey, K. (ed.) (1957) *The Television Annual for 1958*, London: Odhams Press.

Barr, C. (ed.) (1986) *All Our Yesterdays: Ninety Years of British Cinema*, London: BFI.

BBC (1968a) 'Whistle and I'll Come to You', BBC Written Archive Centre, Caversham (hereafter BBC WAC), T53/112/1, Audience Research Report, (17 June).

—— (1968b) '*Late Night Horror*: "The Kiss of Blood"', BBC WAC, T5/1,569/1, Audience Research Report (24 May).

—— (1969) 'Press release on the second broadcast of Jonathan Miller's *Whistle and I'll Come to You*', BBC WAC, T53/112/1, press release (27 July).

Benshoff, H. M. (1993) 'Resurrection of the vampire and the creation of alternative life: an introduction to *Dark Shadows* fan culture', *Spectator*, 13, 3: 50–61.

Bignell, J. and O'Day, A. (2004) *Terry Nation*, Manchester: Manchester University Press.

Bloom, C. (ed.) (1998) *Gothic Horror: A Reader's Guide from Poe to King and Beyond*, Basingstoke: Macmillan.

Born, G. (2004) *Uncertain Vision: Birt, Dyke and the Reinvention of the BBC*, London: Secker and Warburg.

Botting, F. (1996) *Gothic*, London: Routledge.

Branigan, E. (1984) *Point of View in the Cinema: A Theory of Narration and Subjectivity in Classical Film*, New York: Mouton Publishers.

Briggs, J. (1998) 'Night visitors', in C. Bloom (ed.) *Gothic Horror: A Reader's Guide from Poe to King and Beyond*, pp. 101–17.

Briggs, S. (1998) 'Television in the home and family', in A. Smith (ed.) *Television: An International History*, pp. 109–21.

Brunsdon, C. (1981) '*Crossroads*: notes on soap opera', *Screen*, 22, 4: 32–7.

—— (1990) 'Problems with quality', *Screen*, 31, 1: 67–90.

—— (1998) 'What is the "television" of television studies?', in C. Geraghty and D. Lusted (eds) *The Television Studies Book*, pp. 95–113.

Brunsdon, C., D'Acci, J. and Spigel, L. (eds) (1997) *Feminist Television Criticism: A Reader*, Oxford: Oxford University Press.

Brunsdon, C., Johnson, C., Moseley, R. and Wheatley, H. (2001) 'Factual entertainment on British television: the Midlands Television Research Group's "8–9 Project" ', *European Journal of Cultural Studies*, 4, 1: 29–62.

Bundy, M. W. (2005) 'Exquisite corpse: death as an odalisque and the new American gothic in *Six Feet Under*', in K. Akass and J. McCabe (eds) *Reading* Six Feet Under: *TV To Die For*, pp. 34–8.

Caldwell, J. T. (1995) *Televisuality: Style, Crisis and Authority in American Television*, New Brunswick: Rutgers University Press.

Callander, M. (2000) 'Bram Stoker's *Buffy*: traditional Gothic and contemporary culture' [online publication], *Slayage: The On-line Journal of Buffy Studies*, 3, www.middleenglish.org/slayage/essays/slayage3/callander.html, accessed 31 July 2002.

Carlton Productions (1996) '*Rebecca*', BFI Library, *Rebecca* (1997) microjacket, press release (5 June).

Carter, A. (1975) 'And things that go bump in the night', *Radio Times* (20 December), pp. 111–12.

Cashmore, E. (1994) . . . *And There Was Television*, London: Routledge.

Castle, T. (1995) *The Female Thermometer: Eighteenth Century Culture and the Invention of the Uncanny*, Oxford: Oxford University Press.

Caughie, J. (2000) *Television Drama: Realism, Modernism and British Culture*, Oxford: Oxford University Press.

Chapman, J. (2002) *Saints and Avengers: British Adventure Series of the 1960s*, London: IB Tauris.

Cherry, B. (2002) 'Refusing to refuse to look: female viewers of the horror film', in M. Jancovich (ed.) *Horror: The Film Reader*, pp. 169–78.

Chibnall, S. and Petley, J. (eds) (2002a) *British Horror Cinema*, London: Routledge.

—— (2002b) 'The return of the repressed? British horror's heritage and future', in S. Chibnall and J. Petley (eds) *British Horror Cinema*, pp. 1–9.

Coates, P. (1991) *The Gorgon's Gaze: German Cinema, Expressionism, and the Image of Horror*, Cambridge: Cambridge University Press.

Collins, J. (1992) 'Television and postmodernism', in R. Allen (ed.) *Channels of Discourse, Reassembled*, pp. 1–30.

Conrich, I. (1997) 'Traditions of the British horror film', in R. Murphy (ed.) *The British Cinema Book*, pp. 226–34.

Cooke, L. (2003) *British Television Drama: A History*, London: BFI.

Creeber, G. (ed.) (2001a) *The Television Genre Book*, London: BFI.

—— (2001b) ' "Taking our personal lives seriously": intimacy, continuity and memory in the television drama serial', *Media, Culture and Society*, 23, 4: 439–56.

—— (2004) *Serial Television: Big Drama on the Small Screen*, London: BFI.

Creed, B. (1986) 'Horror and the monstrous feminine: an imaginary abjection', *Screen*, 27, 1: 44–70.

—— (1993) *The Monstrous-Feminine: Film, Feminism, Psychoanalysis*, New York: Routledge.

Crisell, A. (1997) *An Introductory History of British Broadcasting*, London: Routledge (2nd edn).

Davenport, R. (1993) 'The knowing spectator of *Twin Peaks*: culture, feminism and family violence', *Literature/Film Quarterly*, 21, 4: 255–9.

Davenport-Hines, R. (1998) *Gothic: 400 Years of Excess, Horror, Evil and Ruin*, London: Fourth Estate Ltd.

Davis, A. (1966) 'Screams behind *The Open Door*', *TV Times* (19 February), p. 8.

Davis, R. A. (2000) '*Buffy the Vampire Slayer* and the pedagogy of fear' [online publication], *Slayage: The On-line Journal of Buffy Studies*, 3, www.middleenglish.org/slayage/essays/slayage3/davis.htm, accessed 31 July 2002.

Dawidziak, M. (1990) 'The horror that wouldn't die: *Dark Shadows*', *Cinefantastique*, 21, 3: 24–30.

Dawidziak, M. and Stevenson, J. (1996) '*Dark Shadows*', *Cinefantastique*, 28, 6: 32–5.

Dickson, A. (ed.) (1990) *The Penguin Freud Library Volume 14: Art and Literature*, Harmondsworth: Penguin.

Doane, M. A. (1981) '*Caught* and *Rebecca*: the inscription of femininity as absence', *Enclitic*, 5–6: 75–89.

—— (1987a) *The Desire to Desire: The Woman's Film of the 1940s*, Bloomington and Indianapolis: Indiana University Press.

—— (1987b) 'The "woman's film": possession and address', in C. Gledhill (ed.) *Home is Where the Heart Is: Studies in Melodrama and the Woman's Film*, pp. 283–98.

Dodd, C. (1995) 'You are invited to a *Pride and Prejudice* dinner party', *Radio Times* (7 October), pp. 24–7.

Dow, B. J. (1996) *Prime-time Feminism: Television, Media Culture and the Women's Movement Since 1970*, Philadelphia: University of Pennsylvania Press.

Dyer, R. (1997) 'Kill and kill again', *Sight and Sound*, 7, 9(NS): 14–17.

Dyer R., et al. (eds) (1981) *Coronation Street*, London: BFI.

Eco, U. (1979) *The Role of the Reader*, Bloomington and Indianapolis: Indiana University Press.

—— (1994) *Six Walks in the Fictional Woods*, Cambridge, MA: Harvard University Press.

Edmundson, M. (1997) *Nightmare on Main Street: Angels, Sadomasochism and the Culture of Gothic*, Cambridge, MA: Harvard University Press.

Eisner, L. (1969) *The Haunted Screen: Expressionism in the German Cinema and the Influence of Max Reinhardt*, London: Thames and Hudson.

Ellis, J. (1982) *Visible Fictions: Cinema, Television, Video*, London: Routledge.

—— (2000) *Seeing Things: Television in the Age of Uncertainty*, London: IB Tauris.

Ellis, M. (1997) '*The Woman in White*', *Televisual* (July), pp. 20–2.

Eramo, S. (1997) 'Shaun Cassidy: singer, sleuth, scribe', *TV Zone*, 24 (Special): 12–15.

Farber, S. (1972) 'The new American Gothic', in R. Huss and T. J. Ross (eds) *Focus on the Horror Film*, pp. 94–102.

Feely, T. (1966) 'My search for the supernatural', *TV Times* (29 January), p. 4.

Ferguson-Ellis, K. (1989) *The Contested Castle: Gothic Novels and the Subversion of Domestic Ideology*, Urbana: University of Illinois Press.

Feuer, J. (2001) 'Situation comedy, part two', in G. Creeber (ed.) *The Television Genre Book*, pp. 67–70.

Fiddick, P. (1971) 'The night when Alan Bromly wished he'd had his glasses on', *Radio Times* (17 April), pp. 4–5.

Fink, E. J. (1996) 'The impact of digital video technology on production: the case of *American Gothic*', *Journal of Film and Video*, 48, 4: 9–19.

Fleenor, J. E. (ed.) (1993) *The Female Gothic*, Montreal: Eden.

Fletcher, J. (1995) 'Primal scenes and the female Gothic: *Rebecca* and *Gaslight*', *Screen*, 36, 4: 341–70.

Freedman, E. (2005) 'Television, horror and everyday life in *Buffy the Vampire Slayer*', in M. Hammond and L. Mazdon (eds) *The Contemporary Television Series*, 159–80.

Freud, S. (1990) 'The uncanny', in A. Dickson (ed.) *The Penguin Freud Library Volume 14: Art and Literature*, pp. 336–76.

Friedman, L. (ed.) (1993) *British Cinema and Thatcherism: Fires Were Started*, London: University of Central London Press.

Fryer, P. A. (1971) 'Science fiction "vacuum" ', *Radio Times* (5 June), p. 5.

Gallafent, E. (1988) 'Black satin: fantasy, murder and the couple in *Gaslight* and *Rebecca*', *Screen*, 29, 3: 84–103.

Garcia, R. T. (1991a) 'Charles Addams', *Cinefantastique*, 22, 3: 35–6.

—— (1991b) 'A retrospect of the "original" *The Addams Family*', *Cinefantastique*, 22, 3: 40–6.

Gardner, C. and Wyver, J. (1983) 'The single play from Reithian reverence to cost-accounting and censorship', *Screen*, 24, 4–5: 114–24.

Gardner, S. N., Kahane, C. and Sprengnether, M. (eds) (1985) *The (M)other Tongue: Essays in Feminist Psychoanalytic Interpretation*, Ithaca: Cornell University Press.

Gauntlett, D. and Hill, A. (1999) *TV Living: Television, Culture and Everyday Life*, London: Routledge.

Gelder, K. (ed.) (2000a) *The Horror Reader*, London: Routledge.

—— (2000b) 'American Gothic', in K. Gelder (ed.) *The Horror Reader*, pp. 253–72.

Genge, N. E. (1997) *The Unofficial Millennium Companion Volume 1*, London: Century.

Geraghty, C. (1981) 'The continuous serial – a definition', in R. Dyer et al. (eds) *Coronation Street*, pp. 9–26.

Geraghty, C. and Lusted, D. (eds) (1998) *The Television Studies Book*, London: Arnold.

Gielgud, V. (1950) 'Reflections upon the present state of television drama', BBC WAC, T16/62/1, memo sent to Norman Collins (Controller of Television) (28 April).

Gitlin, T. (1994) *Inside Prime Time*, London: Routledge (revised edn).

Gledhill, C. (ed.) (1987) *Home is Where the Heart Is: Studies in Melodrama and the Woman's Film*, London: BFI.

Goddu, T. A. (1997) *Gothic America: Narrative, History and Nation*, New York: Columbia University Press.

Gothic Phantom (undated) '*American Gothic* press conference, part one' [online publication], *Gothic Phantom's* American Gothic *Page*, http://members.tripod.com/~Gothic_Phantom/Press_Conference1.html, accessed 21 September 2001.

Grant, B. K. (ed.) (1996) *The Dread of Difference*, Austin: University of Texas Press.

Gray, A. (1992) *Video Playtime: The Gendering of a Leisure Technology*, London: Routledge.

Griffiths, N. (2000) 'House of secrets and lies', *Radio Times* (4 March), pp. 18–20.

Gripsrud, J. (1995) *The Dynasty Years: Hollywood, Television and Critical Media Studies*, London: Routledge.

—— (1998) 'Television, broadcasting, flow: key metaphors in TV theory', in C. Geraghty and D. Lusted (eds) *The Television Studies Book*, pp. 17–32.

Gross, L. S. (1989) *Redefining the American Gothic: From* Wieland *to* Day of the Dead, Ann Arbor: UMI Research Press.

Grunenberg, C. (1997) *Gothic: Transmutations of Horror in Late Twentieth Century Art*, Cambridge, MA: MIT Press.

Gunning, T. (2001) 'The ghost in the machine: animated pictures at the haunted hotel of early cinema', *Living Pictures*, 1, 1: 3–17.

Haining, P. (ed.) (1993) *The Television Late Night Horror Omnibus: Great Tales From TV Anthology Series*, London: Orion.

Hall, S. (1990) 'A word from me', in K. Leigh-Scott (ed.) *The* Dark Shadows *Companion: 25th Anniversary Collection*, pp. 39–41.

Halttunen, K. (1998) *Murder Most Foul: The Killer in the American Gothic Imagination*, Cambridge, MA: Harvard University Press.

Hammond, M. and Mazdon, L. (eds) (2005) *The Contemporary Television Series*, Edinburgh: Edinburgh University Press.

Hammond, P. (1974) *Marvellous Méliès*, London: Gordon Fraser.

Hanson, H. (2000) *Painted Women: Framing Portraits in Film Noir and the Gothic Woman's Film*, PhD thesis, University of Southampton, (November).

Harrison, T., Pojansky, S., Ono, K. and Helford, E. (eds) (1996) *Enterprise Zones: Critical Positions on* Star Trek, Oxford: Westview Press.

Hartley, J. (2001) 'Situation comedy, part one', in G. Creeber (ed.) *The Television Genre Book*, pp. 65–7.

Hartman, M. (2005) '*Twin Peaks*' soundtrack' [online publication], *The City of Absurdity*, www.geocities.com/Hollywood/2093/twinpeaks/tpsound.html, accessed 22 June 2005.

Haskell, M. (1987) *From Reverence to Rape: The Treatment of Women in the Movies*, Chicago: University of Chicago Press (2nd edn).

Hayward, S. (1996) *Key Concepts in Film Studies*, London: Routledge.

Heller, D. (2005) 'Buried lives: Gothic democracy in *Six Feet Under*', in K. Akass and J. McCabe (eds) *Reading* Six Feet Under: *TV To Die For*, pp. 71–84.

Heller, T. (1992) *Dead Secrets: Wilkie Collins and the Female Gothic*, New Haven: Yale University Press.

Hennessey-Derose, C. and McCarty, M. (2003) 'Ladies of the *Dark Shadows*', *Filmfax*, 97: 38–43.

Higson, A. (1991) 'Gothic fantasy as art cinema: the secret of female desire in *The Innocents*', conference paper, *Norwich International Gothic Conference*, University of East Anglia (July).

—— (1993) 'Re-presenting the national past: nostalgia and pastiche in the heritage film', in L. Friedman (ed.) *British Cinema and Thatcherism: Fires Were Started*, pp. 109–29.

—— (ed.) (1996) *Dissolving Views: Key Writings On British Cinema*, London: Cassell.

Hills, M. and Williams, R. (2005) 'Monstrous mothers and vampires with souls: investigating the abject in "television horror" ', in S. Abbott (ed.) *Reading* Angel: The TV Spin-off With a Soul, pp. 203–17.

Hollinger, K. (1993) 'The female Oedipal drama of *Rebecca* from novel to film', *Quarterly Review of Film and Video*, 14, 4: 17–30.

Howells, C. (1978) *Love, Mystery and Misery: Feeling in Gothic Fiction*, London: Athlone Press.

Huss, R. (1972) 'Vampire's progress: *Dracula* from novel to film via Broadway', in R. Huss and T. J. Ross (eds) *Focus on the Horror Film*, pp. 50–6.

Huss, R. and Ross, T. J. (eds) (1972) *Focus on the Horror Film*, Englewood Cliffs, N.J.: Prentice Hall.

Hutchings, P. (1993) *Hammer and Beyond: The British Horror Film*, Manchester: Manchester University Press.

—— (2002a) *Terence Fisher*, Manchester: Manchester University Press.

—— (2002b) 'The Amicus house of horror', in S. Chibnall and J. Petley (eds) *British Horror Cinema*, pp. 131–44.

——(2003) *Dracula*, London: IB Tauris.

Idiart, J. and Schultz, J. (1999) 'American Gothic landscapes: the New World to Vietnam', in G. Byron and D. Punter (eds) *Spectral Readings: Towards a Gothic Geography*, Basingstoke: Macmillan, pp. 127–39.

Jacobs, J. (2000) *The Intimate Screen: Early British Television Drama*, Oxford: Oxford University Press.

—— (2001) 'Issues of judgement and value in television studies', *International Journal of Cultural Studies*, 4, 4: 427–47.

—— (2003) *Body Trauma TV: The New Hospital Drama*, London: BFI.

—— (2005) 'Television aesthetics: an infantile disorder', conference paper, *Screen Conference*, University of Glasgow (July).

James, M. R. (1992) *Collected Ghost Stories*, Hertfordshire: Wordsworth Editions Ltd.

Jancovich, M. (ed.) (2002) *Horror: The Film Reader*, London: Routledge.

Jenkins, H. (1991) '*Star Trek* rerun, reread, rewritten: fan writing as textual poaching', in C. Penley, E. Lyon, L. Spigel and J. Bergstrom (eds) *Close Encounters: Film, Feminism, and Science Fiction*, pp. 172–202.

Jentsch, E. (1995) 'On the psychology of the uncanny', *Angelaki*, 2, 1: 7–16.

Jivani, A. (1996) 'Scared of the dark', *Time Out* (12 June), p. 157.

Johnson, C. (2000) 'Strategies of darkness: industry, aesthetics and *The X-Files*', conference paper, *Screen Conference*, University of Glasgow (July).

—— (2005) *Telefantasy*, London: BFI.

Johnson, C. and Turnock, R. (eds) (2005) *ITV Cultures: Independent Television Over Fifty Years*, Maidenhead: Open University Press.

Jowett, L. (2005) *Sex and the Slayer: A Gender Studies Primer for the Buffy Fan*, Middletown, Connecticut: Wesleyan University Press.

Joyrich, L. (1992) 'All that television allows: TV melodrama, postmodernism, and consumer culture', in L. Spigel and D. Mann (eds) *Private Screenings: Television and the Female Consumer*, pp. 227–51.

Kahane, C. (1985) 'The Gothic mirror', in S. N. Gardner, C. Kahane and M. Sprengnether (eds) *The (M)other Tongue: Essays in Feminist Psychoanalytic Interpretation*, pp. 334–51.

Kaveney, R. (ed.) (2001) *Reading the Vampire Slayer: The Unofficial Critical Companion to Buffy and Angel*, London: IB Tauris.

Kemp, P. (1987) 'Review', *The Independent* (16 February), p. 11.

Kennedy Martin, T. (1964) 'Nats go home: first statement of a new drama for television', *Encore*, 48: 21–33.

Kennedy Martin, T. et al. (1964) 'Reaction: replies to Troy Kennedy Martin's attack on naturalistic television drama', *Encore*, 49: 39–48.

King, S. (1981) *Danse Macabre*, London: Macdonald Futura Publishers.

Lavery, D. (ed.) (1995) *Full of Secrets: Critical Approaches to Twin Peaks*, Detroit: Wayne State University Press.

Lavery, D., Hague, A. and Cartwright, M. (eds) (1996) *'Deny All Knowledge':* *Reading the* X-Files, Syracuse: Syracuse University Press.

Ledwon, L. (1993) 'Twin Peaks and the television Gothic', *Literature/Film* *Quarterly*, 21, 4: 260–70.

Lee, A. R. (1998) 'Southern Gothic', in M. Mulvey-Roberts (ed.) *The* *Handbook to Gothic Literature*, pp. 217–20.

Leigh-Scott, K. (ed.) (1990) *The Dark Shadows* Companion: 25th Anniversary *Collection*, Los Angeles: Pomegranate Press.

Lejeune, A. (1970) 'Hold on to your seats – here comes Sweeney Todd', *TV* *Times* (16 February), pp. 12–13.

Lewin, D. (1987) 'Imperfect heroine', *Observer Magazine* (25 January), pp. 30–3.

Lock, K. (1995) 'Lifting the skirts on *Pride and Prejudice*', *Radio Times* (30 September), pp. 39–40.

Lury, K. (1995) 'Television performance: being, acting and "corpsing" ' , *New* *Formations*, 26: 114–27.

—— (2005) *Interpreting Television*, London: Hodder Arnold.

MacCabe, C. (ed.) (1986) *High Theory/Low Culture: Analysing Popular* *Television and Film*, London: St. Martin's Press.

Madden, C. (1959) 'Re: television programme planning commit-tee meeting', BBC WAC, T16/62/3, letter sent to Michael Barry (29 April).

Mannoni, L. (2000) *The Great Art of Light and Shadow: Archaeology of the* *Cinema*, Exeter: Exeter University Press.

Marc, D. (1997) *Comic Visions: Television Comedy and American Culture* (2nd edn), Malden and Oxford: Blackwell.

Martin, R. K. and Savoy, E. (eds) (1998) *American Gothic: New Interventions* *in a National Narrative*, Iowa City: University of Iowa Press.

Massé, M. A. (1992) *In the Name of Love: Women, Masochism and the Gothic*, Ithaca: Cornell University Press.

Massumi, B. (ed.) (1993) *The Politics of Everyday Fear*, Minneapolis: Minneapolis University Press.

McCarthy, A. (2001) *Ambient Television: Visual Culture and Public Space*, Durham: Duke University Press.

Merck, M. (2005) 'American Gothic: Undermining the uncanny', in K. Akass and J. McCabe (eds) *Reading* Six Feet Under: *TV to Die For*, pp. 59–70.

Milbank, A. (1992) *Daughters of the House: Modes of the Gothic in Victorian* *Fiction*, Basingstoke: Macmillan.

—— (1998) 'Female Gothic', in M. Mulvey-Roberts (ed.) *The Handbook to* *Gothic Literature*, pp. 53–7.

Miles, R. (1994) 'Introduction to special number: female gothic', *Women's* *Writing*, 1, 2: 131–42.

Mirrlees-Black, C. (1999) *Domestic Violence: Findings from a New British* *Crime Survey Self-completion Questionnaire*, London: Home Office Research Study 191.

Modleski, T. (1982a) *Loving with a Vengeance*, New York: Routledge.

—— (1982b) ' "Never to be thirty-six years old": *Rebecca* as female Oedipal drama', *Wide Angle*, 5, 1: 34–41.

Monk, C. (1996) 'Heritage film and gendered spectatorship' [online publication], *Close Up – The Electronic Journal of British Cinema*, 1, www.shu.ac.uk/services/lc/closeup/monk.htm, accessed 15 November 1999.

Moore, H. (1967a) 'To the directors of *Late Night Horror*', BBC WAC, T5/1,569/1, memo (14 September).

—— (1967b) 'To the directors of *Late Night Horror*', BBC WAC, T5/1,569/1, memo (2 June).

Morley, D. (1986) *Family Television: Cultural Power and Domestic Leisure*, London: Comedia.

Moseley, R. (2000) 'Makeover take-over on British television', *Screen*, 41, 3: 299–314.

—— (2001) 'The teen series', in G. Creeber (ed.) *The Television Genre Book*, pp. 41–3.

—— (2002) 'Glamorous witchcraft: gender and magic in teen film and television', *Screen*, 43, 4: 403–22.

Muller, R. (1968) 'How I fell into the monster's clutches', *TV Times* (11 November), pp. 12–14.

Mulvey, L. (1986) 'Melodrama in and out of the home', in C. MacCabe (ed.) *High Theory/Low Culture: Analysing Popular Television and Film*, pp. 80–100.

Mulvey, L. and Sexton, J. (2006) *Experimental Television*, Manchester: Manchester University Press.

Mulvey-Roberts, M. (ed.) (1998) *The Handbook to Gothic Literature*, Basingstoke: Macmillan.

Murphy, R. (1997) *The British Cinema Book*, London: BFI.

Naremore, J. (1998) *More Than Night: Film Noir and Its Contexts*, Berkeley: University of California Press.

Neale, S. (2001) 'Studying genre', in G. Creeber (ed.) *The Television Genre Book*, pp. 1–3.

Nelson, R. (1997) *TV Drama in Transition: Forms, Values and Cultural Change*, Basingstoke: Macmillan.

Newcomb, H. (ed.) (1994) *Television: The Critical View*, Oxford: Oxford University Press (5th edn).

Nicolls, B. E. (1950) 'Note on drama policy by director of home broadcasting', BBC WAC, T16/62/1, memo (5 May).

Nixon, N. (1998) 'Making monsters, or serializing killers', in R. K. Martin and E. Savoy (eds) *American Gothic: New Interventions in a National Narrative*, pp. 217–36.

Pardoe, R. (2005) 'M. R. James on TV, radio and film' [online publication], *Ghosts and Scholars*, www.users.globalnet.co.uk/~pardos/MediaList.html, accessed 4 July 2005.

Parker, L. (1990) 'Out of Angélique's shadow', in K. Leigh-Scott (ed.) *The Dark Shadows Companion: 25th Anniversary Collection*, pp. 14–21.

Parks, L. and Levine, E. (eds) (2002) *Red Noise: Buffy the Vampire Slayer and Critical Television Studies*, Durham: Duke University Press.

Peel, J. (1994) The Addams Family *and* The Munsters *Programmes Guide*, London: Virgin Books.

Penley, C., Lyon, E., Spigel, L. and Bergstrom, J. *Close Encounters: Film, Feminism, and Science Fiction*, Minneapolis: University of Minneapolis Press.

Petley, J. (1986) 'The lost continent', in C. Barr (ed.) *All Our Yesterdays: Ninety Years of British Cinema*, pp. 98–119.

Petrie, D. (ed.) (1993) *Cinema and the Realms of Enchantment: Lectures, Seminars, and Essays by Marina Warner and Others – BFI Working Papers*, London: BFI.

Pidduck, J. (1998) 'Of windows and country walks: frames of space and movement in 1990s Austen adaptations', *Screen*, 39, 4: 381–400.

Pirie, D. (1973) *A Heritage of Horror: The English Gothic Cinema 1946–1972*, London: Gordon Fraser.

Potter, J. (1990) *Independent Television in Britain: Volume Four, Companies and Programmes, 1968–80*, Basingstoke: Macmillan.

Prawer, S. S. (1980) *Caligari's Children: The Film as Tale of Terror*, Oxford: Oxford University Press.

Prior, A. (1968) 'Publicity from BBC and ITV', *Stage and Television Today* (16 May), p. 55.

Probst, C. (1996) 'Mining the macabre', *American Cinematographer*, 77, 10: 46–55.

—— (1997) 'Top-notch transmissions', *American Cinematographer*, 78, 5: 62–78.

Probyn, E. (1993) 'Television's unheimlich home', in B. Massumi (ed.) *The Politics of Everyday Fear*, pp. 268–93.

Punter, D. (1980) *The Literature of Terror: A History of Gothic Fictions from 1765 to the Present Day*, London: Longman.

—— (ed.) (2000) *A Companion to the Gothic*, Oxford: Blackwell.

Ranger, P. (1991) *'Terror and Pity Reign in Every Breast': Gothic Drama in the London Patent Theatres, 1750–1820*, London: The Society for Theatre Research.

Root, J. (1986) *Open The Box*, London: Comedia.

Rowe, K. (1995) *The Unruly Woman: Gender and the Genres of Laughter*, Austin: University of Texas Press.

Russ, J. (1993) 'Someone's trying to kill me and I think it's my husband', in J. Fleenor (ed.) *The Female Gothic*, pp. 31–56.

Savory, G. (1967a) 'Memo to the controller, BBC2', BBC WAC, T5/1,569/1, memo (19 September).

—— (1967b) 'Re: the recording of "Bells of Hell" ', BBC WAC, T5/1,569/1, memo (28 September).

Scharrer, E. (2001) 'From wise to foolish: the portrayal of the sitcom father, 1950s–1990s', *Journal of Broadcasting and Electronic Media*, 45, 1: 23–40.

Sconce, J. (2000) *Haunted Media: Electronic Presence from Telegraphy to Television*, Durham: Duke University Press.

Sedgwick, E. K. (1986) *The Coherence of Gothic Conventions*, New York: Arno.

Seltzer, M. (2000) 'The serial killer as a type of person', in K. Gelder (ed.) *The Horror Reader*, pp. 97–107.

Showalter, E. (1977) *A Literature of Their Own: British Women Novelists from Brontë to Lessing*, Princeton, NJ: Princeton University Press.

Silverstone, R. (1994) *Television and Everyday Life*, London: Routledge.

Singer, D. (1950) 'From clerk to the board: to Basil Nicholls (Director of Home Broadcasting)', BBC WAC, R73/136/1, memo (31 March).

Skal, D. J. (1993) *The Monster Show: A Cultural History of Horror*, Harmondsworth: Penguin.

Smith, A. (ed.) (1998) *Television: An International History*, Oxford: Oxford University Press (2nd edn).

Sobchak, V. (1996) 'Bringing it all back home: family economy and generic exchange', in B. K. Grant (ed.) *The Dread of Difference*, pp. 143–63.

Spigel, L. (1992a) *Make Room For TV*, Chicago: University of Chicago Press.

—— (1992b) 'Installing the television set: popular discourses on television and domestic space, 1948–1955', in L. Spigel and D. Mann (eds) *Private Screenings: Television and the Female Consumer*, pp. 2–39.

—— (1997) 'White flight', in L. Spigel and M. Curtin (eds) *The Revolution Wasn't Televised*, pp. 47–71.

—— (2001) *Welcome to the Dreamhouse: Popular Media and the Postwar Suburbs*, Durham: Duke University Press.

Spigel, L. and Curtin, M. (eds) (1997) *The Revolution Wasn't Televised: Sixties Television and Social Conflict*, New York: Routledge.

Spigel, L. and Mann, D. (eds) (1992) *Private Screenings: Television and the Female Consumer*, Minneapolis: University of Minnesota Press.

Stacey, J. (1994) *Star Gazing*, London: Routledge.

Stevenson, D. (1995) 'Family romance, family violence, and the fantastic in *Twin Peaks*', in D. Lavery (ed.) *Full of Secrets: Critical Approaches to* Twin Peaks, pp. 70–81.

Thomas, H. (1957) 'For your favour', in K. Bailey (ed.) *The Television Annual for 1958*, pp. 8–10.

Tiballs, G. (1996) *Rebecca – Starring Charles Dance, Diana Rigg, Emilia Fox and Faye Dunaway*, London: Chameleon.

Todorov, T. (1975) *The Fantastic: A Structural Approach to a Literary Genre*, Ithaca: Cornell University Press.

Tufte, T. (2000) *Living with the Rubbish Queen: Telenovelas, Culture and Modernity in Brazil*, Luton: University of Luton Press.

Turner, G. (2001a) 'Genre, hybridity and mutation', in G. Creeber (ed.) *The Television Genre Book*, p. 6.

—— (2001b) 'The uses and limitations of genre', in G. Creeber (ed.) *The Television Genre Book*, pp. 4–5.

Vitaris, P. (1997) '*Millennium*', *Cinefantastique*, 29, 4–5: 22–31.

Waldman, D. (1983) ' "At last I can tell it to someone!": feminine point of view and subjectivity in the Gothic romance film of the 1940s', *Cinema Journal*, 23, 2: 29–40.

Walker, M. (1990) *'Secret Beyond the Door'*, *Movie*, 34/35: 16–30.

Waller, G. A. (ed.) (1987a) *American Horrors: Essays on the Modern Horror Film*, Urbana & Chicago: University of Illinois Press.

—— (1987b) 'Made for television horror films', in G. A. Waller (ed.) *American Horrors: Essays on the Modern Horror Film*, pp. 139–60.

Warner, M. (1993) 'The uses of enchantment', in D. Petrie (ed.) *Cinema and the Realms of Enchantment: Lectures, Seminars, and Essays by Marina Warner and Others – BFI Working Papers*, pp. 13–35.

—— (1996) *The Inner Eye: Art Beyond the Visible*, Manchester: Cornerhouse.

Weiss, A. (1993) *Vampires and Violets: Lesbians in Film*, Harmondsworth: Penguin Books.

Weldon, F. (1987) 'A teenager in love', *Radio Times* (14 February), pp. 98–101.

Wheatley, H. (2002) *Gothic Television*, PhD thesis, University of Warwick (August).

—— (2004) 'Putting the *Mystery* back into *Armchair Theatre*', *Journal of British Cinema and Television*, 1, 2: 197–210.

—— (2005) 'Rooms within rooms: *Upstairs Downstairs* and the studio costume drama of the 1970s', in C. Johnson and R. Turnock (eds) *ITV Cultures: Independent Television Over Fifty Years*, pp. 143–58.

—— (2006) 'And now for your Sunday night experimental drama . . .', in L. Mulvey and J. Sexton (eds) *Experimental Television*, pp. 45–58.

Whitehead, C. (1995) 'The Zzzzzz-Files', *Village Voice* (14 November), p. 35.

Whitehead, T. (1980) 'Why our love of Dracula refuses to die', *TV Times* (13 September), pp. 20–1.

Wilcox, R. V. and Lavery, D. (eds) (2002) *Fighting the Forces: What's at Stake in* Buffy the Vampire Slayer, Lanham: Rowman Littlefield.

Williams, A. (1995) *Art of Darkness: A Poetics of Gothic*, Chicago: University of Chicago Press.

Williams, R. (1975) *Television: Technology and Cultural Form*, London: Fontana.

—— (1995) 'Schedulers' tales of the unexpected', *Independent* (Metro) (3 March), p. 17.

Williams, T. (1996) *Hearths of Darkness: The Family in the American Horror Film*, Cranbury, NJ: Fairleigh Dickinson University Press.

Wood, H. (2001) *Interacting With Television: Morning Talk TV and its Communicative Relationship With Women Viewers*, PhD thesis, Open University (June).

Wood, R. (1986) *Hollywood from Vietnam to Reagan*, New York: Columbia University Press.

Yentob, A. and Carter, C. (1996) 'Trust no one', *Guardian* (Media) (6 August), p. 2.

Index

Note: Literary works are indexed separately in this index, as are programme and film titles; numbers in italics refer to illustrations; 'n.' denotes a note